Future titles in the Spellmount Siegfried Line Series

WEST WALL

THE BATTLE FOR HITLER'S
SIEGFRIED LINE
SEPTEMBER 1944 – MARCH 1945

WEST WALL

THE BATTLE FOR HITLER'S
SIEGFRIED LINE
SEPTEMBER 1944 – MARCH 1945

CHARLES WHITING

PAN BOOKS

First published 1999 by Spellmount Ltd, Kent

This edition published 2002 by Pan Books
an imprint of Pan Macmillan Ltd
Pan Macmillan, 20 New Wharf Road, London N1 9RR
Basingstoke and Oxford
Associated companies throughout the world
www.panmacmillan.com

ISBN 1 405 00783 4

A CIP catalogue record for this book is available from
the British Library.

Printed and bound in Great Britain by
Mackays of Chatham plc, Chatham, Kent

Contents

West Wall

The Battle for Hitler's Siegfried Line
September 1944 to March 1945

*Even if we could not conquer, we should drag half the world into
destruction with us and leave no one to triumph over Germany . . .
We may be destroyed, but if we are, we shall drag the world with
us – a world in flames!*

Josef Goebbels, Minister for Propaganda
and Public Enlightenment

Author's Note

It was the biggest battle that the United States of America fought in the 20th century. At times there were up to 2,000,000 American soldiers engaged in just *part* of the great conflict. Among them were some key figures who, in the second half of our century, would make America the superpower she is today – Eisenhower, Kissinger[1], Marshall, etc., writers, entertainers, movie stars, and the great mass of ordinary 'Joes', nameless but vital.

It was no different for that dying superpower, which then still ruled a third of the globe – all that 'red on the map'. Britain might have been overshadowed by an emerging America, but she played a vital role too. At one time she had a single corps, larger than the entire current British Army, some 200,000 men strong, fighting in that epic struggle of the Titans. Among these too were men who would later guide the destiny of their country – Heath, Grimond, Carrington, etc. In one battalion, the Scots Guards, alone there was a future Archbishop of Canterbury, a Deputy Prime Minister, and a Moderator of the General Assembly of the Church of Scotland.

In the end the battle raged for six long, bloody months along a front of 350 miles, and cost over a quarter of a million British, Canadian, American and French casualties. The outcome was on a knife-edge almost to the end. Yet it has never been recognised as a single, cohesive battle. Unlike the Battle for Normandy or the Battle for the Channel Ports, it appears never to have been identified by any historian, military or otherwise, for what it was. For specialist and general writers alike, the tremendous struggles of that winter of 1944-5 have been a series of separate engagements, only tenuously linked.

They have failed to see that not only was the battle the most important of the 1944-5 campaign against Germany, but that it was the *key* battle of the entire war in the west. If the Allies had not won it, there would have been a compromise peace with Germany. And the United States would have retreated into the pre-war isolationism of its own vast continent. The US would not have become a superpower, and the rest of the 20th century in Europe might well have become 'Germany's century'. In the event, the

Allied (for which read American) victory in the spring of 1945 ensured that the future of west and central Europe was settled in America's favour.

On 30 January 1933, as Germany's new leader Adolf Hitler took over power in Berlin, the 'Poison Dwarf'[2] boasted that the new National Socialist Empire (*das dritte Reich*) would last for a thousand years. In fact, its lifespan was a mere twelve years, four months and five days. When that much vaunted 'Thousand Year Reich' finally succumbed to the fury and flames in Berlin, where it had been created, Hitler's empire left behind it little of consequence, save the geographical and political results of the most terrible struggle in history. In tangible terms, there were a few battered examples of 'Neo-classical' (that is, Nazi) buildings, the first of the *Autobahns*, and a couple of those pompous stadia used by the black-clad Nazi masses to demonstrate their cruel, if transitory, power. There was nothing of lasting importance – with one exception.

Even today, sixty years or more since Hitler ordered its construction to begin in secret, *die Hitlerlinie, der Todtwall, der Westwall* (as it finally came to be called) still exists[3]. The 'Great Wall of Germany', which like the Great Wall of China, can reputedly be seen from the stratosphere, crawls across the German countryside like some obscene, grey, primeval reptile.

For hundreds of miles, up and down hills, across swamp and forest, round peasant cottages and through remote villages, the Wall meanders from the Swiss border to the flat, wet plains of southern Holland. Despite all of the efforts of the Allies (and of the Germans too, it must be admitted) to destroy it in war and peace, its various parts are still there to be seen by the wanderer in that lonely border region. The cracked, concrete, military roads that lead nowhere, the moss-covered dragon's teeth, the wrecked bunkers looking like the mindless crudities of modern sculpture, the grotesquely twisted rusty steel spars beneath hedgerows and in ditches, the stark, sometimes (even now) frightening monuments to a terrible past will all still be there when the last survivor of that impossible dream of a Thousand Year Reich is long dead and gone.

In the years 1936–9, when it was being built at tremendous expense[4] and with the massive recruitment of cheap or forced labour from throughout Germany, Hitler's Wall was regarded by some as a great white elephant. Others regarded it as a fake deterrent, not to be compared with the French Maginot Line. What possible purpose could it serve, its critics asked. Germany, with her cardboard tanks and troops armed with WWI rifles, would never succeed in penetrating the Maginot Line; and no one was intending to attack Germany.

In Britain, France and later America, this new concrete wall, which had appeared so startlingly running along the frontiers of France, Belgium, Luxembourg and, in part, Holland, did not appear to be much of a threat. Indeed it became the subject of one of the 20th century's most popular comic songs. For a long time after it had become a hit in 1939, Allied troops went to war singing that mindless ditty about how they would hang their 'dirty washing' on the Siegried Line, 'if the Siegfried Line's still there'.

Ironically, and tragically, many of the thousands, and later hundreds of thousands who would march in September 1939 with that song on their lips were destined to die before the hard steel and concrete fortifications that Tin Pan Alley had so frivolously mocked.

Adolf Hitler, the man who had built that Wall, was not impressed by his enemies' mockery. Whatever others might think of this new 'Wall of Germany', *he* knew that it gave him the freedom he needed to act in the east. For the first time in recent German military history, the Reich need have no fear of conducting a war on two fronts. In the west, the Wall offered protection and a deterrent, while Hitler dealt with the east – Austria, Czechoslovakia and Poland.

Throughout the winter and spring of 1939-40 the Wall continued to afford Germany freedom to act. Hitler absorbed Poland, reached a compromise with his past arch-enemies, the 'Ivans' (the Soviet Russians), and, when his peace offensive in the west failed, made full use of the time given to prepare for his great westwards attack, that would destroy the French Army and send the British fleeing for their lives from Dunkirk, not to return to Festung Europa for another four years. Yes, the silly Siegfried Line, mocked by his foes, had surely paid for itself a hundred times or more.

By the summer of 1940 Hitler no longer needed the West Wall. Now, like Napoleon before him, he was master of Europe. For almost the next three years, he extended his 'Empire of the New Order' until it embraced 300 million people and stretched from the Crimea to the Channel, and from north Africa to Norway. The West Wall no longer guarded Germany's frontier, for that frontier had by now been extended into Alsace, Luxembourg and the *Ostkantonen* of Belgium[5].

From 1940 the West Wall was abandoned to nature, wild life and the local border farmers. Its bunkers were locked shut and, as it later turned out, the keys lost. Equipment such as optical instruments were stored in central depots, while the cannon, machine-guns, etc. were sent to the French coast, where French construction firms laboured (willingly and for good money) to build Hitler's new *Atlantikwall*, which would stop the Allies dead if they dared ever to return to the new National Socialist Europe.

It was not until September 1944 that the 'Great Wall of Germany' came into its own at last. For the first time since its construction nearly a decade earlier, the Wall was going to be tested in battle. A great, khaki-clad tide of seven Allied armies was sweeping through France and Belgium towards Germany's borders. Before that tide, what remained of the shattered *Wehrmacht* fled for its life. Now, there were no natural barriers to stop the enemy, save 'Father Rhine'. In that first panic-stricken week of

September everything depended on Hitler's Wall. Would it hold? Could it stand up to Allied pressure? Was it too late to re-arm the long neglected line of fortifications?

Many Germans thought it was. General Adam of the *Oberkommando der Wehrmacht*, dispatched hurriedly from Berlin in late August to inspect the Wall, gave a negative report. The bunkers were old-fashioned; their firing slits could not be used by the large-calibre German field artillery cannon and machine-guns; fields of fire were overgrown; minefields had been removed – or lost[6].

'The damned bunkers have been taken over by the peasants . . . they store their winter potatoes and beets in the places . . . Totally useless as defensive positions,' General Westphal, Field Marshal von Rundstedt's chief-of-staff, stormed. 'Our only chance – and it's a damned slim one – is to dig new communication trenches and put the men in them, not the bunkers.'

Hurriedly an attempt was made to call up a million civilians, men, women and teenagers, to excavate these new earthworks. In the event only 360,000 turned up. Even the civilians seemed to sense that it was useless. The West Wall was outdated and underarmed. It would not stop one *'Ami'*[7] tank.

However, the doubters were proved wrong. The West Wall turned out to be the impregnable fortified line which Hitler had always maintained it was. Even when manned by third-rate soldiers – 'Christmas tree soldiers', as one of the Wall's first defenders, General Graf von Schwerin, called them scornfully – it held. Third-grade battalions – 'ear-and-nose' regiments, 'white bread' companies, 'booty German' divisions[8] – stopped first-class Allied infantry in their tracks. After all, the defenders, however old, weak or sick, were firing from behind a foot of ferro-concrete.

For six long, bloody months, the British, Canadians, Americans and the French (who could be said to have started the whole thing with their own 'white elephant', the Maginot Line) tried to break through. Time and again they attacked the Wall on four different national frontiers many miles apart. Repeatedly they were repulsed, suffering substantial losses. Platoons surrendered, companies were wiped out, whole battalions fled in disorder. Divisions were decimated in a matter of days, losing thousands of men for a few paltry square yards of useless terrain. In the end the West Wall was conquered because behind it the Allies had taken the Rhine and had cut the defenders off from their base.

But there was no rejoicing in the Allied camp. In fact, it almost seemed as though the top brass did not want it to be known that the final breakthrough had been at such appalling cost.

Finally, after fighting which lasted from mid-September 1944 until mid-March 1945, the Siegfried Line vanished from Allied battle maps. The battle had prolonged World War Two in the west by half a year, and the cost in Allied dead had been greater than the US Army alone suffered in ten years of war in Korea and Vietnam.

This, then, is the story of the 'Great Wall of Germany' – a story written in blood.

Charles Whiting
Bollendorf (Germany), Echternach (Luxembourg),
Etain (France), York (England)
1999

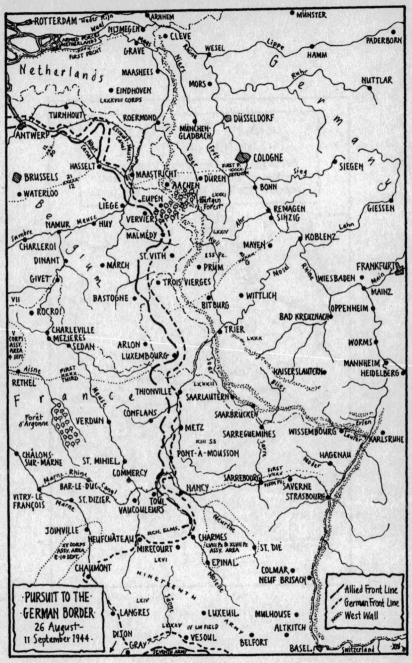

PURSUIT TO THE GERMAN BORDER
26 August–11 September 1944.

Allied Front Line
German Front Line
West Wall

·GERMAN 1940 ATTACK·
·OUT OF THE SIEGFRIED LINE·
Arrows show how the Germans went around
the Maginot Line, through the Ardennes Forest·
and across the Rhine. The Line itself stood firm.

North Sea

Netherlands

Germany

Belgium

Rhine

Ardennes
Forest

SEDAN

Luxembourg

Seine

MAGINOT LINE

WISSEMBOURG

METZ

PARIS

Alsace-Lorraine

Rhine

Danube

France

Switzerland

0   50
·Miles·

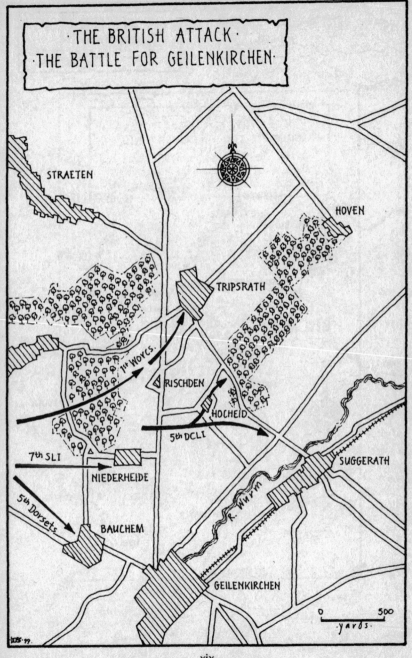

THE BRITISH ATTACK·
THE BATTLE FOR GEILENKIRCHEN·

STRAETEN

HOVEN

TRIPSRATH

1st WORCS.

RISCHDEN

HOCHEID

5th DCLI

7th SLI

NIEDERHEIDE

SUGGERATH

R. Wurm

5th Dorsets

BAUCHEM

GEILENKIRCHEN

0   500
yards.

xix

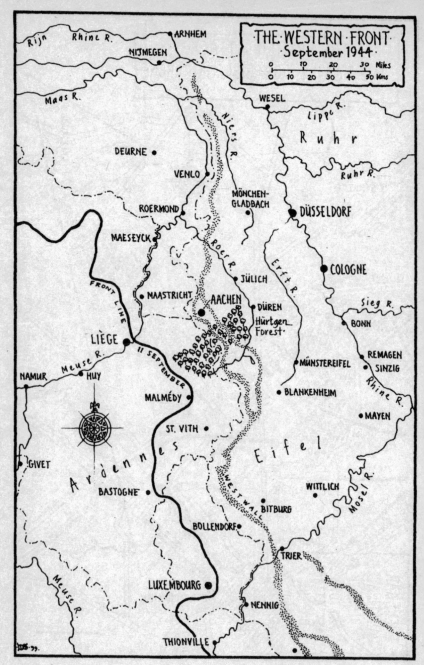

THE·WESTERN·FRONT
September 1944

0   10   20   30 Miles
0 10 20 30 40 50 Kms

Rijn   Rhine R.   ARNHEM
NIJMEGEN
Maas R.   WESEL   Lippe R.
                                              R u h r
DEURNE   Ruhr R.
           VENLO
                    MÖNCHEN-
ROERMOND   GLADBACH   DÜSSELDORF
MAESEYCK
                              Erft R.   COLOGNE
           Roer R.   JÜLICH
  MAASTRICHT   AACHEN   DÜREN   Sieg R.
                              Hürtgen   BONN
LIÈGE   Forest
                                        REMAGEN
NAMUR Meuse R. HUY   MÜNSTEREIFEL SINZIG
                                        Rhine R.
           MALMÉDY   BLANKENHEIM
                                        MAYEN
GIVET   A r d e n n e s   ST. VITH   E i f e l
                                        WITTLICH
    BASTOGNE   WESTWALL BITBURG   Mosel R.
           BOLLENDORF
                         TRIER
    Meuse R.
           LUXEMBOURG
                    NENNIG
    THIONVILLE

FRONT LINE
II SEPTEMBER

xx

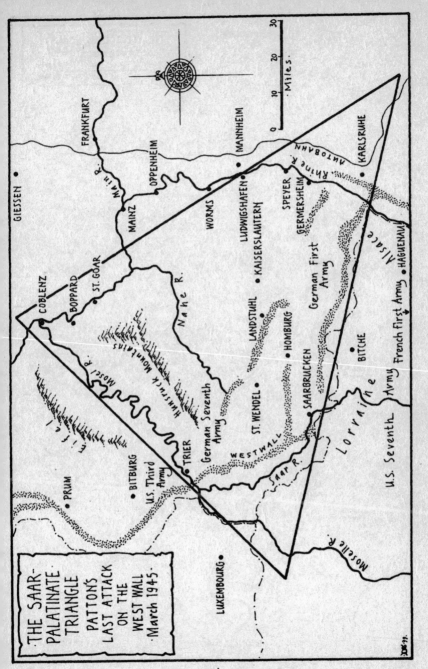

THE SAAR-
PALATINATE
TRIANGLE
PATTON'S
LAST ATTACK
ON THE
WEST WALL
March 1945.

Miles.
0 10 20 30

GIESSEN

FRANKFURT

Main R.

MAINZ

OPPENHEIM

MANNHEIM

WORMS

LUDWIGSHAFEN

SPEYER

GERMERSHEIM

Rhine R.

AUTOBAHN

KARLSRUHE

Alsace

HAGUENAU

French First Army

KAISERSLAUTERN

LANDSTUHL

HOMBURG

German First Army

BITCHE

SAARBRUCKEN

Lorraine

U.S. Seventh Army

ST. WENDEL

WESTWALL

SAAR R.

Moselle R.

Nahe R.

ST. GOAR

BOPPARD

COBLENZ

Hunsruck Mountains

Mosel R.

Eifel

TRIER

German Seventh Army

BITBURG

PRÜM

U.S. Third Army

LUXEMBOURG

DDB '97.

xxi

Prelude to a Battle
1936 to 1944

I can assure you that since 28 May the most gigantic fortification work of all time has been built.

Adolf Hitler, 12 September 1938

I don't care if the guy behind the gun is a syphilitic prick who is a hundred years old, he's still sitting behind eight feet of concrete and he's still got enough fingers to press triggers and shoot bullets, ain't he?

Anonymous GI to *Yank* magazine, September 1944

That Friday night – 'Z-day' minus one – the Führer did not sleep well in his tight, little, white iron cot. This was the second night that, despite the usual sleeping draught, he tossed and turned restlessly, wondering if he had made the right decision. The French were the real problem. What would their reaction be, he wondered.

Naturally, he did not expect any trouble from the 'Tommies', as he still called the English from his days in the trenches back in Flanders. Their new king, Edward, had railed at the 'Huns' (though he was more of a German than Hitler himself, who had been an Austrian citizen until eight years before) throughout World War One. Now the undersized, blond Englishman, whose main interests were married women, cocktails and dancing, was very pro-German and, more importantly, pro-Hitler.

Besides, as he told ex-Captain Wiedemann, his aide and former regimental officer, he had chosen Saturday for the great adventure; for no Englishman worth his salt would 'be found dead in his office' that day. *Das Englische Weekend,* as the Germans called it, was sacrosanct. 'They [the English] will only be back on Monday,' Hitler had told Wiedemann confidently, 'and by then the excitement will be all over.'

Still the Führer was uneasy. His generals and leading ministers were all opposed to his bold move. And since he had announced that the Reichstag would meet on Saturday afternoon, a freezing, snowy Berlin was abuzz

with rumours. Naturally, domestic and foreign journalists were clamour-
ing for details. What was going on? But all that Goebbels' representatives
in the Ministry of Propaganda would tell them was that they were going
on a secret journey the following morning. Until then they were to be held
in custody. And that was that.

Now it was Saturday morning, 7 March 1936. It was just over three
years since Hitler had taken over power in Germany. Since then a lot of
exciting, potentially dangerous events had taken place in the Homeland.
But this was Hitler's first risky venture outside the Reich. How would it
go? Hitler, personally, believed he could pull it off without any problems.
The Army, which would carry out the operation, was not so sure. Right up
to the last moment, the leading generals pleaded with him to back off. But
Hitler stubbornly refused, and my mid-morning on that fateful Saturday
it was already too late. The correspondents were already en route from
Berlin's Tempelhof Airport, and at ten o'clock the German Ambassador,
Hoesch, called on the British Foreign Secretary, Anthony Eden, in London.
The two men were discussing routine matters when the Ambassador
broke off abruptly. 'I have a communication of very great importance to
make. I am afraid that the first part of it will not be to your taste . . . but the
later portions contain an offer of greater importance than has been made
at any time in recent history.'

To Eden's astonishment, the middle-aged, somewhat pompous German
Ambassador started to read out a memorandum to the effect that the 'New
Germany' was taking back that zone of the Rhineland that had been
demilitarised by the victorious Allies at the Versailles Conference after
World War One. In other words, Hitler was starting to revoke the
Versailles-Diktat as he had promised he would ever since he entered
German politics.

Eden, the career diplomat, hid his feelings. He said that he regretted the
German march into the Rhineland, but that he would give careful
consideration to the German proposals. However, nothing could be done
until Monday, as most members of the British Cabinet were away from
London at their country houses and *naturally* could not be disturbed.
Hitler had been right. The 'Tommies' would not react until it was all
over.

Just before noon, when it all started, the Junkers carrying the puzzled
correspondents from Berlin touched down at Cologne-Wahn Airport.
Half an hour later the pressmen found themselves joining thousands of
expectant Germans gathered in the shadow of Cologne's great gothic
cathedral, opposite the Hohenzollern Bridge over the Rhine.

Eighteen years earlier glum citizens of that same Rhenish city had
looked on in silence as regiment after regiment of the field-greys of the
Imperial Army defeated in France marched eastwards over the bridge,
never to return. Now the mood was completely different. The soldiers

were returning. Adolf Hitler's 'New Germany' had thrown off the stigma of defeat. Thanks to the Führer, Germany was a nation to be reckoned with once more.

Suddenly the crowd tensed. They could hear the first regular stamp of steel-shod boots hitting the cobbles in unison. '*Sie kommen*,' the civilians declared with awed, baited breath. Small boys perched on their fathers' shoulders and prepared to wave their paper swastika flags. Women pulled out handkerchiefs. Men straightened their shoulders as if they were young recruits again. What traffic there was rumbled to a halt. Even the barges on the river slowed as the band slammed into a bombastic, brassy march. '*Sie kommen!*'

Things were no different at Trier, the old Roman Imperial city farther south on the Moselle; nor in Saarbrücken on the Saar river, just over the border from France. For nearly ten years these cities and the territory all round them had been ruled by their conquerors – the 'Tommies', '*die Amis*', the '*Franzmänner*'. Then they had gone. But still the Rhineland had remained under their unseen domination. Now *their* soldiers had returned. Nineteen infantry battalions had taken part in the operation, but only three had actually crossed the 'German' Rhine, over which their forefathers had watched so proudly until that terrible day, 11 November 1918, when they had been forced to admit defeat. Still, those three battalions that marched through Cologne, Trier and Saarbrücken, were enough.

In Berlin a nervous, sweating[9] Hitler knew when, after his opening remarks, he told an expectant Reichstag in a suddenly low, controlled voice, 'at this moment German troops are marching', that his gamble had paid off. The deputies, packed into the Kroll Opera House, went berserk. They stamped their jackbooted feet, whistled, clapped, sprang from their seats with faces flushed scarlet, and with outstretched hands screamed, HEIL HITLER! HEIL HITLER! HEIL HITLER! The hoarse cries of triumph, expressing that peculiarly German thirst for revenge, seemed to last for ever.

Sunday came. Paris rushed thirteen infantry divisions into their newly constructed Maginot Line. Hitler's generals begged the Führer to back down. At least, they urged, he should withdraw the three battalions from Cologne, Trier and Saarbrücken. Hitler told his generals to wait. At a pinch he could pull the battalions back the following day. But in the end, although Hitler later confessed to one of his cronies that that weekend had been 'the most nerve-wracking of my life', nothing happened. The French tamely withdrew their thirteen divisions from their Maginot Line fortresses because their men complained that the great underground bunkers were 'too damp'.

Shortly thereafter Hitler made a triumphant tour of the re-occupied Rhineland, where even the local Catholic clergy, for a time the Nazis' chief opponents, blessed the Prussians[10]. Then, resting in 'Amerika' (the code name for his special train) taking him back to Berlin, Hitler remarked: 'Grosser Gott, am I relieved how smoothly everything went!'. Now, as 'Amerika' rumbled northwards, the Führer, who had won his first political battle with his future enemies, turned boastful. 'Yes,' he intoned, 'the world belongs to the courageous. God helps *him*!' He asked one of his adjutants to put on a record of his favourite *Parsifal*, and as the music soared, in one of those noisy, empty phrases of Wagner's, Hitler, carried away by the music, remarked, 'I have built my own religion out of 19th-century opera . . .' He had learned that 'Only as a hero can you serve God'.

As 1936 progressed it really did seem as though God was smiling on His new 'hero'. Hitler brought off coup after coup. He put the one-time pariah nation of Germany back on centre-stage. The Germans' days of being a second-class country were over. But as this new 'hero' knew, God was (to use a hackneyed phrase) always on the side of the big battalions. Not only had he to continue to build up his new *Wehrmacht*[11] – again in contra-vention of the terms of the Versailles Treaty – but he also had to ensure that the frontiers of his new 'Thousand Year Reich' remained protected and inviolate while he did so.

This realisation induced Hitler to authorise a programme on the reclaimed frontiers of the New Germany. This would remain secret until two years later when, on 9 March 1938, Hitler officially announced what he had been doing in those remote villages of the Upper Rhine; and why the local peasantry had been sworn to secrecy about the activities of the (obviously) army men in civilian clothes who had suddenly appeared in their midst out of nowhere. By then it was too late for the coalition, which would declare war on Germany eighteen months later, to do anything about it.

These army engineer officers in civvies had plenty of models for their new assignment from Berlin. Indeed, around 2,000 years earlier, Roman Army engineers had begun their work in almost the same area. It had been their task to construct the *Limes Germanicus*, a series of linked, wooden forts, designed to keep the Germanic tribes from advancing from the east out of Rome's newly acquired Gaul, present-day France. In more recent times it had been the turn of France to construct a new *Limes* on its own soil to prevent the successors of those pagan German warriors from advancing westwards – Hitler's National Socialists.

Back in 1925 a victorious, but exhausted France had already considered building a defensive wall against the Germans on her eastern frontier. Marshal Pétain, the victor at Verdun in 1916 and the acknowledged saviour of the mutinous French Army, had made the suggestion. He wanted no repetition of that battle on the grim heights of Verdun which had bled the French Army almost white. But it was the gigantic ex-Sergeant André Maginot, who had lost a leg at Verdun, who had been the driving force behind putting the plan into action. For years the Minister for War laboured to persuade the Chamber of Deputies, and the French taxpayer (a rare animal in a country where the average citizen hid his money under the bed in order to avoid paying taxes) to spend most of the nation's military budget on a great protective wall.

As Maginot conceived it, the line, which would be named after him one day, would stretch along the Upper Rhine from Basle in Switzerland up through the Saar area to the north, then in stages towards the Moselle and France's border with Belgium. There it would stop, for the French reasoned that Belgium, which had been France's ally in World War One, would come to her aid in any future conflict with the *Boche*; and the Belgians had their own fortified defence system on their border with Germany. In due course, the French would be in for a great surprise as far as Belgian cooperation in war was concerned – but that was much later.

Now as the twenties gave way to the troubled thirties, the building of the Maginot Line began. It was accompanied by alarmist stories in the German press, and (predictably) wild ones in the cheaper British newspapers. In 1933, for example, the *Daily Express* reported that in the Maginot Line 'a whole army corps can live underground, fully provisioned for a year'. In 1935 the *Evening News* used the name 'Maginot Line' for the first time and recorded that, in times of war, men killed in action inside the forts would be placed in huge baths of acid. Here the corpses would decompose almost immediately and the sludge be sluiced away without causing an epidemic.

Still, the Maginot Line (which André Maginot never saw completed as one of the great construction white elephants of the 20th century) was impressive: three great, three-storey, underground forts with reversible surface turrets through which cannon, machine-guns, even flame-throwers could be fired automatically from far below, supported by a myriad pillboxes and forward defensive works. They were manned by the cream of the French Army, many of them specialists, who were treated to special rations and, more importantly for the French *poilu*, an increased ration of strong *pinot noir*; sunray sessions, underground gyms and fitness rooms, etc. They even grew their own mushrooms in the bottom of the forts.

But as cynics remarked at the time, there were *two* Maginot Lines: the impregnable fortresses that the French General Staff liked to boast about; and the other Line which was nowhere near as strong as the generals claimed. For the Maginot had two fundamental weaknesses: it had an open flank on the Franco-Belgian border, and it was too shallow. Once its flank was turned, or was actually penetrated, it would be rendered ineffective.

So, it was not to be the model for Hitler's wall now under secret construction just over the German border. A German cynic of the time stated, when he first heard of the Führer's secret plan to build a line of his own: 'France has her line and so Hitler has to have one too.' But vain and boastful as he was, that was not the reason for which Hitler began his West Wall.

He had already assessed the weakness of the Maginot Line more quickly than his own General Staff. As a result, he decided that his (as yet unnamed) fortified line would stretch the *whole* length of Germany's borders with Belgium and France (in all some 560 km) from Holland to Switzerland. These last two nations were traditionally neutral, and were not linked to the former entente powers by any form of treaty.

Moreover, Hitler's line would be in depth – up to thirty kilometres in parts. Key spots, where an enemy would be likely to strike in time of war, would be covered by a double line of fortifications. The line would be designed around strongpoints, surrounded by weaker fortifications, that Hitler hoped would lure an attacker deeper and deeper into his defences until they became completely bogged down. Finally, Hitler would add one further feature, not thought of by the French for their Maginot Line: an air defence zone that would prevent an attacker from the air from stopping the supply of reinforcements being brought up to the line.

Essentially, by 1936 Hitler had learned from France's decade of planning and building. He had spotted the weaknesses, and was determined not to repeat them. But he had already become aware of one major weakness in his own plans for the West Wall – money. The French had financed their Maginot Line at the expense of the rest of the French Army. Vast funds had gone into its construction, and the country's mobile troops were now suffering from a lack of modern arms, in particular armoured vehicles. And armoured vehicles would be vital if the French were, in the event of war, to cover that open Belgian flank. Hitler knew that he would have to plough enormous sums of money into his West Wall, but he was not prepared to allow the line to consume his entire military budget. He needed funds to create the tank divisions that would one day be the vital component of his planned *Blitzkrieg*.

So, what was he to do? In the final analysis he resorted to lies and propaganda about the strength of the line he had begun to create, so far in secret. As the Poison Dwarf had always maintained: 'If you are going to tell a lie, tell a big one.' That was what the Führer was going to aim for. Soon the propaganda war would begin. General Gerd von Rundstedt, the author of the Allies' defeat in the west, would laugh cynically when he saw the line for the first time. He would laugh even louder when he opened Rudolf Kuehne's propaganda book about the line, *Der Westwall*, and read:

No enemy can approach this bulwark of steel and concrete unpunished. Even an attack with the strongest means will, despite the greatest sacrifice, collapse under the power of the defensive armament.

And the reason for the future field marshal's laughter? Simple. The illustrations were not even German. They were photographs of the deep forts emplaced in what was called the 'mini-Maginot' on Germany's eastern frontier. They were in fact Czech.

But back in 1936, when Hitler secretly began the great project, naturally no attempt was made to publicise it. On a future date a proud Führer would boast to German General Guderian: 'Believe me, General, I am the greatest builder of fortifications of all times . . . I built the West Wall.'

But for the time being the world, as far as was possible, was not to know of Hitler's achievement as the 'greatest builder of fortifications'. In fact, Hitler could not lay claim to that distinction. The honour went instead to a tall, heavily built ex-World War One flier, Doktor Fritz Todt, who had exactly five years to live when *he* began the great secret project.

DOCTOR DEATH ENTERS THE PICTURE

Fritz Todt ('death' in German) was to go down in history as the civil engineer responsible for the bulk of the major construction work associated with Germany's war. Indeed, the two major German building programmes of the twentieth century – the *Autobahn* network and the Siegfried Line – will always be linked to the name of the big, hulking engineer who today lies buried in the shadow of the 'Eagle's Nest' at Berchtesgaden, where Hitler had made his pre-war home.

Cast in the mould of those great English and American organisers of mass labour in World War Two, Ernest Bevin and Henry Kaiser, Todt was also a fervent Nazi who, thanks to the party machine, had almost unlimited power at his disposal. Using the Nazi Party *Gauleiters*, he mobilised huge columns of unemployed men (and women) from all over the Reich. Without too much discussion, these virtual serfs were sent into the unknown at Todt's bidding to work on the great and still secret project. Used to a more modern German industrial scene, these forced labourers were shocked and dismayed to find themselves in the remote, poverty-stricken villages of the Eifel and the Black Forest.

Here the peasants still worked their land using the medieval strip system. They ploughed their tiny fields, spread out all over the place, with oxen. When they could not afford a 'beast', their barefoot women-folk and undernourished children did the work, sweating and straining to haul the plough through the heavy, red-clay earth.[12]

Such considerations did not worry the tall Nazi engineer, whose Todt Organisation now ran the construction project with ruthless military efficiency, working from dawn until dusk and, if necessary, through the night too.

In the tiny, rundown villages, where Todt billeted his forced labour, there was no running water, indoor sanitation or other, normal sanitary facilities. Typhoid was rife, as was tetanus. Due to the lack of flushing lavatories, the locals and those allotted to share their hovels (called 'Welch', the peasant dialect name for 'outsiders' or 'foreigners') used earth privies next to the animals' stalls. Both human and animal waste was then used as manure to cultivate the poor crop of turnips, potatoes and clover (for the animals). As a result, anyone suffering from the slightest cut or skin break ran the risk of contracting tetanus, or 'neck stiffness' as the peasants called it. But again Todt, here, there and everywhere in his riding breeches and high, polished boots, consulting his plans and bellowing orders, was unconcerned. There was always replacement labour available from the great pool of unemployed – there were six million in 1936. Todt's motto was one occupied Europe was to learn to fear: *'marschieren oder krepieren'* ('march or croak').

In fact, waste (*Jauche* as they called it) was highly prized. 'Rich' peasants piled it high under their windows in what the GIs later called 'honeydew mounds' to demonstrate how wealthy they were. More animals meant more waste. It was one of the indicators young peasants of marriageable age looked for when they went on *Brautschau* (looking for a bride). As they crudely put it, 'Shit means money.'

Soon, however, the imported labour got used to the conditions in which they had to live: no radio, cinema or dances (these areas were strictly Catholic), in many cases not even a local *Gasthaus*. For the first time in years, they were earning good money. And among their ranks were plenty of nubile and willing wenches. Often the barns and animal stalls in which they slept were little better than makeshift brothels. The local birthrate rose dramatically.

The imported workers and the youths of the new, compulsory labour service (*der Arbeitsdienst*) worked amazingly hard. Bunkers began to spring up all along the German frontier. Every fifty to one hundred metres there was a small bunker (unlike those in the Maginot Line) – simple and unsophisticated, the size of a small house, arranged in a front line between half and one-and-a-half kilometres deep, protected from armoured attack by prefabricated tank traps – the notorious 'dragon's teeth' as they came to be known.

Kilometre after kilometre the new fortifications ran the length of Germany's border. Up and down hills, across farm tracks, through deep forests, round swamps, even round large country estates and through villages they progressed, looking for all the world like the scaly, concrete spine of some ugly, primeval dragon.

Here and there the line was broken by a deep, multi-storey underground bunker in the style of the Maginot Line. The second largest of these was the *Panzerwerk Katzenkopf* (Cat's Head Armoured Fort) situated above the border village of Irrel in the south Eifel, dominating the Sauer river and the main road from Ettelbruck (in Germany) to Luxembourg Ville (the capital of Luxembourg).

The Cat's Head position was started in the spring of 1937 under conditions of the greatest secrecy. Thousands of men were brought in to start burrowing, mostly with pick and shovel, into the mountain overlooking Irrel, to a depth of thirty-six metres. The diggers, hidden by boards, camouflage nets and reed matting, cleared the tons of earth and rock, then started pouring concrete at the rate of 32,000 tons and a cost of 6 million German Marks.

Once that gigantic task was completed, the great underground cavern was fitted out in three storeys with reversible turret cannon, machine-guns, even automatic flame-throwers, all protected against poison gas by huge filters and oxygen. It was to be held by a garrison of eighty-four men of the Düsseldorf Fusilier Regiment who would serve for four to six weeks. Then they would be relieved by their comrades of the same Rhenish regiment. So, by the time it was finally completed in January 1939, the Cat's Head, which joined the other 22,000 smaller bunkers and pillboxes of the line, was regarded as virtually impregnable.

But, as we shall see, it was not. Nevertheless, it had begun to worry Anglo-American Intelligence mightily, as it was positioned so that it dominated the undefended left flank of the Maginot Line. Indeed, the whole new German complex, now officially known as the West Wall[13] was becoming a major headache for those secretive upper-class British gentlemen whose task it was to ferret out the secrets of 'Twelveland'[14].

COTTON'S FLYING CIRCUS

On 12 September 1938 Hitler strode imperiously to the platform at the annual party conference in Nürnberg, the 'city of the movement'[15] and thundered into one of his customary rabble-rousing speeches. But for once this was not just a melange of party platitudes and vague philosophy. This time the Führer, already sweating and continuously thrusting that unruly lock of dyed black hair back from his forehead, had some hard-faced and worrying facts to reveal. He told the quarter million listening to him the details of the the tremendous building project currently being undertaken by a million of their fellow citizens on the borders with France and Belgium.

'I ordered the immediate building of our fortifications in the west,' he thundered, staring round at the rigid ranks of his SA, the Brownshirts, and the teenagers of his *Arbeitsdienst*, who were carrying burnished shovels, gleaming like silver on their skinny right shoulders. 'I can assure you that since 28 May the most gigantic fortification work of all time has been built.'

He paused for breath and allowed his audience to gasp with surprise at the momentous secret the Führer was revealing to them, before they burst into spontaneous cheering and hysterical shouts of HEIL HITLER! which seemed to go on for ever.

But those enthusiastic Nazis were not the only ones taken by surprise at Hitler's revelations that day. Allied Intelligence was too. And with the Germans erecting their West Wall bunkers just across the Rhine from their own Maginot Line fortifications, the agents of the French *Deuxième Bureau* knew something was afoot. However, neither they nor their British opposite numbers in MI6 (the London Intelligence agency also known as SIS) had been able to obtain accurate details of the Nazis' much vaunted new fortified line. Twelveland, as Nazi Germany was known, had, as far as Allied Intelligence was concerned, been virtually sealed off for the past two years.

It had become one of British Intelligence's principal targets immediately after Hitler marched into the Rhineland in 1936. Until then, Germany had been an easy and not too worrisome field of activity for London's spymasters. They had their agents everywhere, some at the very top and dating back to 1919 when the disillusioned, defeated citizens of the new Weimar Republic had been easily bought for hard currency.

They had included members of the million-strong German SPD (the country's socialist party), bitter opponents of the Nazis; renegade officers; Catholic nuns who hated the 'godless' followers of the 'anti-Christ', Hitler; even professional cyclists, unable to compete outside Germany on the European racing circuit because the authorities would not allow them to take money out of the country.

Hitler had always feared the machinations of the 'English Secret Service' as he called it. In 1939 he told SS General Schellenberg, head of the SS's own intelligence apparat:

> The English Secret Service has a great tradition. Germany possesses nothing comparable with it ... Therefore, each success means the building up of such a tradition and requires even greater determination. The traitors who would stab Germany in the back during this most decisive struggle must be ruthlessly destroyed. The cunning and perfidy of the English Secret Service is known to the world, but it will avail them little unless Germans themselves are ready to betray Germany.

Schellenberg's Gestapo and 'Santa Klaus'[16] *Abwehr* had taken the Führer at his word. In the closing years of the 1930s they *had* 'ruthlessly destroyed' network after network of British espionage. Moreover, the authorities had declared the West Wall area to be a *Sperrgebiet* (a restricted area), where the locals needed special passes to enter the immediate neighbourhood of the new fortifications. Rapidly, the British spymasters in Queen Anne's Gate were becoming 'eyeless in Gaza'.

As the Nazis closed down one spy network after another, the British were growing desperate. The recruited the aid of Hungarian-Jewish movie mogul, Alexander Korda. He persuaded the staid British Jewish Board of Guardians to draw up a questionnaire for Jews still living in the Reich. Cunningly concealed in these documents were questions about what these would-be immigrants to Britain knew of the border area, and in particular the West Wall.

Other Jews from among the sizeable Rhineland population being forced out of the country of their birth fooled the Gestapo into believing they were trying to smuggle out *valuta*. At border checkpoints they were given the customary castor oil treatment, and the guards duly found the jewels they had swallowed or the gold coins they had hidden in the stainless steel *Kassiber*, which they then inserted into the rectum. But in their excitement the border guards completely overlooked the information being carried about the West Wall.

In Berlin, protected by his diplomatic immunity, young Major-General Kenneth Strong of The Royal Scots, Assistant Military Attache at the British Embassy, was also trying to puzzle out the various problems associated with the West Wall. In particular, he was concerned with the number and quality of the troops manning it. Would they, like those garrisoning the French Maginot Line, be from first-class divisions? Or would they be second-raters from reserve divisions, leaving Hitler, in time of war, to deploy his first-class troops in mobile operations elsewhere?

In June 1939 Strong (who would one day be Eisenhower's Chief of Intelligence and, six years on, still concerned with the mysteries of the 'Siegfried Line') struck lucky. There was a grand parade scheduled in Berlin in honour of the Regent, Prince Paul of Yugoslavia. The night before the parade Strong received a telephone call from an officer friend in the German War Ministry. In a roundabout way, the 'friend' (whom Strong never named) suggested that Strong might take a walk later on. It was going to be a fine evening in Berlin.

'I thought this a curious message,' the tall, dark-haired Scot recalled many years later, 'but I decided to go. To my astonishment I found that the Germans had marked on the pavements the names of the units that were to assemble that evening and take part in the parade the next day. It was a real bonanza.'

Later the young Scottish officer was confronted by 'an army' of plump, middle-aged *Putzfrauen* (cleaning ladies) equipped with 'buckets and mops . . . to wash away the secret information. Someone in authority had discovered the blunder. But I already knew now what units manned the Siegfried Line.'

At about the same time, the SIS resorted to even more direct methods in an attempt to find out what was happening in the West Wall. Up to that time, the British spymasters had paid willing stewards and stewardesses flying over Germany in British planes to take photographs of the Wall and other key targets on their way into Berlin-Tempelhof.

The French had done the same. Commandant Georges Ronin of the *Deuxième Bureau* had bribed Air France personnel to take hurried snapshots of the West Wall as their aircraft crossed the Rhine, and this information had been passed on to his opposite number, Fred Winterbotham, himself an ex-pilot, of the SIS's Air Intelligence Section. The French had even hired a splendid old man with a flowing beard, who was normally a portrait photographer in Paris, to fit his enormous and ancient wooden camera into a very old aeroplane, and fly up and down the French side of the Rhine taking photographs of the West Wall fortifications.

But by the spring of 1939, when Hitler had begun his preparations for war in earnest, the overflights, and even those along the Rhine, were becoming increasingly difficult. German fighters were forcing suspect aircraft ever higher over German air space. The result, as German *Luftwaffe* Intelligence had intended, was that the lenses of the spy cameras fogged up in the colder air, making photography impossible. Suddenly, the Anglo-French Intelligence experts were in trouble, especially as Britain did not now have a single agent of any quality in 'Twelveland'.

It was now that Winterbotham, tall, blond and handsome, and soon to be guardian of the secret Ultra decoding operation at Bletchley, had a brilliant idea. Together with an Australian pilot, adventurer, and well known philanderer, Sidney Cotton, he persuaded his bosses to buy a new American Lockheed 12A, a twin-engined executive aircraft capable of flying at 22,000 feet, higher than any known German fighter of the time. Although Winterbotham disliked the Australian, who was 'too big for his boots'[17], they worked closely together to adapt the new acquisition for flights over German air space.

A hole was cut in the Lockheed's frame and three cameras installed. One pointed straight down, with the other two at angles so that the spyplane could get the maximum coverage of the object being photographed. Now came the surprise. On the Lockheed's first trial in England it was discovered that, when the concealed shutter on the outer frame was opened from the heated cabin, the hot air was immediately drawn out of the hole and across the cameras' lenses. As Winterbotham stated many years later, when the U-2 successors to Cotton's Lockheed were already flying over Soviet Russia doing the same job, 'Wonder of wonders, they [the lenses] did not fog up, even at a height of 20,000 feet. It seemed too simple to be true.'

From that time (spring 1939) on, Cotton, sometimes accompanied by the ancient French portrait photographer with his flowing white beard, flew *up* and *over* the Rhine, capturing vital pictures of the Siegfried Line, while German fighter pilots, sent to intercept anything crossing the prohibited 'Red Zone', as it was called, fumed far below in angry impotence.

On a couple of occasions, the 'skirt-chaser' Cotton took his current girlfriend on these spying missions, and even crossed the frontiers of neutral Belgium to take shots of the West Wall running along the Belgo-German border. These would be the first photographs of the area, and they must have come as a considerable shock to Allied Intelligence, when they saw evidence of the extent of the Siegfried Line, now running for nearly 500km from Switzerland to Holland.

On 24 August 1939 Cotton and his new Canadian assistant, Bob Niven, made their last overflight. Unknown to them, this was the day Hitler had decided on for his attack on Poland, the event that would lead to the outbreak of World War Two. The two young adventurers seemed to realise that the balloon was about to go up. Cotton obtained permission from the German air controllers to fly over German territory, but he was warned that he had to stick to a ceiling of 300 metres, and that if he deviated from this by so much as a metre, his Lockheed would be shot down without warning. It was obvious to the happy-go-lucky Cotton that the Germans were on to him at last. Still, the two men managed to get in some swift shots to their rear once they had crossed the German border. Two hours later they landed at Croydon, from where the year before Prime Minister Chamberlain had flown (for the first time in his life) to Munich 'to save the peace'. Here they were asked by customs officials where they had come from.

'Berlin,' Cotton replied.

'Left it a bit late, haven't you?' the customs man snapped.

Cotton did not rise to the quip, though he knew better than most just how 'late' it really was that day. And so, the great aerial spy game, focussed on Hitler's West Wall, and the forerunner of all those spy satellites that are, at this very moment, orbiting the earth and recording our every move, came to an end.

Six days later Germany was at war with Poland, and three days after that Britain and France joined in on Poland's side. Whatever the Allies intended for the West Wall could now be put into effect. Britain's struggle with 'Twelveland' could begin in earnest.

Nothing happened – nothing at all! Although France had put her Maginot Line on a war footing on that same 24 August, the French Army of the Frontier made no immediate attempt to attack the Wall which lay only a couple of miles away. Why should they, the French generals seemed to be saying. As General Maurin, War Minister in 1935, had expressed it: 'How can we still believe in the offensive when we have spent thousands of millions to establish a fortified barrier? Who would be mad enough to advance beyond this barrier on goodness knows what adventure?'

So it was that in the first week of September 1939, while Hitler drove ever deeper into Allied Poland, sixty-seven French divisions faced a skeleton force of nineteen weak German divisions in their own fortifications within hailing distance, and did nothing. As for the Führer, he apparently did not share his generals' fears. He thought he had the measure of the Anglo-French Allies, those appeasers who had rolled over so tamely at Munich the year before to have their bellies scratched. They would do nothing in the west. Even if they did, he told his valet, Linge[18], 'they will break their teeth on my West Wall'.

The veteran American correspondent in Berlin, William Shirer, observed as he travelled the length of both fortified lines between Karlsruhe and Basle on the German side of the Rhine:

> No sign of war, and the train crew told me not a shot had been fired on this front ... We could see the French bunkers and at many places great mats behind which the French were building fortifications. Identical picture on the German side. The troops seem to be observing an armistice. They went about their business in full sight and range of one another ... Queer kind of war.

It was. As General Spears, chief British liaison officer with the French, remarked after observing a German hoarding that stated to 'Soldiers of the Northern Provinces' that 'the perfidious British soldiery were sleeping with their wives and raping their daughters', the French unit opposite replied with another hoarding that maintained, 'We don't give a bugger. We're from the south.'

However, the French General Staff knew that *something* had to be done. In his General Order I, 8 September 1939, General Edouard Requin expressed it thus: 'The time has come to hit hard and answer with guns and machine-guns all attempts at fraternisation. Any of the enemy who show up will be killed or captured ... Everybody must be convinced that the present war will know neither weakness nor pity.' It was not a very rousing or inspiring general order, but it did indicate that the French were prepared to attack. (The British Expeditionary Force had not yet arrived in France in strength[19].)

Awareness that the French were at last going to do something sent shivers of fear down the spines of the German generals who knew. General von Mellenthin, corps commander, inspecting the West Wall defences opposite the Maginot Line, was appalled by the quality of the German troops holding the line. They were 'second-class, badly equipped and inadequately trained, and the defences were far from being the impregnable fortifications pictured by our propaganda. The more I looked at our defences, the less I could understand the completely passive outlook of the French.' And now the French were on the move.

On the move, perhaps, but without much enthusiasm or their famous Napoleonic *élan*. Eight divisions, two of them motorised, five battalions of tanks and artillery started to move on 9 September heading for one of the hardest sectors of the West Wall to defend – the flat, industrial district around Saarbrücken. On the night of 8/9 September one of the guns in the Maginot fortress at Hochwald fired the first shot of the war in the west into Germany. It was a symbolic gesture and remained so, for the Hochwald never fired another shot in anger for the rest of the war – at least against the Germans. When it did fire again, it would be German fire directed at the advancing Americans.

In due course the French offensive 'captured' some two hundred square kilometres of forest and field, which the Germans had carefully evacuated before war actually broke out as part of their plan for the 'Red Zone'. The British and French press had a field day.

The offensive was 'methodical' and 'limited', the papers maintained. All the same it was a great victory. All of the ground leading to the West Wall defences had been taken. Everywhere the Germans had 'fled in panic', etc. etc. In fact, the German evacuation of the Red Zone had been planned back in 1937, and by the time the triumphant communiques were issued and had been mulled over by the pundits (who were already predicting that Nazi Germany would not be able to resist this warfare on two fronts for much longer), the French were digging in to the captured areas of woodland and fifty villages in the poverty-stricken Saar, that were all completely deserted. Even the local dogs had been evacuated.

On 30 September, with the Poles defeated, the commander of the French North-East Front, General Alphonse Georges, arrived in the Saar to explain to his subordinates something they already knew: to remain in enemy territory in front of the Maginot Line without a plan for an attack on the West Wall was a recipe for disaster. There was only one thing to do – withdraw.

Thus, *l'Offensif Sarre* ended with a whimper. The road to the Reich had been more or less wide open for two or three weeks, but the French had failed to take it. They had not attacked so much as a pillbox in the West Wall. And as the British and French press fell silent, and hardly referred to the Saar, the French quietly withdrew, followed by the eager Germans, now reinforced by the first fighting units from the east, which had been 'blooded' in Poland.

SITZKRIEG ON THE SIEGFRIED

As September gave way to October, and Hitler prepared for his next move, they too settled down for the next stage of the *Sitzkrieg*[20]. An uneasy peace reigned in front of the Siegfried Line, disturbed only by the bloody-minded 'Anglais' who had moved up. It seemed these 'English' (in fact mostly Scots from the 51st Highland Division) wanted to have a crack at the Line, on which they were going to hang their 'dirty washing, Mother dear'. They engaged in offensive operations of which the French strongly disapproved. Live and let live was the French motto now. Besides, men got killed in offensive operations. Unfortunately this was true. However, the first casualty caused by the activities of these over-eager 'Englishmen' was French. He was deaf, and had not responded quickly enough to the British sentry's traditional challenge 'Who goes there?' He was shot dead because of his tardiness and lack of knowledge of English. Typical of the British. Meanwhile the front in the Saar and Alsace went back to sleep.

Things were not much different in neutral Belgium. That dangerous left flank of the Maginot Line was still open as 1939 gave way to 1940. The Belgians had done nothing in their part of the Ardennes, even though they knew that the West Wall was filling up with troops from Echternach to Monschau. And in addition, on 10 January 1940 they had warning of German intentions when a courier plane crashed at Mechelen (Malines) near Brussels. It was carrying two majors, one of whom had on him the top secret plans for the Führer's invasion of the Low Countries. After that, the Belgians gathered more evidence that Germany intended to infringe Belgium's neutrality for the second time in a quarter of a century. Top-ranking members of the 'Father Christmas' *Abwehr* warned the Belgians of what was to come, even giving them the date of the expected German attack. Still nothing was done.

The *Ardennenjäger*, recruited locally, German-speaking, and in many cases German-born (the regimental area had been part of Germany until 1919) warned that the West Wall was filling up with troops, and that at night the Eifel forests just over the border were alive with military activity. All of their friends and relatives on the German side had been evacuated with the rest of the population of the Red Zone. And that could mean only one thing: the Germans were going to attack.

Some of the more adventurous of the Light Infantry's commanders volunteered to take patrols across the frontier in and around St Vith, where the 'Black Man'[21] section of the West Wall lay closest to Belgian soil. But they were forbidden to do so. Their king, Leopold III, who was also their commander-in-chief, was resolutely opposed to any action that might antagonise Hitler.

Even when Colonel Hans Oster, Chief of Staff of the *Abwehr*, told the Dutch Military Attache in Berlin (who passed the news on to his Belgian Intelligence colleagues), 'That swine [Hitler] has gone off to the Western Front', and followed up with a signal to The Hague, 'Tomorrow [10 May] at dawn. Hold tight', the Belgian king did nothing. It was almost as if he wanted the Germans to win. And they did.

Early on the morning of 10 May 1940 Adolf Hitler, with his General Staff in attendance, took up his position at the *Felsennest* (Eyrie) outside the picturesque, walled Eifel township of Munstereifel[22] and waited. Twenty-five miles away on the Belgian border, his armoured troops burst from their positions in and around the West Wall, and began their major drive through neutral Belgium and Luxembourg. Here and there, in the same forests the Americans would fight through nearly five years later, the *Ardennenjäger* fought skirmishes in an attempt to halt the juggernaut. They hadn't a hope in hell.

By the 14th the Germans had reached the border with France. Here they ran up against one of the outlying forts of the Maginot Line, La Ferte. This lay a few miles outside the Germans' main objective, Sedan, where, in 1870, the Prussians had won their great victory that led to the downfall of Napoleon's Imperial France. A lucky shot scored a direct hit on a key observation slit. Temporarily blinded, the defenders could do nothing to stop the German infantry shoving smoke bombs, high explosives and grenades through the gaping, jagged hole. The 266 defenders fought on wearing their gas masks. Earlier the fort's commander had written to his wife: 'We know our mission requires us to die on the spot.'

That commander, a lieutenant in the elite Maginot Line fortress troops, did not die in battle at La Ferte. Indeed, he continued to fight, even supporting French counter-attacks by the Foreign Legion and the hard-bitten Moroccan 'interval' troops, that is those whose job it was to defend the 'intervals' between the Line's forts. He fought to the very end. When the Germans finally accepted the surrender of La Ferte from a subordinate officer, they found to their shock the bodies of 210 French soldiers. Most had been wounded and had then died of asphyxiation when the Fort's ventilation system failed. As the German infantry were making their gruesome discoveries in the heart of the wrecked fortification, they started when they heard a single shot. It was the commandant. He had not died in battle as he had suggested to his wife, but had taken the soldier's way out. In defeat, rather than surrender to the Boche, he had shot himself.

Not many of the Allies followed the example of that brave young officer when it was clear that they had been defeated. The Germans had won. Most acted like King Leopold, who declared on 25 May, 'I have decided to stay [in Belgium[23]]. The cause of the Allies is lost.' Meekly he surrendered to the German invaders.

Come what may, there was one prominent member of the Anglo-French Alliance who would not surrender. Just after Hitler had confidently assured Field Marshal Kleist, 'We shall not hear much more of the British in this war', the new Prime Minister, Winston Churchill, made the first of his classic wartime broadcasts. Today the rhetoric seems old-fashioned, more 19th- than 20th-century. Those born after the war, on hearing it now, would consider the delivery bombastic. But in that bleak summer nearly sixty years ago, it provided a spark of light and hope.

Churchill made his speech at midnight in a cold, dimly lit room in London's Broadcasting House. He thundered in the style he had learned as a young man in the previous century: 'We shall not flag or fail. We shall go on to the end . . . we shall defend our island whatever the cost may be . . . WE SHALL NEVER SURRENDER.' After those defiant words, Churchill paused, an old man gasping for breath before he started to speak again. He rattled off his carefully chosen phrases faster and faster, his voice a drumbeat, charged with a faith in the nobility of his cause: ' . . . and even if – and I do not for a moment believe – this island, or a large part of it, were subjugated . . . then our Empire beyond the seas . . . would carry on the struggle.'

Again the great man paused. Then his closing words expressed his only realistic hope for the future vanquishing of Europe's new master, Adolf Hitler: ' . . . until in God's good time, the New World, with all its power and strength, might step forth to the liberation and rescue of the Old.'

On that bleak June day of defeat and despair, Churchill knew it would be a long time before this 'liberation' might come about. Perhaps at that moment, slumped at the microphone, with the sound of traffic outside subdued, he wondered if America would ever enter the struggle against Hitler. In the end, however, he pulled himself together. He clapped his hand over the mike and said to American correspondent, Ed Murrow[24] : 'And if they *do* come, we shall have to hit them on the head with beer bottles, for that is all we shall have to fight them with.'

HALF TIME AT HITLER'S WALL

Now the troops had gone. The *Wehrmacht* used the West Wall as the springboard for their great westward attack. It succeeded, perhaps beyond the Führer's wildest dreams. The British, the last remaining foe, had been turned head-over-heels out of Europe. The continent was at peace at last. Hitler's new Reich reigned supreme from Cracow to Calais, from the Arctic Circle to the Mediterranean. Already the Führer was beginning to demobilise his fighting divisions. They would not be needed in the 'New Europe'.

Things were little different on Germany's western front, which had changed radically since May 1940. Now, Alsace-Lorraine, Luxembourg and the East Cantons of Eupen, St Vith and Malmédy were German again, incorporated into the Greater Reich, inhabited by German citizens as before. Great parts of the West Wall, and of the Maginot Line, were now well *behind* Germany's new frontiers. What need was there now for a Wall running deep inside Germany, in a Europe that was at peace?

So it was that, as the Eifel and Black Forests peasants returned to their homes in the former Red Zone, the thousands of bunkers had their weapons and expensive fittings removed. The doors were locked and the keys taken away to be stored in central depots. The military roads that linked them were cracked and neglected. The barbed wire rusted or was removed by local farmers, who used the wooden partitions built into the concrete walls of the pillboxes to store their potatoes and *Runkelruben* (a type of turnip fed to animals) over the winter. Rapidly the bracken (known locally as *Eifelgold* because of its gold-coloured flowers), and the brambles took over. One by one the man-made structures were reclaimed by nature, finally to disappear as if they had never been there in the first place.

The years passed. The Todt Organisation and the Nazi Labour Service dismantled more and more of the forts' equipment. This was stored in depots in case of an emergency – but what emergency? Nazi Germany was winning the war on all the fronts that had opened up since the great 1940 victory in France. The Reich was packed with booty from a dozen countries. And Germany had the great industries of half of Europe working all-out and willingly for a German victory. Household names – Skoda of Czechoslovakia, Phillips of Holland, Renault of France, Arbed of Luxembourg – were only too eager to supply the new masters of Europe with guns, electrical equipment, tanks, trucks, and so on. The West Wall receded further and further into the distant past.

The Allied landings in Normandy on 6 June 1944 changed all that dramatically. The Atlantic Wall, Dr Todt's other great creation just before his death in 1942, failed to hold the Anglo-American forces back. They broke out of Normandy, advancing across that same flat, defenceless northern French plain that Hitler's armies had swept through so rapidly in what now seemed like another age. It was now clear that, if the *Wehrmacht* failed to halt the enemy, it would not be long before they reached the border of the Reich itself.

Reichsminister Albert Speer, who had taken over from Todt, warned Hitler of the danger on 9 August, and persuaded him that all available civilians should be put to work rebuilding or strengthening the West Wall. At first Hitler hesitated. He thought that if he took action, it would appear that his army in France had been defeated. By the third week in August, he knew that it had. On the 24th he signed an order entitled *Befehl über den Ausbau der deutschen Westellung*. This could be translated as 'Order for the Enlargement of the German Western Positions' – apparently innocuous, and calculated not to cause panic among the civilian population. In reality it meant the rearmament of the West Wall. The writing was on the wall, in both senses. Unlike in 1939, this time Germany really was going to come under attack. At last, the West Wall was to be properly tested. Some seven Allied armies – British, American, Canadian and French – were on their way, heading for a last confrontation. And this time the 'Tommies' might just fulfil that old boast of 1939 and really hang their 'washing on the Siegfried Line, Mother dear'.

Shaken as they were by events in France, the German authorities reacted with draconian measures. All theatres, music halls and cabarets were shut. Every publisher, save only those publishing school textbooks and the Führer's own *Mein Kampf*, were closed down. The universities (apart from the medical faculties) followed suit.

The services were not exempt from these drastic cuts. Pilot training came to an abrupt halt. In the *Kriegsmarine* all capital ships were ordered to be mothballed. Their crews, and those of the U-boat arm, now without ships, were ordered into the infantry.

Throughout the Reich military hospitals and reserve depots were combed for 'bodies'. Men with severe stomach problems were combined into 'white bread battalions'. 'Ear and nose' battalions followed, in which orders were often given in sign language. Woe betide any guard commander who did not make his presence known well in advance at night. He ran the risk of being shot by his own men.

Civilians were caught up in the great *levée en masse*. Boys over the age of 15, girls over 16 and all men up to 59 were ordered to report immediately for duty at depots close to the West Wall. From there they were to be sent to schools close to the border area – the Red Zone was being evacuated again and the schools closed – where they would be issued with picks and shovels[25].

Meanwhile, immediately behind the West Wall, in cities such as Cologne, Aachen, Trier, and Saarbrücken, deserters, stragglers, lightly wounded soldiers and elderly men from the German Home Guard (the *Volkssturm*) were hurriedly prepared to man the long, empty fortifications. In the old Roman city of Trier alone, 40,000 men were rounded up but, being leaderless, only one battalion was made immediately available. Urgently the 'Trier Battalion' was shipped to the Eifel front under the command of an ex-priest who thought his men 'a lot of soft tits'.

This commander was not alone in his estimation of the calibre of the newly created emergency battalions charged with preparing the West Wall for the first attack in its ten years of existence. In the first week of September a young German soldier wrote to his fiancee (the unposted letter was found on his body): 'Today I was transferred to the 42nd Machine-Gun Fortress Battalion as a messenger, destination West Wall. The battalion is composed of Home Guard, soldiers and half cripples. I found many among them who were obviously off mentally. Some had their arms amputated, others were one leg short. A sad sight!'

These desperate measures to man the West Wall against the coming Allied attack were announced by Radio Berlin and in the 'Poison Dwarf's' news media, in an attempt to encourage the German people. The announcements were picked up by the Allied press. In London and Washington, the British and American editors had a field day, mocking the *Volkssturm*, the old men, the stomach cases, and cripples with wooden legs and glass eyes.

However, the Tommies and the GIs who would soon be attacking the West Wall were unamused. As one of them told the US Army magazine, *Yank*: 'I don't care if the guy behind the gun is a syphilitic prick who is a hundred years old. He's still sitting behind eight feet of concrete, and he's still got enough fingers to press triggers and shoot bullets, ain't he?'

THEY'RE HERE!

On the afternoon of Monday 11 September 1944 the *Burgermeister* of the little hamlet of Sevenig on the Our river, on the border of Germany and Luxembourg, was taking a short break. The old man had been helping his few able-bodied neighbours with the harvest. Now he sat on a bench in front of his beamed, white-washed cottage, smoking what the Germans call a *Shagpfeife*. His mix was home-grown, sprayed with 'Virginia Aroma'. It was years since he had smoked real tobacco. Still, it tasted better than his usual dried peppermint tea leaves.

It was warm and there was a little sun. There was the promise of a long *Altweibersommer*[26] in the air. As he sat there, *Burgermeister* Michel Weber thought how peaceful everything looked. The cut corn was turning to gold in the stooks arranged round poles in the Eifel style. The birds were singing, and the little river, which anyone could wade across at this time of year, bubbled merrily. Weber took a contented puff at his little yellow pipe, at peace for a short while with the world. Perhaps things were not so bad for the Fatherland after all.

Suddenly he was startled by the sound of someone splashing through the shallows from the Luxembourg side of the Our. He sat up and removed his pipe from his mouth. He stared with his weak old eyes. A German captain, in a tattered uniform, was heading his way, with two shabby privates in tow, both as dusty and ragged as their officer. The *Hauptmann* paused when he saw Weber. He appeared not to have been expecting to find anyone left on the German side of the river. *'Was?,'* he rasped, his face red and angry, *'Sie sind noch hier?'* ('What? You're still here?')

The *Burgermeister* looked puzzled. What did the officer mean? He rose to his feet stiffly, pipe in hand, and waited. The officer was in a hurry, and he wasted no time in enlightening the confused old man. 'Save yourself,' he snapped. 'We're the last. After us it's the enemy.'

Before Weber could ask any questions, the three soldiers moved off. Moments later they were clambering up the steep slope from the river valley, and vanished into the pine forest, leaving the old man to ponder the captain's words.

Had the officer meant that he was the last of some decimated infantry battalion? Or something worse – that he was the last of the entire German Army, beaten in France and fleeing *Heim ins Reich* (home to the Reich) through Belgium and Luxembourg. Could things really be that bad?

The *Burgermeister* sat down again. He stared across at Luxembourg and at the slope leading up from the main road. There was no sound, save for the chirping of the birds, and the sigh of a gentle September breeze in the trees. There was no longer the clatter of gunfire they had been hearing recently in the far distance.

Then he saw them. They were filtering through the trees, slipping in and out among the tightly packed firs, avoiding the open fire breaks. He knew immediately that they were not Germans. If they had been, he would have recognised the grating of their steel-shod boots on the rocks that were always close to the surface of the poor, thin soil in this area. But the men advancing towards the river were making hardly any sound. They were wearing some kind of rubber-soled shoes. They had to be American!

Moving quickly for a man who was so old and, in the peasant way, taking everything in his stride, *Burgermeister* Michel Weber hurried back to the hamlet to find the *Dorfschreier* – the man who for many years had summoned the villagers with his bell to hear important announcements. He found him and gasped out his startling news. '*Schnell. Die "Amis" sind da.*[2]7'

NOTES

1   Then a Private First Class in the US 84th Infantry Division, the 'rail-splitters'.

2   Goebbels, so-called because of his small stature and vitriolic tongue.

3   Later to be known in the west as the Siegfried Line after the mistaken identification of a WWI German position on the Western Front.

4   But not as expensive as the French Maginot Line which swallowed up so much of its military budget that France was never able to field those mobile armoured forces that might have dealt with the German *Blitzkrieg* of 1940.

5   Even today these nations have German-speaking populations on their borders with Germany. The *Ostkantonen* (East Cantons) are the St Vith, Eupen and Malmédy regions of Belgium, taken from Imperial Germany at the Treaty of Versailles. Apart from most of Malmédy, they are German-speaking, with their own schools, parliament, etc.

6   Some had been dug up by farmers. The plans of others laid down in 1939 had been mislaid.

7   A contemptuous name for an American.

8   Deaf soldiers, those suffering from stomach complaints, and ethnic Germans.

9   He often lost as much as seven pounds in the course of making a long speech.

10   Because of the special regionalism of Germany, and the antagonism between the Protestant north and the Catholic south, north Germans were often called 'the blue ones' (the old Prussian uniform had been dark blue), or simply 'the Prussians'.

11   Which replaced the *Reichswehr* of the pre-1933 Weimar Republic.

12   When the author first knew the area ten years after the war, they were still using oxen, and had no electric lights or sewage system. They did not even have metal roads.

13   Since 1936 these defensive fortifications had been known variously as 'the Hitler Line', 'the Führer Line' or 'the Todt Line' (after Dr Fritz Todt). It received its official German title on 19 November 1938.

14   The British, at this time, gave target countries code numbers.

15   So called because the annual conference of the Nazi Party was held here.

16   Admiral Canaris, head of the German Secret Service, and known as 'Father Christmas' because of his shock of white hair and benign appearance, was in charge of it.

17   Cotton always sold his services to the highest bidder. As soon as war began and the new lieutenant of Naval Intelligence, Ian Fleming (of James Bond fame) heard of 'Cotton's Circus', he tried to bribe Sidney into joining Naval Intelligence. The RAF were quicker off the mark – hence no mention of Cotton in the Bond saga.

18   A colonel in the SS. In Hitler's household even servants held officer rank in the elite Black Guards.

19   Montgomery's regular 3rd Division was forced to use Pickford trucks, rented from the well known removal company, to ship its infantry to their positions in France. It was typical of a BEF, well equipped with mobile cinemas for the troops, but lacking trucks and tanks.

20   The German term for the 'phoney war' had been coined by the Americans, but after World War Two the Germans themselves used it to describe this period of inactivity.

21   *Der schwarze Mann* line of fortifications north of Trier, of which we shall hear more.

22   In 1944 Field Marshal Model, 'the Boy Field Marshal' as von Rundstedt called him contemptuously, set up his HQ in this same town during his six-month attempt to prevent the Western Allies from penetrating the West Wall.

23   Both of his royal neighbours, the Queen of Holland and the Grand Duchess of Luxembourg, fled to Britain.

24   Murrow, with his charactersitically mischievous grin, would do much to turn an isolationist United States in Britain's favour.

25   Speer anticipated that 1,000,000 labourers would be recruited in this manner. After a week, just 235,000 turned up for duty.

26   'Old woman's summer', i.e. Indian summer.

27   'Quick. The Yanks are here.'

BOOK 1

September to December 1944

Maybe there are five thousand, maybe ten thousand Nazi bastards in their concrete foxholes before the Third Army. Now, if Ike stops holding Monty's hand and gives me the supplies, I'll go through the Siegfried Line like shit through a goose.

General Patton, US Third Army, September 1944

1

The Line is Reached

Soldiers of the West Front, I expect you to defend the sacred soil of Germany to the very last. HEIL HITLER!

Field Marshal Gerd von Rundstedt, September 1944

Victory was in the air. First, the defeated Germans had retired in small groups. They had been disciplined and organised, if dusty and unshaven. But by the first week of that terrible September, they had degenerated into a panicked, disorderly rabble. Each man was out to save his own skin. There was no longer any unit cohesion. They fled France in tanks, trucks, armoured cars, some towing lines of other armoured vehicles that had run out of fuel. In anything with wheels, they abandoned that country where they had lived 'like God in France' as they described it. They packed into ancient buses, horsedrawn farm carts, French *'gazogènes'* (automobiles powered by coal- or charcoal-gas and carried in rubber containers on the roof). One infantry group was spotted fleeing in an antique fire engine, looted from some provincial *pompiers*.

As these wretched convoys streamed back through Belgium, Holland and Luxembourg towards the supposed protection of the 'Thousand Year Reich', every part of the German Army was a hotch-potch. There were 'Hiwis' (Russian volunteers in German uniform), 'blue boys' (sailors from the *Kriegsmarine*, a navy with no ships), 'grey mice' (the dowdy female auxiliaries in their grey uniforms – 'officers' mattresses' as the German footsloggers cynically called them), sullen young men bearing those fearsome insignia, the skull and crossbones and the runic SS of the *Waffen SS*. There were even renegade Sikhs of the 'Indian Legion', still wearing their turbans.

With them fled the 'collabos', the French, Belgian, Dutch and Luxembourg collaborators who, for personal gain and belief in Hitler's 'New Europe', had thrown in their lot with the German 'New Order'. In due course, they would be back as the founding fathers of the Common Market, those who survived. But now, watching them go, the Flemish peasants pretended to whet knives, and told each other with a wicked grin that, for them, it would soon be *'bijltesdag'* ('hatchet day').

27

Behind them came the victorious Allies, British, American and Canadian. The last two were divided into two armies: General Courtney Hodges' First US Army, and General Patton's Third Army. Now, after the crazy dash across France, their advance was starting to slow a little. Supplies – still being transported from the invasion beaches – were slow to reach them, and gas was running out. Nevertheless, the great armies, including Hodges' First which was advancing in a zone some sixty-five miles wide, were still on the move.

They had to be, for the Allied leaders were sticking to a strategy worked out long before D-Day. Its objective was to drive as speedily as possible for the borders of Hitler's Third Reich. Once there, they were to 'undertake operations aimed at the heart of Germany and the destruction of her armed forces'. For this to be accomplished, the Ruhr, the industrial heart of Germany, would have to be taken first. That would be followed by the capture of the enemy's 'political heart', Berlin. Back in the UK it had all seemed so easy. Now, with the German Army in the west in full retreat, it seemed even easier.

In the first week of September 1944 geography offered four exits from northern France. For the British and the Canadians the route selected was Flanders and the plain that stretched all the way to Germany in the north. To the south, Patton's Third Army had been allocated a route through the industrial region of Metz, Saarbrücken and on to Frankfurt – not the swiftest way to reach the Ruhr and Berlin.

Between these there was a central route through the Belgian Ardennes and into the German Eifel. This route could also be divided into two: on its northern flank General Hodges' VII Corps was faced with the relatively flat and unwooded terrain leading to the old Imperial German border city of Aachen. From here the Corps Commander, the bold and dynamic 'Lightning Joe' Collins, might well make the running and push straight across the Rhine to the Ruhr.

On the southern flank, below Collins' corps, there was General Gerow's V Corps. He was faced by terrain that was wooded and rugged all the way. It was basically a series of steep hills leading from Belgium and Luxembourg down to the German border rivers, Our and Sauer.

By the second week in September Gerow's three divisions – the US 5th Armored and the 28th Infantry, together with the veteran 4th Infantry, which had landed on Utah Beach on D-Day – were making good progress. Already the veterans and the thousands of reinforcements they had accepted into their depleted ranks since Normandy were talking of being 'home in the land of the round doorknob'[28] before Christmas.

Not all of them were in a hurry to go home now that the 'Krauts' were in full retreat and the fighting had slackened. The weather was fine, disciplined had relaxed, and there were easy pickings. There was plenty of booze and 'oo-la-la'. The locals were grateful, and the girls in particular were eager to express their gratitude in the most delightful and natural ways.

How could those excited young men, working their way, often half-drunk on alcohol and high spirits, down the forest trails towards the Reich, have known that they were on their way to their deaths? The war in Europe would not end that month, nor the next. It would, in fact, drag on for a further long and bloody *eight* months. This remote border area between Belgium-Luxembourg and Germany, of which most of them had never heard until a few days earlier, would be the setting for the most bitter fighting in western Europe. Before it was over, the 4th Infantry and their running mate, the 28th, would be decimated – not once, but twice. Before they cleared this forest and what lay waiting for them in it, it would be spring 1945. By then most of them would be dead, wounded, or mad.

On Monday 11 September 1944 one of the most famous Americans joined the chase. He was a writer familiar now to many people, as his face had appeared on the cover of *Life* magazine. With his New York GI jeep driver, a couple of French 'Irregulars', and Peter Lawless, a British war correspondent, the little band of civilians arrived in the Belgian border town of Houffalize, ten kilometres from the Reich as the crow flies. Here they paused on the high ground, drank the wine they had brought with them, and waited to see what would happen. In the warm September sunshine, they appeared to be what a 19th-century German observer might have called '*Schlachtenbummler*' ('battlefield tourists'), especially the big man in a helmet, who seemed to be their leader.

Middle-aged and heavily bearded, he looked like what one of his acquaintances called a 'khaki-clad teddy bear'. He mixed cocktails from the gin he carried in one water bottle at his ample waist and bitters from another bottle. It was still early, but that meant nothing; he regularly drank a bottle of champagne for breakfast.

This man's name was Ernest Hemingway, but he was known to his intimates as 'Papa', as if he had already reached his 'three score years and ten'. In fact he was 44. The years of dissipation had taken their toll – his juices, creative and sexual, had dried up. Despite the fact that he had a new mistress, fellow correspondent Mary Walsh, waiting for him back at the Hotel Ritz in Paris, he was impotent. His 'Mr Scrooby' as he called it refused to perform. Now the man who had been voted 'America's Most Popular Writer' the month before had come to the war. He was to join his favourite US infantry division, the 4th, otherwise known as 'the Ivy League', to report on the impending battle for Germany.

On this warm September day, as the last of the German V2 rockets to be launched from the area headed for the stratosphere above him, Hemingway, who had made 'battle' his 'speciality' (and how jealously he guarded that 'speciality'), drank his martinis and enjoyed the battle below from his ringside hilltop viewpoint. A small party of the 2nd SS, 'Das

Reich', retreating for the fortifications of their native country[29] a mere ten kilometres away, had decided to make a last stand before the men of the 'Ivy League' arrived.

Their opponents were easy meat for the SS, veterans of Russia and the debacle in Normandy. They were Belgians of the Resistance's Armée Blanche[30]. Confident that they were moving into an open city, the Belgians were neatly trapped by the SS dug in round the cobbled main square.

It was over in a matter of minutes. Happily drinking on the heights above, imbued with that particular schadenfreude he had made his own, Hemingway and his companions enjoyed watching the Belgians 'ripping off their armbands' and 'fleeing for their lives'. The little skirmish over, the SS slunk away into the forest that lined the Luxembourg-St Vith road, just before Colonel 'Buck' Lanham's 22nd Infantry Regiment of the 4th Division arrived to inform the Colonel's crony Hemingway that on the following day the 4th would be 'the first American division to pass into Krautland'.

It was not to be. For a time Hemingway played his usual games, telling the locals that he was not a general (as they had assumed on account of his age and imposing figure), but a mere captain (he was not one of those either) 'because I never learned to read and write'. Other US troops had already crossed into the Reich twenty kilometres to the south.

On that same Monday afternoon, Lieutenant Vipond of the US 5th Armored Division's 85th Reconnaisance Squadron's Troop B had briefed one of his NCOs in Luxembourg. The 5th had liberated the little Grand Duchy within hours, hardly knowing they had passed through it. Now, high on the wooded heights above the Our river, Vipond told his staff sergeant, Warner L Holzinger, soon to return to the home of his forefathers, that if he wished to claim credit for being the first enemy soldier to enter Germany in wartime 'since Napoleon' a century and a half before, he had better hurry.

Already men of half a dozen US units were racing to claim that distinction. Indeed, the gunners of America's premier infantry division, the 1st ('the Big Red One'), which had fired the first shots of both World Wars, and had been the first to land in north-west Europe at 'Bloody Omaha', had achieved a first again. They claimed to have pumped the first shells into Germany in the region of Aachen.

As that September Monday drew to a close, and dark shadows raced down the tight, mysterious valleys like silent black hawks, Holzinger and his small band set off into the unknown. They came down the steep hillside from the road on the heights: one day the GIs would call it 'Skyline Drive'. They moved cautiously towards the Our. To their right lay the Luxembourg hamlet of Stolzembourg; to their left another hamlet,

Gmuend, on the German side of the river. There was no sign of life, not even a farm dog barking. The only sign that there ever had been life here was the little, blown 18th-century bridge spanning the fast-flowing, shallow stream.

For a while, the four Americans and the one French officer who had accompanied them as interpreter crouched on the narrow road that wound its way in and out of the valleys on the Luxembourg side. What went through their minds at that historic moment is not recorded. Perhaps they were preoccupied with thoughts of danger. After all, they were venturing – just the five of them – into Hitler's much vaunted '1,000-year Reich'.

In the end they decided to risk it. Holzinger led the way, wading into the shallows, his carbine at the ready. Behind him came Corporal Ralph Diven, T/5 Coy Locke, Pfc George McNeal and their French interpreter, Lieutenant Lille. But, though they eyed the cliff-like opposite bank continuously and nervously, nothing happened. Then they were on the track on the other side, wet to the hips and wondering whether they should press on to Gmuend. They decided they would, and it was only then that they discovered they had been standing directly in front of a cunningly camouflaged bunker, the slit in its zigzag-striped front overlooking the very spot where they had just crossed[31].

Now they began to find more and more bunkers. And it was no different once they had passed through an abandoned Gmuend and climbed the steep hill beyond it. On their right, the woods were full of them. Unwittingly these first GIs to cross into wartime Germany had stumbled into Hitler's West Wall – the notorious 'Siegfried Line' of 1939 – and it was completely, absolutely *empty*. The Germans appeared to have vanished off the face of the earth.

At the top of the hill, panting and puffing from the climb, the intrepid little patrol discovered another twenty or so pillboxes. They too were abandoned, and it was obviously a long time since they had been occupied. The dust was thick on the floor, and where there had once been machine-guns and cannons, there were now long-established spiders' webs. Round one bunker, a local farmer – now, like everyone else, long gone from that remote place – had built a chicken coop, and had made a well-worn path through the rusting, barbed wire entanglements.

By now it was getting dark and a chill wind was blowing across the bare heights above the Our river. Holzinger and his companions had no wish to linger in what they now realised was the Siegfried Line. The Krauts might come back[32]. Although they had been promised medals by Lieutenant Vipond if they brought back significant information, they valued their hides more. They beat it, back the way they had come, across the river and to the safety of Allied Luxembourg.

The American Generals had been competing to be the first to reach

31

Germany and 'the Line'. That night General Hodges' HQ proudly announced: 'At 1805 hours on 11 September a patrol led by Staff-Sergeant Warner L Holzinger crossed into Germany near the village of Stolzembourg, a few miles north-east of Vianden, Luxembourg.'

Later that same night, patrols from the 5th and 28th Divisions slipped over the Our at half a dozen places. A reinforced company of the 28th Infantry Division went over between the Luxembourg village of Weiswampach and the German village of Sevenig. They brought back some worthless German paper Marks, a farmer's black, peaked cap, and some German soil in bottles to prove that they had actually set foot on the sacred ground of the 1,000-year Reich. Perhaps today, more than half a century later, those bottles have pride of place on the mantelpiece of some suburban parlour – if, that is, their original owners lived to take them home.

While Hemingway watched and listened, Colonel 'Buck' Lanham organised a strong reconnaissance patrol from his 22nd Regiment to cross over into the Reich. It consisted of the 'scouts and raiders', plus two self-propelled tank destroyers and five jeeps. Their mission was to collect information about the enemy's defences, and a jar filled with German earth. This was to be sent to no less a person than Roosevelt (part of whose family had come from this very area[33]), the ailing President of the United States. The 4th Infantry Division had always had a keen eye for publicity.

The patrol set off. It reached the Luxembourg-St Vith road. Here it was in territory that had been German up to 1919 and had become German again in 1940. The men knew nothing of the complexities of recent European history, but one of them, Lieutenant George Wilson, did at one point notice a change in the expressions on the faces of the locals. The day before they had been greeted by cheering, warmly smiling civilians; today 'the faces by the side of the road grew much tighter and the smiles became rare. . . . Nearly everyone stared straight ahead with frozen faces, too afraid to look us in the eye.' The men of the Ivy League Division did not know it, but 27,000 of the males from this 80,000-strong German-speaking enclave of Belgium were currently serving in the German Army.

They left the road and started to descend to the Our river. The little convoy had got half way down the steep forest track that led to the tiny German hamlet of Hemmeres on the other bank, 'when there was suddenly a quick flash and a ripping explosion'. The railway bridge across the Our vanished[34]. Now the tank destroyers opened fire with their mighty 90mm cannon. The handful of 2nd SS left in the hamlet on the German side of the river started to retreat. Their half-tracks scuttled back and forth down the single, steep village street, picking up the infantry. The Germans were getting away.

However, the commanders of the two tank destroyers were more concerned with their own safety. They hesitated on the Belgian side of the river. Neither wanted to risk his vehicle in the shallow water. The Krauts could have laid mines in it. Lieutenants Manning and Shugart tossed a coin to decide who would go first. Shugart lost. Meanwhile they told a bespectacled officer named Dawson (who had thought he would never see combat on account of his poor eyesight) to go on ahead with the jeeps. As one of the few survivors of those first moments on German soil, Dawson long afterwards commented: 'The tankers and TD men argued that the jeeps were faster, more manoeuvrable – and more expendable. I didn't like that word "expendable".'

Still, Dawson was a good, steady officer. He pushed on with his little jeep force. Carefully, taking a handful of prisoners as they went, he crawled through the small border town of Bleialf, now virtually deserted, but soon to be the scene of months of bloody fighting, and on up the heights beyond. He stopped at the top and surveyed the valley below. It seemed empty. Then he spotted them, two German soldiers, busy chopping wood like boy scouts at some peacetime camp site in the forest. Just then it happened. 'One guy picked up an armload [of wood] and disappeared behind a door that seemed to open into the side of the hill.' Dawson was puzzled. Where had the German vanished to?

'I fixed my eye on the spot and saw the door open again. The man came out for more wood. Now I could clearly make out a mound of earth and the outline of a gun emplacement. This fortification was just across the valley and only about one hundred yards from the road. Suddenly my stomach turned a little, and I got a slight chill as I realised I might well be the first American to set eyes on a pillbox in the famous Siegfried Line.'[35]

A little while later Lieutenant Dawson was recalled, and his being the first to spot the Siegfried Line was forgotten. Credit for being the first on to German soil on 12 September went to 'another outfit in the 22nd Regiment. Unit pride was important in those days.'

It was. Captain Stevens, the 4th Infantry's PR man (the American Army had them even in those far off days), was quick off the mark in reporting the news. Under the headline, CRACKERS OF THE HINDENBURG LINE FIRST TO BREAK SIEGFRIED LINE, the US Army newspaper, *The Stars and Stripes*, reported: 'The US 4th Infantry Division, the first US Army outfit to crack the Hindenburg Line at Meuse-Argonne in the last war and first to enter Paris in this one, also was first to penetrate Germany through the Siegfried Line in force, it was disclosed today.'

In fact, Dawson in the van with his handful of infantry had not penetrated the Siegfried Line; he probably would not have lived to tell the tale if he had. But that Tuesday morning, 12 September 1944, his regimental commander, Colonel 'Buck' Lanham, was determined that the 22nd Infantry would do so – at the double.

'Papa' Hemingway, with his 'Irregulars' was determined to 'join in the fun'. In an article titled 'War in the Siegfried Line' that he wrote for

Collier's magazine on the exciting events of that day, he stated that, as Allied planes came zooming in at zero feet to strafe the retreating Germans, he saw 'two enemy half-tracks tearing up the white road that led into the German hills'. US guns began lobbing shells at them. 'You watched one half-track slither sideways across the road. The other stopped on the turn of the road after trying twice to move like a wounded animal. Another shell pounded up a fountain of dust and smoke alongside the crippled half-track, and when the smoke cleared, you could see the bodies on the road. That was the end of the rat race.'

Some time later Hemingway and the rest crossed the Our, 'brown over brown mossy stones'. It was 4.27pm and they had reached the hamlet of Hemmeres.

It was a typical, dirty, run-down Eifel village of the time, where the poverty-stricken farmers still ploughed using oxen. There was no running water, and typhoid was rampant in the summer. To Hemingway's eye, the people did not look any better than the place. 'Ugly women and squatty, ill-shaped men' came sidling up to the Americans bearing bottles of schnapps. As they approached, they drank some of the fiery, home-brewed spirit to prove to the '*Amis*', as they called '*die Amerikaner*', that the liquid was not poisoned. Not that Hemingway would have worried; he was well used to that sort of 'poison'.

Hemingway and his 'Irregulars' wasted no time. They commandeered what had been a farm-cum-post office (it is still there), built in 1732, and set to making themselves comfortable. That done, they invited Colonel Lanham and his staff to dinner, and Hemingway was going to ensure that his guests would not dine on the same C-rations they had subsisted on for weeks. He had 'liberated' (for which read looted) a score of the villagers' chickens. He shot the heads off the squawking fowl and ordered the first crone he saw to fricassee them for his guests. As always, Hemingway regarded all Europeans (except aristocrats) as servants, there to obey his commands. Naturally, the old peasant woman, in her drab, black, ankle-length dress, was in no position to defy him.

So it was that 'Buck' Lanham and his staff came to dinner in the tumbledown, dirty-white-painted, timbered, 18th-century house, whose roof sagged with age. They dined in style, for the time at least. As Lanham later recalled, there was 'chicken, peas, fresh onions, carrots, salad and canned fruit'. There was wine, good company, a few high jinks, common among soldiers, especially when they were with 'Papa', and relief that they had finally entered Germany without loss. It was a happy night. In Lanham's words:

The food was excellent, the wine plentiful, the comradeship close and warm. All of us were heady with the taste of victory as we were with the wine. It was a night to put aside the thought of the great West Wall, against which we would throw ourselves within the next forty-eight hours. We laughed and drank and told horrendous stories about each other. We all seemed at the moment like minor gods and Hemingway, presiding at the head of the table, might have been a fatherly Mars, delighting in the happiness of his brood.

Little did these young men, most of whom would be dead or wounded before the year was out, know that this the last happy day. Hitler's wall of death was waiting for them. Now the bad times were about to begin.

NOTES

28   In Belgium, Luxembourg and Germany, the doorknobs were square or wedge-shaped.
29   Not strictly true. One third of the division, responsible for the massacre in the French town of Oradour-sur-Glans, were Alsatians and former French citizens themselves.
30   'White Army', so called because of the white overalls dropped to them by the RAF and which they wore as a uniform.
31   The bunker and the trail are there to this day. Nothing much has changed in that zone of death since 1945.
32   An hour later, another patrol from the 5th Armored spotted Germans being dropped off from trucks in little groups to take over the long abandoned bunkers.
33   President Franklin Delano Roosevelt was in part descended from the Delannoy family who, as the de Lannoys, had held the castle at nearby Vianden in Luxembourg. Now rebuilt, the castle was defended against the Germans by GIs during the 'Battle of the Bulge'.
34   The unrepaired bridge is still there, a silent witness to the first crossing in force of the US Army into Germany in World War Two.
35   He probably was. George Dawson is long gone, but those pillboxes he spotted that September day still run the whole length of a German ski ridge, today called 'der schwarze Mann' ('the Black Man').

2

First Blood

Goddamit! Let's get those Krauts. Come on! Nobody's going to stop here now.

Colonel 'Buck' Lanham, 14 September 1944

On the evening of Wednesday 13 September 1944, Colonel 'Buck' Lanham, commander of the Fourth Division's 22nd Regiment, assembled his officers. The three battalion commanders and their staff met him in the one-horse German village of Schweiler, just across the border with Belgium. There in the hissing white glare of a Coleman lantern[36], the wiry, bespectacled West Pointer with literary ambitions briefed his officers. Hemingway, who had established himself and his little band of followers, looked on.

Lanham's scouts had discovered that the enemy held the 'Black Man' ridge some three miles from their position that evening. The ridge had become part of the Siegfried Line, as had the hamlet of Brandscheid to the right of the feature. Brandscheid – a church, an inn and half a dozen houses lying on a slight rise – was defended by eighty concealed bunkers, all difficult to attack. Indeed, by the time the US Army finally captured the wrecked hamlet, it would be known as 'the German Verdun', a place that had been taken and re-taken several times in the six-month battle for it.

Lanham's plan, to attack the Siegfried Line pillboxes on the 'Black Man' and then move right to Brandscheid and its pillboxes, was simplicity itself. His 22nd Regiment, of which he was so proud, would attack at 1000 the following morning. The Regiment would assault the positions in a column of battalions. The Third Battalion, under the command of the veteran Lieutenant Colonel Teague, was this time to jump off in a column of companies. Once they had broken through the Line, the other two battalions would move after them and complete the assault. As Lieutenant George Wilson, a 22nd veteran, wrote after the war: 'The vulnerable part of the pillbox was to the rear. The crossfire support did not reach back there, and all they had was some barbed wire and whatever rifles and machine-guns could be transferred to the rear trenches. The trick was to get behind the pillbox quickly.'

To Lanham it all seemed cut and dried. He hoped that after the breakthrough here in the Eifel, the whole division would be heading straight for the Rhine. The 'boys' would be 'home for Christmas after all'. But Colonel Lanham, who wrote poetry in his spare time, would not have been so sanguine if he had known what was waiting for him on the morrow.

Kampfgruppe Kuehne (Battle Group Kuehne), named after the man in command of it, was one of those ad hoc units that always seemed to have saved the Germans' bacon in desperate moments. It was a collection of young recruits, gathered from the Adolf Hitler Kaserne (barracks) in nearby Wittlich, and rushed to the front in the half-tracks of the 2nd SS 'Das Reich'. There they had occupied the line around Brandscheid and prepared to fight the first battle for Hitler's great war – and *nomen est omen*. In German *kühn* means 'bold', and Major Kuehne was a very bold commander. The men of the 22nd Regiment were heading for trouble.

At first things went well. Teague took his men forward from the hamlet of Buchet which was below the line of West Wall positions on the heights. His men of the Third Battalion took advantage of every depression and hollow, keeping away from the narrow, winding road that led up to the 'Black Man'. They were all heavily armed, with some of the GIs carrying specialised weapons: flame-throwers and satchel charges to be used in close combat. And all the while, the artillery kept throwing shells above their helmeted heads and plastering the German positions[37].

The Yanks got closer and closer. Was this going to be the walkover Colonel Lanham had promised? As Hemingway and the Colonel watched through their binoculars, there was no movement from the German positions. Perhaps Lanham was already planning his next move? Hemingway did not know. As usual, he was half drunk from the two canteens of looted German cognac he was now carrying.

Suddenly, startlingly, it happened. Even though they knew it might, the two observers were taken unawares as fire erupted from the German positions. Mortars howled – the characteristic throaty twang, followed by the obscene sound mortar bombs make when they come hurtling out of the sky. Moments later the German MG42 machine-guns joined in. The German 'stubble-hoppers' (infantry) called them '*Hitlersägen*' ('Hitler's saws'), and they did sound a bit like high-pitched saws as their slugs scythed through the air to left and right.

GIs started to fall. As Hemingway later described it for *Collier's*: 'They started coming back down across the field, dragging a few wounded, and a few limping. Then the tanks started coming back, and the TDs [tank-destroyers] and the ones whose men coming back plenty. They couldn't stay in that bare field, and ones who weren't hit started yelling for the medics for the ones who were hit and you know that excites everybody.'

Captain Howard Blizzard of the Third, watching the battle with the two older men, snapped, 'Sir, I can go out there and kick those bastards in the tail and take that place.'

Lanham shouted back over the racket, 'You're an S2 [operations officer] in a staff function and you stay where you are.'

Blizzard fell silent. But, as more and more started to drift back, he said half-aloud, 'We're going to lose this battle.'

Lanham must have felt the same, for suddenly he exclaimed, 'Let's get up there. This thing has got to move. Those chickenspitters[38] aren't going to break down this attack.'

The Colonel drew his .45. Followed by Blizzard, he moved forward to where some of his men were taking cover in a fold in the ground. 'Let's go up there,' he yelled, 'and get this place taken.'

Indulging in a little show of melodramatics, Lanham fired a couple of shots in the general direction of the German defenders. He thought that might encourage his reluctant heroes. 'Goddam,' he yelled against the high-pitched *burr-burr* of the enemy machine-guns, 'Goddamit! Let's get those Krauts. Come on! Nobody's going to stop here now.'

Lanham went on shouting, threatening and cajoling until his men rose and advanced up the body-strewn slope. Thereafter, the Third Battalion moved 'smoothly southward until they hit the heavily defended village of Brandscheid' as George Wilson recalled. Here Kuehne's men finally stopped them with the help of the 2nd SS and, as it was growing dark, Lanham told Teague to get his men to dig in. They would attack Brandscheid the next day.

Lanham did not know it then, but, as Wilson recalled, 'this little burg [Brandscheid] was circled by pillboxes and it was just not worth the cost of storming it'. Indeed, Teague's men would be attacking Brandscheid – without much success – for a further two weeks.

Hemingway did not mind. He had established himself in a rambling, early 19th-century farmhouse in Schweiler, just above the cobbled track that ran through the tumbledown village. As his billet, he had chosen the house of the richest farmer, Herr Margraff (a man who, before the war, had owned all of *fifteen* cows). Here in 'Schloss Hemingstein', the writer drank with his cronies, played poker, boasted (naturally), and told his tales of derring-do to anyone who would listen. There was a constant stream of visitors to the farm, from the 4th's Assistant Divisional Commander, General George Taylor, to the humblest GI autograph hunter.

What the old farmer (he was 73 at the time) made of Hemingway and his loud-mouthed, drunken companions is not recorded. But he was much concerned about the virtue of his 18-year-old daughter. American war artist John Groth, who spent a couple of weeks at 'Schloss Hemingstein', described her as a 'typical German peasant girl with a flat, red face framed by yellow hair', whose 'eyes were always afraid'. Her worried father knew why. Every night, when the GIs locked the Germans in their own barn, the daughter slept between her parents – just in case. Not that Hemingway himself would have posed any threat. 'Mr Scrooby' was still acting up[39].

Every morning when it was not raining, Hemingway left his 'billet' and jeeped up to the front, which had now become static, some three and a half miles away. It was almost as if he were going off to some dangerous job, from which he would return, completely unscathed, to the home comforts and jolly comradeship of his 'castle'.

By now the 22nd Regiment was tackling individual bunkers methodically, one by one, reducing them by the use of a violent and deadly (for both sides) system. The bunkers lent themselves to systematic treatment, as they all seemed to conform to the same design. John Groth described them:

> [They] had a roof of concrete six feet thick, the walls four feet. They had been equipped with air-conditioning and with three-tiered bunks. On the walls were posted warnings against smoking during the day or on clear nights, and against showing light near open doors or apertures. There were notices on how to seal them completely in case of gas alarms. Over the door was the nameplate that occurred in most: THIS PILLBOX WAS BUILT IN 1939 BY LEWIS WOERNER.

The destruction of Woerner's creations delighted Hemingway. It seemed to appeal to his taste for grand guignol and juvenile bloodlust. He described the capturing of one of them:

> The Krauts wouldn't come out when we talked to them, so we pulled the TD right up to the back of the steel door we had located by now, and that old Wump gun fired about six rounds and blasted the door in and you ought to have heard them wanting to come out. You ought to have heard them yell and moan, and moan and scream and yell 'Kamerad' . . . They started to come out and you never saw such a mess. Every one of them was wounded in five or six places from pieces of concrete and steel. About eighteen men came out and they got down on their knees on the road. They expected to get shot. But we were obliged to disappoint them . . . There were legs and arms scattered all over the goddam place.

Then, after witnessing another day of mayhem and slaughter, Hemingway would set up an impromptu bar with his two canteens of looted cognac and invite anyone available for a 'snifter', before returning to 'Schloss Hemingstein' for another evening of boozing and bragging.

But while Hemingway celebrated, enjoying the life of the ordinary 'dough' but without the unpleasant business of having to spend the night in a muddy foxhole alone and without 'classy chats about the cosmos', things were starting to go seriously wrong for Colonel Lanham's Regiment fighting the first battle of the Siegfried Line.

Already the 22nd Regiment had suffered 800 casualties. And Kuehne's men were resisting as fiercely as ever. Not only were the Germans hanging on to their West Wall positions tenaciously, but they were also counter-attacking. One *Kampfgruppe Kuehne* assault out of their pillboxes caught Lanham's 1st Battalion completely by surprise. Its commander, Colonel Dowdy, was killed in the attack and one of his companies retreated in some disorder, after suffering fifty percent casualties, and with only two company officers left on their feet.

The first cases of 'combat fatigue' – the term was a delightful euphemism for the terrible reality – made their appearance. Soon that affliction would be the major bugbear of the US Army in Europe that winter. The terrain, the weather, and the sheer tenacity of the Germans defending the Line soon started to take their toll. After the headlong flight from France of the *Wehrmacht* the month before, the average GI had not expected anything like this kind of bitter resistance from the enemy.

The US Defense Department's official history of the Siegfried Line campaign notes for 17 September, when the 1st Battalion under its new commander, Major Latimer, resumed its attack: 'Enemy shelling so unnerved several officers, including the Commander of the attacked tank platoon, that they had to be evacuated for combat exhaustion'; another shelling so upset the Company Commander (of 'A' Company) that he too had to be evacuated. 'The attack fizzled away to nothing.'

By Sunday of that week, Lanham's attack was effectively stalled. Casualties were mounting, the weather was getting worse, and so far his men had not gained any key roads leading beyond the Eifel and on to the Rhine. He ordered his First Battalion to pull back.

There was another consideration, or so it seemed. Colonel Lanham and his men believed they were being hampered by a lack of supplies. As Lieutenant Wilson put it: 'I found out later that we were really handicapped by a lack of supplies, having only enough gas to move each vehicle in the division five miles, and we had only one day's supply of ammunition.'

In the case of the 22nd Regiment, the men blamed Patton for the shortages. As Wilson stated: 'There were ugly rumours that Patton's Third Army was getting more than its fair share, sometimes even through pirating. It was also believed that the High Command favored Patton, not expecting that Patton would be stopped cold in the Metz-Nancy region.'

In his turn, Patton blamed Montgomery in the north for having hogged all the vital petrol, oil, ammunition and rations needed for the attack through the Siegfried Line and on to the Rhine. 'Ole Blood 'n Guts' was quoted as snarling that if he got the 'green light' from Eisenhower, 'I can go through the Siegfried Line like shit through a goose'. Instead, the key supplies had been given to that 'little fart Monty'.

After the war, it would be a major contention among American historians of the campaign in Europe that the war on that continent had not ended in September 1944 because Eisenhower had allocated the bulk of the supplies to Montgomery's abortive attempt to turn the flank of the Siegfried Line at Arnhem. If Hodges' First Army and Patton's Third had been given their heads – *and supplies* – they certainly would have done the 'ordure trick' and rushed the Rhine, Germany's last major line of defence.

But at the time things seemed very different. At Chartres on 2 September both Hodges and Patton maintained that they *could* drive into Germany with the tonnage of supplies they were receiving. 'We have an excellent plan,' Patton told Eisenhower, 'for a drive through the Nancy-Epinal Gap.' There was no suggestion that this drive might be halted due to lack of supplies. Indeed, both Hodges and Patton encouraged their corps commanders to keep up their drive towards the Siegfried Line. A week later, they were still doing so, and again there was no mention of supplies being diverted to Montgomery in the north, which might have halted their advance.

So what was happening with the vital supplies in that crucial third week of September 1944, when Patton and, in particular, Hodges and his First Army were finding it so difficult to crack the nut of the Siegfried Line, and Montgomery was about to launch his bold airborne invasion of Holland?

Both the Americans and the British were still being supplied from the Normandy beaches. All POL (petrol, oil and lubricants) was still flowing through the British PLUTO pipeline; and both Hodges' and Patton's armies were using that POL, brought up to the front by the 'Red Ball Express', a constant stream of trucks, driven by black drivers and each carrying five tons of supplies.

But what of the British? Were they too being supplied by the 'Red Ball Express', as American historians still seem to believe more than half a century later? In fact they were not. Instead, four days after Hodges and Patton reported to General Bradley on 12 September that both of their armies had sufficient gasoline and ammunition to carry them to the Rhine, British supplies were being delivered by their own 'Red Lion' convoys. And it would be these convoys that would supply Montgomery's Anglo-American airborne army in Holland.

The 'Red Lion' was organised by the British Army and was staffed by British drivers, except for those provided by eight American transportation companies. The 'Red Lion' performed a little better than the 'Red Ball', delivering 650 tons per convoy to the US average 500. In addition, the 'Red Lion Express' was quicker and more efficient, due to the fact that all of its supplies had been organised to be picked up from only *one* dump and to be delivered to only *one* dump, whereas the 'Red Ball' used several. The American official history states: 'Red Lion convoys exceeded their target . . . and handled a total of 18,000 tons. Almost half of this consisted of supplies for the two US Airborne Divisions participating in the Holland operations, a statistic often ignored by the partisans who so heatedly criticised this "diversion" of US resources. Furthermore, the operation took place *after* the pursuit had definitely been halted, and both the First and Third US Armies had come up against the prepared defense of the West Wall.'

So what was stopping Hodges' First Army, and farther south Patton's Third Army in this first attack on Hitler's Wall? Not a lack of supplies, nor the machinations of the little 'limey fart', Montgomery who was allegedly hogging the supplies. No. What was stopping the drive into Germany was simply the stubborn defence being put up by the Germans fighting from prepared positions on German soil for the first time. Hitler's 'white elephant' was paying for itself at long last.

On the Fourth Division's right flank in the Eifel, the US 28th Infantry Division was also making its first attack on the Siegfried Line out of Luxembourg. One of the three divisions of General Gerow's V Corps, part of Hodges' First Army, it was known as the 'Bloody Bucket', supposedly on account of its divisional patch, that did look like a bucket filled with blood. The thousands upon thousands of young men who served with the National Guard outfit in World War Two knew different. It had acquired that nickname because of its blood-soaked reputation for suffering horrific casualties. Twice in the eleven-month campaign in north-west Europe, it would have a virtually total turnover of personnel because of those casualties.

Now the two regiments of the 'Bloody Bucket' attacking (the 109th and 110th) faced some of the best German troops on the Western Front, the *Panzergrenadier Regiment der Führer* of the 2nd SS Division. The SS made the Americans pay heavily for every foot of ground won. On the first day of the American attack on the Siegfried Line, the SS stopped the enemy dead 700 yards from the first pillboxes. Towed tank-destroyers were brought up to blast the German-held bunkers. But, as one observer cynically remarked later, they did little 'but dust off their camouflage'.

Still the doomed young men of the 'Bloody Bucket' division continued their attack. They fought their way through minefields, covered by German mortars and machine-guns. The fields were littered with their bodies. The pitiful cry, 'Medic!' rose on all sides, and soon the aidmen too were suffering heavy casualties. Still the infantry fought on. They reached the first line of 'dragon's teeth'. One Lieutenant Joseph Dew, in an attempt to help the infantry, brought his Sherman to within a few yards of the obstacles. Although the German guns zeroed in on him, Dew stuck it out. With his 75mm cannon, he blasted a path clear through the 'dragon's teeth' and minefields, before scuttling rapidly to the comparative safety of the rear.

Again the infantry advanced. They moved forward slowly, bodies bent as if against a great wind. The Germans poured on their fire. Men went down by the dozen. Finally darkness fell and the attackers could go to ground – but not the SS.

That night Private Roy Fleming of the 'Bloody Bucket's' 110th Infantry was alerted by a sudden, strange lull in the nightly artillery fire. As he reported later to the regimental commander, Colonel Seely: 'Suddenly everything became quiet. I could hear the clank of these vehicles. I saw a flame-thrower start up and heard the sounds of a helluva scrap up around Captain Schultz's positions.'

A few minutes later, another company intercepted a frantic radio message in clear, not in code as was usual: 'King Sugar to anybody . . . King Sugar to anybody . . . HELP . . . We are having a counter-attack.' But before the Regiment could go to the aid of their comrades struck by a surprise SS attack, the noise subsided. Moments later the radio went dead.

Nothing was ever discovered about what happened to the Regiment's 'F' Company. There was a rumour that the SS had attacked with improvised flame-throwers mounted on half-tracks. But that was about it. Nearly 110 men had disappeared without trace. Even after the war, nothing was found out about them. But the fact that a whole company (quarter of a battalion) had vanished overnight took the heart out of the 'Bloody Bucket's' attack.

By 16 September the 'Bloody Bucket' had managed to push forward on a narrow front. There it had captured most of the high points, and so commanded the ground all around, even though the SS still held it. As the official history correctly states: 'Though the penetration was narrow and pencil-like, the 28th Division had for all practical purposes broken through the West Wall.'

But this was a pyrrhic victory. The 28th had lived up to its nickname. In a matter of a week, it had suffered 1,500 casualties, all riflemen. And riflemen were in very short supply that autumn. On the same day that the 28th broke through the Siegfried Line, General Gerow, the hollow-eyed commander of the V Corps to which the 4th and 28th Divisions belonged, ordered the offensive to be wound up. Both divisions, it seemed, were in no shape to continue the attack. In effect, the first sizeable American attack on the West Wall was coming to an end. As already suggested, the US top brass would later ascribe their failure to Montgomery and the lack of supplies. But the truth was different. Hitler's already obsolescent Wall, manned by determined men, had done the trick – it had stopped them. In the long bitter and bloody months to come, it would continue to do so until, in the end, the Supreme Commander, General Eisenhower, would despair of ever breaking through that 'damned Siegfried Line'.

Surprisingly, it was the secondary attack, carried out by Gerow's third division, the Fifth Armored, that proved the most promising. Supported by a regiment of infantry, the 112th Regiment of the 28th Division, the 'Victory Division', as it was known, had crossed the Our-Sauer rivers at the small town of Wallendorf. Here German resistance was minimal, and the enemy was taken by surprise.

The following morning, the Germans hurried a company of Mark IV tanks, supported by infantry, towards the river, where they bumped into American Shermans. For once, the Americans were quicker off the mark than the gunners of the Panzerlehr Division. One by one the men of the Fifth knocked out the first three Mark IVs. As one of the triumphant American gunners exclaimed, 'It was just like an old-style turkey shoot.' It was certainly too much for the remaining German tanks. They scurried for cover. The Americans did not hesitate. They pushed on into the unknown, heading for a feature known as 'Dead Man's Creek'. By nightfall they were six miles inside German territory, the Siegfried Line well behind them.

The news that the 'Amis' had broken through at this remote border spot threw German higher HQ into a panic. By chance, Fifth US Corps had picked the place where two German armies met. Now the battle would be conducted by two German higher HQs, Field Marshal Model's Army Group B and General Blaskowitz's Army Group, who were some 150 miles from each other.

The veteran Field Marshal von Rundstedt, now 69, given to drink, and far away at his own HQ near the *Autobahn* above Koblenz, was shocked when he heard the news. He called General von Knobelsdorff, who was in charge of the area, personally and rasped in that harsh Prussian voice of his: 'How is it possible that the Americans could break through [the West Wall] like that?'

The Commander of the German 1st Army stuttered, 'They crossed the Sauer in tanks and used flame-throwers to block the pillboxes' slits and smoked the defenders out. They weren't very experienced.'

Von Rundstedt was not interested in the fate of those inexperienced stubble-hoppers. He snapped, 'But only eight US tanks have been reported.'

Von Knobelsdorff agreed, but said, 'Others have crossed since.'

The fact that the Americans were reinforcing this minor thrust worried the veteran commander greatly. He realised something, which at the time the Americans perhaps did not. If the 'Amis' managed to break out of their little bridgehead, they might well advance on Bitburg, the county town only twenty miles away. Here they could make use of the road network out of the Eifel and on to the Rhine. And that could spell disaster[40].

A now greatly worried von Rundstedt decided to take personal control of the whole operation. So it was that General Oliver, commander of the

5th Armored, confronted in battle no less a figure than Germany's most renowned field marshal in World War Two.

While Rundstedt sought *den Knueppel aus dem Sack zu holen* (to pull the club out of the sack) as he put it, and launch a massive counter-attack on the unsuspecting 'Victory Division', the local German commanders threw in what reserves they could find.

Another Alarm Battalion Trier[41], commanded by a former Catholic priest, Captain Karl Kornowski, was rushed to the Sauer front. At the first village they came to, a defeatist fellow priest advised Kornowski to 'take off your grey uniform and put on your priest's robe', in other words, desert. Kornowski replied, 'It's too early for that.' And so he went to the front.

But he had great difficulty finding it. He came across a major cowering in a foxhole. Kornowski asked where he was supposed to attack. The frightened major did not answer for, as the ex-priest put it contemptuously, in terms not normally expected from a man of God, 'He was too busy crapping his pants to show us.'

Finally, however, he found it at Dead Man's Creek. The mixed battalion of dodgers, ex-deserters and defeatists was pushed into action by the forceful priest. They succeeded in recapturing eight bunkers. Then their luck ran out. Kornowski was ambushed and captured. Taken back to Wallendorf, where his possessions were, as he put it, 'looted', Kornowski first had to surrender his precious bottle of schnapps. 'First, I had to take a slug to prove it wasn't poisoned, then it went the round of the victors' throats. But they did give me back my tobacco pouch, rosary and picture of the Virgin Mary. Nice of them!'

Perhaps the ex-priest's comment was meant to be sarcastic. But at least he survived to be a parish priest in the Eifel for the next forty years. Ironically, several of his parishioners were Americans stationed at the nearby US Air Base at Bitburg.

Now von Rundstedt piled on the pressure. He threw in the remnants of two infantry and one armoured division on the Americans' right flank. On the left he attacked with an armoured division and an armoured brigade, while the point of the 'Victory Division's' advance was held by another infantry unit. These divisions were largely the survivors of the ones that had fled France the month before, but they still outnumbered the Americans. And due to the increasingly bad weather in that third week of September, Oliver, commanding the 'Victory Division', could not call up air support as often as he wanted to.

The Fifth Armored Division's situation worsened rapidly on 19-20 September, when General Gerow, V Corps commander, ordered the Division and the US 110th Infantry to begin a planned withdrawal. The Germans, sensing victory, intensified their attacks on the American flanks. The remaining twenty-five tanks of General Bayerlein's *Panzerlehrdivision*, plus infantry, were thrown into the attack. They were covered by twenty-five *Luftwaffe* fighters, which swept in at tree-top height, cannon and machine-guns pumping sudden death. Bayerlein ('an old hare' as the Germans called their veterans) had fought in France, Russia, Africa and France again. He was a master of his metier. His tanks took on double their number of American Shermans and forced them back. After the day-long tank battle, sixty wrecked Shermans dotted the battle area along with all of Bayerlein's remaining tanks from the debacle in France. They had been knocked out too. But he had won. The 'planned' American withdrawal turned into something of a panic-stricken flight.

Hidden in a barn in the hamlet of Nausbaum, and peering through a slit in the blackout shutter, Hermann Puetz watched the '*Amis*' depart. 'They had already whipped down the cooks' tent. Most of the infantry had vanished too. As our tanks rumbled ever closer, they'd had enough. They abandoned the rest of their gear, took their hind legs in their hands and fled.'

They did, almost everywhere. But in the triangle of the three villages of Gentingen-Kewenig-Wallendorf, the men of the 'Victory Division' hung on grimly to their bridgehead – virtually to the bitter end. On 22 September American infantry attacked on a key height, named Romersberg, time and time again. The first assault was made in thick fog. Just when it seemed they might make it to the top, the fog lifted. Immediately German artillery took up the challenge. Their shells bombarded the open fields below. The Americans reeled back. But half an hour later they came again. Again they were thrown back. Soon the slopes were littered with their khaki-clad bodies. But still they attacked again, five times in all. In the end they gave up and the jubilant Germans took over the pillboxes of the Siegfried Line that the Americans had captured. It is recorded that on that day an American captain stripped off his uniform and fled back to Luxembourg in civilian clothes.

The victorious Germans had a field day. There was loot to be had, the like of which they had not seen for many a day – Hershey chocolate bars, Virginia cigarettes, *real* coffee in place of the usual ersatz junk, known contemptuously by the German soldier as 'nigger sweat', even drink (US officers got a special monthly ration of hard liquor). Further back the men of the 'Poison Dwarf's' Propaganda Ministry celebrated this first German West Wall victory too.

They used the recapture of a dozen or so German villages, and what had happened there during the '*Ami*' period of occupation as a warning to the German people of what would happen if the enemy broke through the West Wall again and overran the Reich. Under alarmist headlines, such as THE RAPED VILLAGE and WOMEN AND CHILDREN USED AS HUMAN SHIELDS, the propagandists in Berlin detailed how 'the swineish Americans' aided by 'Belgian, Polish and Luxembourg criminals', had mounted 'a reign of terror'.

Using 'chocolate as bait', they had beaten 'a mother in the Hamlet of Kruchten senseless' and had then stolen her four infants. Why was never explained. Wallendorf had been the target of '*Amis* who were trained arsonists'. In vain the local citizens had pleaded on their knees for mercy. But the '*Amis*' still set every house in the riverside village alight, crying 'this is what we'll do with every German village we capture – burn it to the ground'.

It was clear that the war was entering a new phase. During the retreat from France, the more fanatical Nazis had refrained from reprisals – they had been afraid of retribution if they lost the war, which then looked likely. Now they had achieved their first victory on German soil. They had thrown a whole American corps (some 40-50,000 soldiers) out of their positions on the Siegfried Line. The '*Amis*' could be beaten, as long as the will to fight was there. At last the gloves were off.

On that same 22 September 1944, when the remnants of the 'Victory Division' withdrew across the Sauer to lick their wounds, a kind of uneasy peace fell over the Ardennes. This would last until the enormous tragedy of the following December, when the Germans retaliated.

At dawn a group of heavily armed SS men, under the command of a hard-faced 'old hare' (veteran), appeared suddenly out of the early morning mist on the other side of the Our at the Luxembourg hamlet of Kalborn. It was obvious that they had crossed by boat during the night. Now, before the slow-witted villagers could react, the menfolk were rounded up by the SS in their camouflage tunics, and with stick grenades thrust down the sides of their jackboots. The captain mustered his prisoners, then bellowed, '*Habt ihr Waffen*? (Have you got weapons?). '*Nein*' (No) came the reply.

Naturally the villagers were lying and the SS officer knew it. Behind his back, the women were signalling to their menfolk. They had hidden the handful of antiquated hunting rifles in the straw in their barns.

'You know what happens to people who lie?' the SS officer threatened. Then he yelled an order, '*Los!*' (Go!). His men shouted and started to drive the villagers down the little cobbled street towards a large pond. Most of them did not reach it. A machine-gun swung into action. At that range the gunners could not miss. Villagers, hurt and unhurt, went down in a chaotic, confused mass of flailing arms and legs.

But the drama was not yet over. From the village of Heinerscheid, farther up the hilltop road that the GIs would later call 'Skyline Drive', two youngsters appeared. They were paying a quick visit to their home village to feed their animals. Unfortunately for them, one wore the badge of the Belgian Resistance, and the other carried a revolver at his hip.

Swiftly the SS sprang into action. They disarmed the boy, who whispered to his companion, 'I think I am going to be shot.' He was right. Just as the pair reached the pond, the SS opened fire again. The kid who had carried the revolver slumped over a barbed wire fence, dead.

At that same moment an unsuspecting American jeep came trundling down the slope into the village. The SS swung round, weapons at the ready. The jeep driver saw them too late. An SS man gave him a burst with his Schmeisser. The windscreen shattered into a shining spider's web. The driver gave a shrill scream. The jeep ran into the kerb and came to an abrupt halt, the dead driver sprawled over the hood. Behind him his two passengers raised their hands in surrender.

The SS acted with some urgency. They believed they had been detected. They looted their two prisoners, snatching their cigarettes and other valuables. Then, as an afterthought, they ripped off their dogtags – something no one could explain until much later. But by now it was too late to react to this surprise raid from the nearby Siegfried Line, and all the others that followed during the weeks to come, when the Ardennes had become the 'Ghost Front'[42]. Then the SS were away, doubling back down the river bank, seeking the safety of the hamlet of Dahnen and the protection of Hitler's Wall.

NOTES

36 The place had no running water or electricity. It only acquired both comparatively recently.

37 To this day they can be seen between the ruins of the bunkers. In the depths of the wood, the 'battlefield tourist' can find old, rusting US rifle grenades and jagged, dangerous-looking fragments of those self same shells.

38 Naturally, he did not use the term 'chickenspitters', but *Collier's* was a family magazine.

39 When, a few years ago, the author asked this woman if she remembered Hemingway, she in turn asked if he had been 'a comrade' of his. So much for the average German's knowledge of America's Nobel Laureate.

40 In fact, it was from Bitburg that Patton started his armoured thrust to the Rhine six months later. His 4th Armored covered the ground in exactly fifty-two hours.

41 An ad hoc military formation, formed from whatever men were available.

42 So called because it seemed that nothing happened.

3

Stalemate

'Im Westen nichts neues' (In the West, nothing new)

Standard German Army daily communique, late autumn 1944

Now it was October, nearly winter. The pine-crested ridges of the Eifel-Ardennes were wreathed in mist. Much of the time a steady, grey, cold drizzle fell. Mournfully the raindrops dripped like tears from the trees. Often there was no other sound.

In a long stretch of the front opposite the Siegfried Line, from Echternach in the south to Monschau in the north, nothing happened. From time to time there was an apparently unnecessary German raid across the river. One day three doctors disappeared; all that was found of them was their uniforms next to their abandoned and wrecked jeep; a battalion commander was snatched; sometimes the Germans simply sneaked into the border farms, to sleep with the local women – or so US Intelligence thought.

To the south in the Saar, General Patton, who had boasted that he would go through the line 'like shit through a goose', had still not reached it. He was bogged down in the fighting around the Lorraine town of Metz. To the north, the US premier division, 'the Big Red One' (1st Infantry Division) were still fighting bitterly from street to street in the old German city of Aachen. Nowhere was much progress being made. The steam had gone out of the initial American attack. The Siegfried Line defences were becoming more formidable by the day. There seemed to be no way of breaking through the fortifications without employing major resources; and the manner in which Eisenhower had spread his troops over a front from Switzerland to southern Holland militated against this.

Along the 'Ghost Front', tours in the line were reminiscent of those in quiet sections of the trenches in France during World War One. The planners' greatest concern was how to get the troops into the line safely, not what they would do once they were there. Captain Charles MacDonald, who would one day be the doyen of military historians specialising in 'America's 20th-century Gettysberg' (the approaching 'Battle of the Bulge'), recalled 'going up' on the 3rd of the month:[43]

Our truck convoy wound its way back through the thick forest into Schoenberg the next morning and out again over the highway leading east. As we neared the German border, the road began a steep ascent into the mountains to our front. A big white signboard with glaring letters told us what we were near. YOU ARE NOW ENTERING GERMANY, AN ENEMY COUNTRY. BE ON THE ALERT.

Now the 'new boys' left their trucks and marched. A guide told MacDonald to remove his captain's silver bars, something unthinkable in the British Army, or he might attract snipers. Then the 22-year-old captain, who had never been in action before, saw the West Wall for the first time:

We crossed a slight knoll and the anti-tank wall of the Siegfried Line came into view. It looked like a prehistoric monster coiled around the hillsides; the concrete dragon's teeth were like scales upon the monster's back – or maybe headstones in a kind of crazy cemetery.

Now they ran over some broken ground until the 'new boys' finally reached their position – a farmhouse set right inside the Wall just below the 'Black Man' positions:

We found the company commander in a small low cellar illuminated only by a dim kerosene lamp that needed its shade washing. There were men in every conceivable sleeping position all over the floor . . . When we reached the light of the first floor, I saw the lieutenant's eyes were bloodshot and half a week's beard covered his face. His voice trembled when he talked, and he would start at the slightest noise.

Captain Charles MacDonald of Company I, 23rd Infantry, 2nd Infantry Division was 'in the line' for the first time. It was to change his life.

Surprisingly, the 2nd 'Indianhead' Division (so called for its divisional patch) and the other US divisions entering the Siegfried Line that October were not thrown into life-or-death combat as many of the men had feared.

As already mentioned, the fighting had virtually ceased. Even the static warfare that they, the 'new boys', might have anticipated was reduced to not very energetic patrolling to within a thousand yards of the German-held pillboxes of the West Wall. The American brass appeared to reason that their patrols did not stand a chance of penetrating the maze of barbed-wire entanglements, minefields and forward German infantry positions defending the enemy's main line of defence. Why waste precious infantrymen's lives? Leave intelligence gathering to the high-altitude reconnaissance flights that photographed the entire length of the Siegfried Line every day. If the Germans were planning anything behind their fortifications, the 'flyboys' would find out about it.[44]

Instead of fighting, the GIs spent cold, boring days improving their billets, keeping warm, and dreaming up new ways of preparing their 'K' and 'C' canned rations. An unfortunate few were housed in foxholes that functioned as a home, a defensive position, a latrine (when under constant enemy shelling), even as a grave. But the majority lived in wooden 'squad huts' made from the plentiful timber of the Eifel-Ardennes. Little by little, refinements were added, such as iron stoves, and bedding looted from the abandoned houses. One later described his 'squad hut': '[there were] bunks, blankets and a wood-burning stove . . . It was like being in a boy scout camp, not the front line.'

With time on their hands, the cooks prepared good meals, often baking cakes from a range of canned goods, and preparing roasts from the plentiful game of the area. There were even women available, or so it was rumoured. One excited teenager reported to his comrades that during his wanderings (soldiers have always been great 'wanderers' in such situations), he had come across a small, isolated artillery outfit that 'kept a broad – a *private* broad'. According to this soldier, the gunners had chipped in 'forty bucks' a week, and on pay day, the 'broad' would come secretly into the line and 'service them guys, one by one'. He had thought of 'chipping in to buy a piece of the action', but had decided against it. After all, the woman was their 'private' broad.

But all was not sweetness and light on the Siegfried Line. At both ends of the long, static front, US casualties were mounting rapidly, both in the US VII Corps attacking Aachen on the First Army front and Patton's two corps assaulting Metz in the Third Army area to the south.

Daily, the 'meat wagons' would arrive at the new US military cemeteries at Henri-la-Chapelle in Belgium and Epinal in France, skidding and bouncing their way down the muddy, rutted tracks with their cargoes of dead GIs. Hastily the 'stiffs' would be unloaded, without much dignity, for there were more to be transported away from the front. It was Army policy to dispose of the dead as quickly as possible; they had served their purpose, and the sight of their bloody, shattered bodies did nothing for the morale of the living.

The 'sorting sergeants' would go to work on the corpses. Expertly, the NCOs would slit the dead man's uniform up both sides and pull out what possessions remained with the body. Personal effects were placed in a little canvas bag to be sent home to the next of kin. 'Dirty' French postcards, condoms, anything that might offend the dead soldier's grieving relatives were got rid of.

Next came the dogtags. One was cut off to be sent to the Graves Commission staff in the rear; the other was placed in the dead man's mouth and the jaw firmly closed. This would assist any further identification at a later date.

It was not always easy. Many of the bodies were mutilated. Parts had been blown off by shells or mines. These terrible 'X bodies', as they were called, were hated by the men who worked on them. Often they stank. Sometimes they moved and twitched, the guts still rumbling as the gas generated by their last meal escaped.

If an 'X body' still had a head, the sergeant on the 'stripping line' had to force open the jaw to make a dental identification chart, based on induction records. If there was no head, but hands, the icy, cold, dead fingers were injected with a special fluid to bring the whorls on the tips into relief. This allowed fingerprints to be recorded – a nauseating task.

On occasions both head and hands were missing. Then, the corpse became that of 'an unknown American soldier'. In time, before the terrible Siegfried Line campaign was over, there would be thousands of 'unknown American soldiers' in the cemeteries springing up everywhere behind the Eifel-Ardennes front.[45]

But the living, those young men who might themselves soon be brought in as 'stiffs' in the 'meat wagons' could not allow themselves to be weighed down by thoughts of their dead comrades. They felt an overwhelming, almost electric, desire to live and enjoy life while there was still time.

Showered and shaved, with the stink of death and mud eradicated from their uniforms, they would take the 'deuce-and-a-half' (two-and-a-half-ton truck), that would carry them from the killing fields for a seventy-two-hour pass in the fleshpots of Belgium, Luxembourg and Paris. There, what they called the 'feather merchants' awaited them – organisations whose primary task was to maintain the morale of the fighting soldier.

Rest camps had been established, where the front-line troops could shower, sleep and relax. There were 'donuts and Java' (doughnuts and hot coffee), as much as they wanted; shows from the States; even 'spelling-bees' and ping-pong. But the men from the front did not want ping-pong, and they did not on the whole like the 'feather merchants' who would never have to lay *their* lives on the line.

They wanted 'booze and broads' in that order. At the front they were condemned to short, brutish lives. Doughnuts and coffee were not enough. As General Patton put it (and he, like most of the top brass, including the Supreme Commander, kept a mistress for most of the campaign): 'The man who won't fuck won't fight.' These men, for whom time was probably running out fast, were certainly ready to do that.

Drunk, and their back pay bulging from the pockets of their 'Ike blouses', they cruised the blacked-out streets of the major cities, looking for the whores, amateur and professional. These, for the most part skinny and dressed in jackets made from rabbit fur or black market GI blankets, offered their undernourished, sometimes raddled bodies for sale in doorways. At night they pressed their blue-disked flashlights against the base of their stomachs to advertise exactly what was on offer.

Not surprisingly, what was then called a 'social disease' was endemic. Men who had unprotected sex and caught VD were often punished with imprisonment in the stockade. But riflemen were in too short supply to have them confined. The new wonder drug, penicillin, was used in great quantities and cured the disease in a matter of two to three days. Then the unfortunate soldier faced the terror of what they called the 'umbrella' – a catheter that could be opened inside the penis so that its sharp plates could clear away any lesions. After that, as the GIs put it, 'you pissed blood in ten different directions' for a few days.

In October 1944 Ernest Hemingway had returned from his stay with the 4th Division in the Siegfried Line to his 'headquarters' in the swish Hotel Ritz in Paris which, naturally, he had personally liberated the previous August. There he entertained the 'Kraut' (Marlene Dietrich) and four of 'Buck' Lanham's battalion commanders on leave in the French capital, together with his new love, fellow correspondent Mary Walsh.

At first the young majors were very restrained. Awed by having the star of 'The Blue Angel' and 'Destry Rides Again' in their midst, they behaved themselves. Politely one of them asked Dietrich if she would pose with him for a photograph. She agreed to do so on the hotel bed so that he could send the photo to the States 'to impress the folks back home'. 'Warily,' as Mary Walsh recalled, 'the blushing officer arranged himself as stiff as at attention beside her.'

By the time they came to eat, they were mostly drunk – 'eyes were becoming glazed and speech a bit slurred'. One of the young infantry officers found himself next to Clare Booth Luce, a self-opinionated Congresswoman, wife of the owner of *Time Life*, and Mary Walsh's boss. Luce told the drunken officer that she was impressed by the work of the Army Air Corps in the current campaign and suggested – stupidly in that company – that in Belgium and Germany surely the infantry had to be 'of some use'.

'You're darned right, babe,' one of the 4th Division's officers snarled. 'And don't put your mouth on it.'

'The infantry,' the misguided Congresswoman persisted, not noticing the danger signs, 'they pinpoint the advance, don't they?'

'Pinpoint it? Sweet Jesus,' the officer exploded. 'You ought to read a book you dumb broad. What are you doing here anyway?' Thereafter, he seemed too drunk or preoccupied to listen to whatever answer she gave to his question.

That night Mary Walsh took Hemingway to task about his guests. 'Your friends are drunks and slobs,' she raged at him. 'They threw up all over my bathroom. They probably lost me my job. They drove Marlene away. They may be heroes in Germany, but here they stink, stink, stink!'

Hemingway, voted the USA's greatest writer the previous August, punched her.

But, just like Hemingway's 'drunks and slobs', the men mostly went back. Their pay gone, heads throbbing, hollow-eyed and morose, they wondered whether they were taking a little 'souvenir' with them in the form of 'gontac' or 'siff'. Sick of the 'feather merchants', the 'canteen commandos' with their 'donuts and Java' they headed for the cleaner air of the front and those killing fields. And there it would be waiting for them in those sombre-green, wet-dripping ridges and silent fields – Hitler's Great Wall of Germany.

In the only novel he wrote based on his experiences in Europe in 1944-45, *Across the River and into the Trees*, Hemingway made his protagonist, Colonel Richard Cantwell[46], explain what happened next in the Siegfried Line that early winter. Cantwell's account is bitter, confused and naturally 'faction', but Hemingway did succeed in depicting the situation better than any subsequent military historian. Here is Cantwell speaking:

> General Walter Bedell Smith [Eisenhower's Chief of Staff] explained to all of us how easy the operation that later took the name of Hürtgen Forest would be. . . . In comes the General [Eisenhower]. He is no pistol-slapper, but a big businessman: an excellent politician, the executive type. The Army is the biggest business, at that moment, in the world. He takes a half-assed pointer and he shows us, with complete conviction, and without forebodings, exactly what the attack will be, why we are making it, and how facilely it will succeed. There is no problem.
>
> This high pressure salesman, and I say this with no disrespect, but with admiration for all his talents, or his talent, also told what we would have of the necessary. There would be no lack of anything.

For the 'factional' Cantwell, acting as Hemingway's mouthpiece, there was only one fly in the ointment as Eisenhower, in the guise of the 'big businessman', explained this new plan to break through the Siegfried Line. The Army would attack 'to the east of Aachen, a distance of some 380 kilometres from where they [HQ] were based'.

> An army can get to be huge; but you can close up a little bit . . . I understand the necessity of the big executive being removed from contact with his working people. I understand about the size of the army and various problems. I even understand logistics, which is not difficult. But no one commanded from that far back in history.

Hemingway had Cantwell call a coming battle in the West Wall 'Passchendaele with tree bursts'. For once, despite the cynicism, the bitterness and the hyperbole, Hemingway had got it right. That was what it was going to be for thousands upon thousands of GIs who would die there (more than in the whole of the Vietnam war). 'Passchendaele with tree bursts', though neither they nor their masters called it that. The brass gave the place and the battle the neat, tidy, non-emotive name 'The Battle of Hürtgen Forest'.

The apprehensive GIs, division after division of them, waiting there to go into the attack, called it more dramatically, but truthfully, the 'Death Factory'. And for the few correspondents who ventured up there to report on it (very few did; it was a battle that could not be won and, besides, even news correspondents got killed there), it became the 'Green Hell of the Hürtgen'.

The forest lies just south of Aachen. It is twenty miles long and ten miles wide. Riven by steep gorges, the sides of which are thick with pines and firs, it is an easy place in which to get lost – even today, when there are marked trails (courtesy of the various local tourist boards) everywhere.

It is the kind of place that is a little frightening, associated with those dark, unpleasant, so-called 'fairy tales' collected by the Grimm Brothers in the 19th century. Indeed, an imaginative type might be inclined to drop a trail of things behind him in the woods to mark his path, just as Hansel and Gretel did in the hope of finding the way home, but instead coming upon that dreadful *Pfefferkuchenhaus* with its cannibalistic witch. In October 1944 there were plenty of bodies lying in those woods to satisfy that horrid creature's craving for human flesh.

The Battle of Hürtgen Forest had begun in September. By then General 'Lightning Joe' Collins' VII had succeeded in breaking through the first line of defences in the West Wall around Aachen. But once through, Collins' infantry and armoured had become bogged down; the cocky Irish-American General's drive for the Rhine had become sticky and slow.

He had tried a new tack. He would attack through the forest, even though it had Siegfried Line defences to both front and rear, and head for the Rhine, leaving Aachen to be dealt with at his leisure. That had been the plan, but it turned out to be far from easy.

Collins had ordered General Craig, commanding the veteran 9th Infantry Division, to start the ball rolling by sending one of his regiments into the attack. They would have to attack through the first line of West Wall defences, but, Collins reasoned, once they had broken through, the advance through the forest, which the Germans did not seem to be defending in any strength, would not be difficult.

In the event, it had taken five solid days to take the first pillboxes. One of them, Bunker 116, located at a feature known as '*Ochsenkopf* (Ox-head)'[47] would cost nearly a whole battalion of infantry, killed, wounded and captured, before it was finally taken. For five days the 9th, attacking from the direction of the Eifel village of Zweifall, battered its head on the German defences. Unable to manoeuvre in the tight confines of forest trails and fire-breaks, covered by mines and fixed-line machine-guns, the infantry took appalling casualties.

The last time American soldiers had fought under such terrible conditions had been in 1918 in the Argonne. They were totally untrained for this sort of combat. 'Then the enemy seemed to be everywhere,' a frustrated 9th infantryman told a correspondent, 'and in the darkness of the thick trees and the confusion, the firing seemed everywhere too.'

'If anyone – from private right on up to myself,' one company commander complained bitterly a few days before he was killed in action, 'said he knew where he was at any one time, he was a damn liar.'

Overnight, in order to survive, these GIs, trained only in attack, had to learn new techniques. If they did not, they might well be dead by the next day. The kind of foxholes they had dug until now were of no use. Here shells did not explode on the ground with the shrapnel flying upwards relatively harmlessly. Instead they burst overhead in the trees (they were known as 'tree-bursts'). Now the shrapnel showered downwards. So the GI learned to cover his foxhole with logs and sods, as the Germans did. If he did not, the foxhole might well become his grave.

Movement at night was taboo. In the confusion of the forest, both enemy and friendly formations fired first and asked questions afterwards. It was safer to stay put. If you felt the need, and did not have an empty shell-case to defecate into, you cleared your bowels in your foxhole. Better defiled than dead.

Right from the start of the six-month Battle of Hürtgen Forest, the hard-pressed infantry and their commanders longed fervently to escape the frightening, vice-like grip of the forest and its tightly packed trees. Here the most senior officer and the humblest doughboy felt like blind men. They craved open ground. But each time they managed to break out from the lethal, green embrace of the forest, they found their way barred by yet another hill and gorge in which the German Mark IV tanks and self-propelled guns roamed. And back it would be, in a panic-stricken flight for the cover of those damned trees.

The days blurred into one never-ending hell. No one noted the passage of a single day any more. The slaughter and the misery went on relentlessly. Each dripping dawn among the shattered firs, with the trees snapped like matchsticks, brought new replacements – bug-eyed young GIs who had barely started to shave. In clean uniform, even wearing neckties, weighed down like pack animals with their full equipment, they were assigned to platoons of men who did not really want to know them. They were death's men already. Inexperienced, they were lucky to last the day before a 'million dollar wound' or sudden death took them out of that terrible forest on a litter.

Even the Germans, more familiar with this kind of warfare after their experiences in the great forests of the Russian steppe, felt the horror of those killing woods. Colonel Wegelein, commander of a German battle group, Kampfgruppe Wegelein, was spotted by an American sergeant. He had left his foxhole, unarmed and accompanied only by his dog. The NCO promptly shot him dead. Swiftly he riffled the body and snatched the battle group's plans for a counter-attack that day.

Later, US Intelligence tried to deduce something about German morale from the dead colonel's strange behaviour. Why had an experienced senior officer, with five years' combat experience, and who had served in the German Army since 1921, been wandering around the forest in that way? Was he, too, perhaps sick of the wholesale slaughter? Had he been deliberately courting death as a way of putting an end to it all? Or had he simply lost his way?

They never came up with a satisfactory explanation. But what did it matter? Colonel Wegelein was just one of many. In the Hürtgen Forest the fate of individuals no longer counted. Wegelein followed the rest in the 'meat wagon' for that last journey to Henri-la-Chapelle and the new cemetery being opened at Margraten in Holland. The miltary undertakers were doing a roaring trade, at least. When the two regiments of the 9th Infantry Division withdrew from the battle of the 'Green Hell' in mid-October, they had lost half their strength. 4,500 men were killed, wounded or missing. The Americans estimated that the German defenders had suffered 2,000 casualties, with about 1,200 taken prisoner.

Had anyone won, an innocent observer might have asked, watching the bodies of dead Americans and Germans being piled up the whole length of Zweifall's Hasselbackstrasse, waiting for transportation to the rear through the West Wall breach.

Yes, would have been the answer. There could only be one victor this grey, wet October – the West Wall.

NOTES

43 MacDonald jealously guarded 'his' battle against other historians. Naturally, as an American he regarded the battles for the Siegfried Line as purely American affairs. Little reference is made in his books to the British, and when it is, scorn is usually poured on Montgomery and his 'tea-drinking soldiers'. But MacDonald had his defects; he was an 'official' government historian who did not know the people who lived in the border region, nor their history; he spoke none of the local languages and had to rely on partisan locals for assistance and guidance. In many ways he was given a false impression of the situation in the area in 1944-5. The result was something of a stereotype – brave Americans, treacherous Nazis, interfering British, and American generals fighting all comers to maintain the pride and prestige of the US Army.

44 For once the brass may have been right. Back in 1936 the locals were puzzled by German Army teams in civilian clothes who arrived with the reoccupation of the Rhineland. These teams explored every height in detail, then, when

satisfied, erected a large white stone (occasionally they can still be found to this day). These were 'trig points'. But from the positions erected later on these heights, the German defenders could survey every inch of ground, making it extremely difficult for enemy troops to penetrate the Line.

45 Even today, more than fifty years later, the authorities are still working on the identification of 'new' skeletons being found in the remoter forests of the Eifel-Ardennes.

46 The character was probably based on a mixture of Hemingway himself, Colonel Lanham, Commander of the 42nd Infantry Regiment, and a few officers the writer met during his time with the US 4th Infantry Division.

47 Today the ruined bunker is part of a peaceful parking lot next to the German country road L160, south-east of Aachen.

4

The Plotters

The whole art of war consists of guessing what is on the other side of the hill.

The Duke of Wellington

On the morning of 21 October 1944 Colonel Wilck, the Commander for the last seven weeks of the old Imperial German city of Aachen, made his decision. Earlier that Saturday morning, with an American 155mm blasting away at his HQ over open sights, he had sent a last radio signal to Field Marshal Model, Commander of Army Group B, responsible for the whole of the Siegfried Line almost as far as the French border. It had been a bold message, belied by the suffering all around him. It had read: 'All forces committed to the final struggle ... The last defenders of Aachen, mindful of their beloved German homeland and with firm confidence in final victory, donate 10,468 Reichsmarks to the Winter Help[48]. We shall fight on. Long live the Führer!'

Wilck had not meant a single word of that stirring message. But he knew it had to be sent if he were to save his wife, a hundred miles away in the Rhineland, from imprisonment in a concentration camp. Hitler had instituted *Sippenhaft* (arrest of kith and kin), under which the relatives of anyone who failed in his military duty could be arrested and punished in his place. Wilck did not want his wife to have to suffer for his failings.

At dawn Major Rink, a former theology student who had become a member of the elite 1st SS 'Adolf Hitler Bodyguard Regiment' and had been the backbone of Wilck's resistance in Aachen, had reported to Wilck. He had told the middle-aged colonel that he was not prepared to 'fight to the last bullet and last man', as Model had ordered. He and his survivors were 'going to do a bunk'. And that was that.

If the SS were prepared to desert the sinking ship, Wilck told himself, he would be justified in doing what he had been preparing for all this long, terrible week. In open and clear, so that anyone and everyone could hear it, Wilck dispatched a radio signal to his old division, the 246th Volksgrenadier. This stated: 'All ammo gone after severe house-to-house fighting. No water and no food. Enemy close to command post of the defenders of the Imperial City. Radio prepared for destruction. *Ende.'*

Five minutes later the radio went off the air for good, and in the suburbs German artillery shells started to fall on American soldiers and German civilians alike. Wilck knew that Model had given him up. It was time for him to surrender. But how?

Already two German officers, trying to surrender independently under a makeshift white flag, had been shot dead by the '*Amis*'. Perhaps that had been due to the terrible confusion of the street-to-street fighting outside his bunker. Or perhaps it was sheer bloody-mindedness on the part of the '*Amis*' who had lost 3,000 men in the battle for Aachen.

In the end Wilck asked for volunteers from the thirty or so POWs from the American 1st Division in the bunker. Two stepped forward, Sergeant Ewart Padgett and PFC James Haswell. They were each given a sandwich and a home-made white flag. At the door of the bunker an English-speaking officer wished them a hoarse 'Good luck'. Then they were on their own on the outside, blinking in the bright light after the gloom of the bunker.

Bullets started to cut the air all around them. Furiously they waved their white flag as if their lives depended on it – which they did. The firing stopped. A scruffy, unshaven rifleman eyed them suspiciously for a moment; then he waved them forward – slowly.

Two hours later it was all over. Aachen had surrendered at last, and across the border the Belgian newspaper *La Nation* headlined the event with the bold words AIX-LA-CHAPELLE N'EXISTE PLUS.

The officer who had received those final messages from Colonel Wilck, and would survive to tend his beloved rose garden on the Rhine into our own times, was Field Marshal Walter Model, about to become one of the key figures in the history of Hitler's Wall. Commander of the German Army Group B, he looked like the Hollywood stereotype of the Prussian officer – somewhat run to seed, arrogant in manner, a monocle screwed into his left eye, his cap at a jaunty angle. In fact, he was not from a long line of aristocratic Prussian military officers, Rather, he was the scion of three generations of music teachers, all pious Protestants, unwarlike and firmly middle-class. The community into which Model was born was far removed from those East Prussian estates, where the *Junkers* treated their farmworkers like serfs and which had traditionally produced Germany's officer class.

Despite his pious, middle-class upbringing, Model nevertheless displayed all the virtues and habits of that class. Unlike most of the American generals, against whom he would fight until his death, he had seen a lot of the war. He had been wounded in action four times, twice in World War One. On one occasion a bullet passed straight through his body. The surgeons pronounced him a 'medical wonder'. During its passage the slug had not touched a single vital organ. It was not long before, in his characteristic fashion, Model was making life hell for the doctors and nurses in attendance on him. He was impatient to return to front-line combat.

He was as ruthless as those old Prussians, too. Most of his staff officers hated him for his overbearing manner and incessant demands. When he departed for one of his rare leaves, his Chief-of-Staff gave out the signal, '*Schweinfurt*', a pun on the German city of that name, that could be translated as 'the pig's gone'.

One day in 1942, when the German Ninth Army had reached breaking point on the Eastern Front, Model arrived unexpectedly at Army HQ. Sporting a fur-collared greatcoat that reached his ankles, and with old-fashioned ear muffs sheltering him from the biting Russian chill, he flung his cap on the nearest chair and, ignoring the salutes of the surprised staff officers, he strode to a map of the front.

'Rather a mess,' he declared after studying it for a moment. He then proceeded to bark out a series of orders. The officers stared at each other in amazement. Where in the devil's name was Model going to find the men to carry out those orders?

Finally, Colonel Blaurock, the Ninth's Chief-of-Staff, plucked up the courage to venture: 'And what, Herr General, have you brought us for this operation?'

Model surveyed his new Chief-of-Staff quizzically through his monocle before answering, 'Why, myself!'

This answer was typical of Model's arrogant, overbearing vanity, which made him so disliked by his staff. He frequently threatened them with court-martial[49]. But if he was unpopular with some of his officers, he was widely liked by the ordinary 'stubble-hoppers', as the infantry called themselves. He spent up to eight hours a day at the front, sometimes taking over command of badly led battalions, even companies, when the situation had become 'ticklish'. Time and again between 1943 and 1944 he saved the front in the east from breaking down completely.

Although he hated the '*Monokelfritzen*', as he called his Prussian generals, Hitler thought highly of Model. He called him 'my fire brigade', sent to wherever a conflagration had broken out. He promoted him over the heads of more senior officers, to the extent that Field Marshal von Rundstedt nicknamed him 'the Boy Field Marshal'.

At his HQ at Munster-Eifel, Model, who had previously signalled Wilck in Aachen to 'fight to the last bullet . . . and allow yourself to be buried in the ruins', must have pondered his own position now that the Imperial City had finally surrendered. He probably realised that the enemy attack into Aachen had been a bad move on the part of the Americans. It had tied down a whole corps and allowed the West Wall to be got ready for what was to come – an all-out attack on the Line.

But for the time being, the Americans were wasting men and effort on comparatively useless attacks on the Hürtgen Forest and the Metz-complex to the south. To do this, they had replaced their experienced divisions facing the Wall in Belgium and Luxembourg with inexperienced ones (and soon also with those shattered in the Hürtgen Forest). Model must have concluded that there would be no danger to face from that quarter. Indeed, two months after it had seemed that the enemy would sweep unhindered through the West Wall, the Line was holding firm against elements of three American armies, with a new one, the US 9th Army, about to enter the fighting.

To Model's way of thinking, there was only one fly in the ointment – the 'Tommy', Field Marshal Bernard Law Montgomery. In the north, on the Dutch-Belgian border, the British were still licking their wounds after the debacle of Arnhem. But Model knew that the little British field marshal would not let matters stay as they were, even though winter was approaching. He would make another attempt to circumvent the West Wall, up there where the German defences ended. He would outflank it, just as the Germans had managed to do to the Maginot Line back in 1940.

By nature the British were slow-moving; they would take their time. But Model's Chief-of-Staff, the cunning General Westphal, who, alone of all his staff had fought Montgomery in the Western Desert under Rommel, had told him often that, although the Englishman took his time, he was very thorough – almost like a German. He would only strike when he was completely sure that he had the men and materiel to achieve victory.

On that Saturday in the third week of October 1944, Model must have told himself that a race to save the West Wall – and the Reich – was about to begin. If they were to be saved, Hitler would have to strike before Montgomery. But *where* and *how*?

On the day after Wilck's surrender of Aachen to the Americans, Generals Westphal and Krebs, both amongst the highest ranking staff officers in the *Wehrmacht*, were summoned to Hitler's remote, gloomy headquarters in East Prussia. The generals thought they had been asked to attend a routine briefing. They were in for a surprise.

Since the attempt on his life on 20 July 1944, Hitler was taking no chances with any of his generals, some of whom had been the moving force behind the assassination attempt. As soon as they arrived, Westphal and Krebs had their side arms taken from them. They were searched, as were their briefcases, then ordered (before they had even seen the Führer) to sign an undertaking binding them to the utmost secrecy – on pain of death. They were told bluntly that, if they revealed anything of what they heard that day, they would be shot without trial. Tamely swallowing this insult to their status as German officers, both men signed that they would never reveal the details of an operation coded '*Wacht am Rhein*' ('The

Watch on the Rhine'), named after a well known song from the jingoistic, monarchist period prior to World War One. Even as they signed, they must have wondered what all the fuss was about. The codename of the operation seemed to imply that this was to be a defensive move. Why should that be top secret? After all, both of them had been conducting a large-scale defensive operation in the West Wall since early September.

In due course Westphal and Krebs were summoned to the presence of the Führer himself. Hastily Hitler and his cunning, pasty-faced adviser, Colonel-General Jodl, set out the plan for 'The Watch on the Rhine'. It appeared to have been worked out in some detail by Hitler and his General Staff. Now he wanted the two staff officers to have their superiors, Field Marshals von Rundstedt and Model, prepare a strike force of thirteen infantry divisions, two parachute and six panzer divisions, some 250,000 men in all, to march west from the West Wall positions between Monschau and Echternach.

The aim was to split the Anglo-American armies, capture the key supply port of Antwerp, and put Britain (a country already scraping the barrel of her manpower) out of the war for at least a year. In that time, Hitler would, he maintained, achieve a separate peace with the West and be free to turn his full attention on the real enemy, Russia.

Hitler told the two shocked staff officers, who could not believe that at this eleventh hour a hard-pressed Germany could muster such a huge force, that everything depended on two things – secrecy and surprise. As soon as the Allies realised that he was going to attack through their weakly held 'Ghost Front'[50], they would rush in their reserves (the Americans had at least three divisions in Britain alone, waiting to be shipped to the continent) and that would be that. 'The Watch on the Rhine' would certainly fail.

Like his two staff officers, Model did not like the plan. He thought it was too ambitious. However, he did agree with a surprise offensive. In his opinion, it would catch the Americans (who thought they had already won the war) off balance. But he wanted it to be a more limited attack. An offensive, aimed at capturing Aachen and cutting off the ten or so US divisions in the Aachen-Hürtgen-Eifel area, had a better chance of success.

But Model knew that once the Führer made up his mind there was no way of changing it. He also knew that whatever plan was finally adopted, his own 'small solution' or Hitler's 'large solution', success depended on the 'Amis' facing the West Wall on the 'Ghost Front' not becoming aware of what was afoot until it was too late. Security, as the Führer had stated, was of paramount importance.

Had he known what was going on in the enemy camp as October gave way to November and the start of the great offensive grew ever closer, Model would not have worried so much. If the 'Boy Field Marshal' had been privy to the thoughts of the enemy's top generals, it would have seemed that they would positively *welcome* a German offensive on the 'Ghost Front'. Two of those generals went on record to say they would; and one – the most important one – did not seem to care that they did.

There is in existence a US Army Signals photograph, showing US VIII Corps Commander, General Troy Middleton, in a small office near the Luxembourg town of Wiltz in the late afternoon of Wednesday 8 November 1944. On his left is General Bradley, his boss, Commander of the US 12th Army Group, complete with shoulder holster and combat jacket. To his side is General Leonard, leader of the newly arrived 9th US Armored Division. Sitting at the only desk in the corner, sipping coffee out of a chipped mug, is the Supreme Commander, General Eisenhower. Naturally, he has one of the sixty Lucky Strike cigarettes he smoked every day clenched in his right fist.

Middleton, fat, bespectacled, who had been a college president before the war, has his head bent slightly to the side. His right hand is raised as if he is making a point. For their parts, Eisenhower and Bradley are listening to the VIII Corps Commander. But what is the point Middleton is making?

It must have been important, but neither senior officer ever revealed what it was. Nor did the Supreme Commander file a message for his tour of that front between 8 and 10 November. General Bradley, in two volumes of autobiography, does not mention it. Yet these two men were responsible for the lives of hundreds of thousands of soldiers. Normally, scores of messages passed through their hands every day. For those seventy-two hours they appear to have done absolutely nothing. Since then, historians of the campaign must have often wondered what went on when 'Ike' and 'Brad' visited the 'Ghost Front' for the last time before the drama to come in December.

One thing that *is* known about this period is this. By early November, America's top generals in Europe were heartily sick of banging their heads against the defences of the Siegfried Line. There had been no real success anywhere – no decisive breakthrough. Advances against the Wall, won at a high cost in young American lives, could be measured in metres.

It was understandable that General Bradley could explode to Eisenhower's Chief-of-Staff, Bedell Smith: 'If the other fellow would only hit us now. I'd welcome a counter-attack. We could kill more Germans with a good deal less effort, if they would only climb out of their holes [in the Siegfried Line] and come after us for a change.'

We know too (from Middleton) that on that afternoon in Wiltz, Eisenhower asked him: 'How serious a problem would we have if Hitler were to attack through the Ardennes?'

Perhaps it was here, just as the army photographer took a shot of Middleton with his hand raised, that the latter replied fervently: 'It would be the best thing that could happen to us. I have nothing of value that I can't afford to lose between the front and the Meuse river. If they come through, we can trap them and cut their head off, shortening the war by several months.'

If anything is clear about the totally confused question of what the Americans knew in advance of the great German 'surprise' offensive, it is this: the 'Ghost Front' was the most likely place for the enemy to attack – at least in the opinion of the US Army's top brass.

If that is so, why did Eisenhower and Bradley not do something to reinforce and strengthen Middleton's VIII Corps, instead of removing his battle-experienced infantry divisions and replacing them with weak and exhausted men, and with others with no battle experience at all? Indeed, from what is now known about the 'surprise' attack, which finally cost the American Army 80,000 casualties, it appears that not only did Eisenhower welcome an attack from the Siegfried Line on Middleton's 'Ghost Front', but *he knew it was coming*.

But as Eisenhower took command of all Allied ground forces on 1 November 1944 (the first time in his long army career that he had ever commanded troops in the field), he seemed completely confident and gave no hint of being worried about what was to come. The British King, George VI, visited the US front and distributed medals to the top brass. Eisenhower talked to his troops in the field and, to their great amusement, slipped in the mud and fell on his elegantly clad butt. The troops loved it, and the Supreme Commander shrugged it off with a smile.

A new US Army, the Ninth under the command of General Simpson, arrived at the front, and General Bradley decided, with Eisenhower's agreement, that it should go to strengthen Montgomery in the north. Otherwise, 'Monty might wangle it', and 'as Simpson's Army was still our greenest, I reasoned that it could be the most easily spared.'

Needless to say, Eisenhower did not visit his troops slogging away in the 'Green Hell of the Hürtgen'. Nobody of importance ever did. Besides, the Hürtgen was dangerous. Even generals could get killed there. Instead, Eisenhower, in excellent humour despite the problem of how to break through the Siegfried Line being still unresolved, visited General 'Big' Simpson and his new Ninth Army on his quiet front.

'Big Simp', who kept his head shaved – Patton said of him: 'When he's not fighting, he works as an advertisement for a hair restorer' – had invited a British guest to meet 'Ike' and his fiery Chief-of-Staff, 'Beetle' Smith.

This was General Brian Horrocks, Commander of the British XXX Corps, and known universally as 'Jorrocks'. The tall, ascetic-looking general, who had seen more than enough of war (he was wounded in both World Wars, and had been a prisoner of both the Germans and the Russians), liked the Americans. He got on famously with the Supreme Commander and his two generals over an excellent dinner (for which

Horrocks had supplied that rare commodity, whisky). Now Eisenhower asked him jovially: 'Well, Jorrocks, are you going to take on Geilen-kirchen[51] for us?'

Horrocks replied that 'the spirit was willing, but the flesh was weak'. The only division he had available was the 43rd Infantry, which had suffered tremendous casualties. Its commander, General 'Butcher' Thomas, had never spared his long-suffering men, and by the time the campaign was over, the division would have suffered 12,500 battle casualties – a complete turnover of its fighting personnel. Horrocks felt, therefore, that his only available division was too weak to take on one of the strongest positions in the West Wall.

Eisenhower did not hesitate. In his easy, relaxed manner he said to Simpson, 'Give him one of ours, Simp.'

Simpson suggested the 84th Infantry (the 'Rail Splitters'), which had just arrived in Europe.

Horrocks protested that the task ahead would be very tough for 'the new boys'. It did not seem right that a US division should be launched into its first battle by a British general.

Eisenhower overrode his objections, and the conversation then ranged over the recent abortive operation at Arnhem, which had involved two US airborne divisions, the 82nd and the 101st. They had now been withdrawn to France, where they had shown themselves to be seriously indisciplined. There had been scores of desertions, a lot of drunkenness, and some rapes. Eisenhower had been tempted to order the public execution of convicted American rapists to show the French that the Americans meant business. Angrily, the Supreme Commander declared that 'they [the airborne troopers] were a disgrace to the whole US Army'.

Horrocks, who had come to admire the US paras during Arnhem, retorted hotly that it was a shame the whole US Army did not consist of such 'disgraces'. His angry outburst provoked a roar of laughter from Smith, who was not notably pro-British. He commented: 'Well, well, I never thought I'd hear a Britisher standing up for US troops against an American general.'

So the new plans for the attack on the Siegfried Line were formulated. In the end, these plans would involve practically all of the Allied front from Simpson's Ninth in Holland, General Hodges' First Army in the Hürtgen Forest on the Belgo-German border, right down to Patton's Third Army in Metz and the Saarland.

Only one stretch of that long front seemed destined not to play a role in the events to come – the 'Ghost Front'. No American patrols probed the Siegfried Line positions on the other side of the Our-Sauer river border. Even the former, daily reconnaissance flights over the entire length of that front seem to have been suspended, for no apparent reason[52].

Naturally, the local peasants, with relatives living on the German side of the border, had plenty of rumours to pass on. They had stories of German activity on practically every part of the Siegfried Line. But the '*Amis*' were not listening to the peasants' stories any more. Perhaps they assumed that the locals would be pro-German, and just wanted to spread alarm.

So, while Model prepared for the great 'surprise' German counter-offensive (which perhaps was not such a surprise after all), the Allies prepared too, for their last great all-out attack on the Siegfried Line. This time, if they were successful, they knew that the war in Europe might after all be over by Christmas 1944. With luck, the 'boys' would be tucking in to 'Mom's' turkey 'with all the trimmings' before the year was out.

Unfortunately, 'luck' was not going to be on the side of the Allies.

NOTES

48 The Nazi relief fund used to provide warm winter clothes for the poor before the war. Since 1939 it had been used to do the same for the German Army.
49 Model's son told the author that his father had to behave this way to keep waverers toeing the line.
50 A sixty-mile front held by a four-division US corps, outnumbered four to one.
51 Where the British 2nd and American 9th Armies linked up at the extreme northern end of the Siegfried Line.
52 The overlays of those flights are kept in the UK at the University of Keele. There are none for the period in question. The usual explanation for the strange absence of the vital photo-recce pictures just before the German 'surprise' offensive is the bad weather normal at that time of year. However, air-recce was already using air-to-ground radar, which would have enabled it to pick up major areas of new activity.

5

The Limeys take a Hand

Silent cannon, soon cease your silence. Soon unlimber'd to begin the red business.

Walt Whitman, 'Drum Tap', 1865

Dawn, 2 November 1944

It was a typical early morning for that time of year in what the GIs were now calling 'the awful Eifel' – cold, damp and grey. A thin mist curled like a silent, skinny cat in and out of the shattered, dripping lines of firs in the Hürtgen Forest.

On all sides there was pent-up, controlled tension. Up front the assault infantry of the 'Bloody Bucket', the 28th Infantry Division, crouched in and around the battered bunkers of the Siegfried Line, their shell-pocked, concrete sides looking like some loathsome skin disease. Most of the men urinated a lot – a sure sign of nerves. Some prayed – but not many.

Further back the gunners, standing next to the heaps of shells, detonators already in place, took a last 'draw' before it all started. Behind them came the battalion and regimental aid stations, mostly tented and improvised, with sheet-metal 'reflectors' made from fuel cans hanging over the waiting, scrubbed tables. Already the surgeons had laid out their gleaming instruments for the bloody work ahead of them. The ambulance drivers stood in front of their box-like vehicles, the dreaded old legend fixed in their windows, PRIORITY – CARRYING CASUALTIES. The scene was set; the players were in place; the drama could begin.

At 0800 hours precisely, the morning stillness erupted into an ear-splitting roar. The 12,000-round initial bombardment was under way. It was the Western Front, circa 1917, all over again. Suddenly everything was noise, fire, flames and fury.

Just as their fathers in the Imperial Army had done the men in field grey cowered at the bottom of their log-covered pits and in their bunkers, as the earth trembled like something alive. The concrete dust rained down in a grey sheet. They would wait for the bombardment to stop, as it surely must, then they would man their machine-guns. The 'Amis', it seemed, had not learned much about infantry assaults since World War One.

At 0830 precisely the artillery bombardment stopped. It left a loud, ringing echo behind, that seemed to go on for ever. Still, the defenders started cautiously to raise their heads. They stared out of their slits at the transformed landscape: the snapped trees, the brown, steaming pits, the piles of green vegetation. They waited. But the '*Amis*' did not come. Was this some kind of new tactic, the Germans asked themselves. In a way it was. But it failed.

General 'Dutch' Cota, the divisional commander, had requested air support to follow the artillery bombardment and cover his advancing infantry. But now, as the minutes ticked by with leaden inexorability, the TAC Air Force dive bombers did not arrive. The weather was too bad. They were 'socked in' on their airfields back in Belgium and France. Gradually the Germans began to relax. Whatever the '*Amis*' were up to, it did not look as though it was going to affect their miserable, damp existence this particular November morning.

At noon Colonel Petersen, a slender, wiry officer who had grown up in Pennsylvania among the miners, oilfield workers and tradesmen who still made up the hard core of his outfit, the 119th Infantry of the Twenty-Eighth, ordered his men into the woods. They were to take the key village of Schmidt.

Everything seemed relatively easy after the pounding their predecessors, the ill-fated 9th Infantry Division, had taken. The long lines of cautious infantry pushed their way through the lunar landscape, covered with water-logged shell holes, smashed trees and battle debris. They forded the Kall river, climbed the slope beyond, and routed a bunch of second-rate German infantry who had attempted to stop their advance. By day two, they were well on their way to capturing Schmidt. It had been easy . . . all too easy.

During the second night of the 'Bloody Bucket's' attack, the 28th's engineers started to check out the winding, hilly 'Kall' trail that led to the infantry dug in at Schmidt. Behind them a troop of tanks from the 707th Tank Battalion followed.

Climbing the trail at night was difficult for the tankers. Everything went well until the lead tanks under Captain Hostrup ran into trouble. The right shoulder of the trail, with a 100-foot drop, started to give way under the weight of his Sherman. Swearing and sweating, Hostrup backed off until he reached the engineers still working on the trail. He told them what had happened, and both parties agreed they would wait where they were until dawn, when the engineers would make a proper start on shoring up the trail so that the tanks could advance.

Meanwhile at his HQ, 'Dutch' Cota was receiving telephone calls from commanders all along the Siegfried Line congratulating him on his breakthrough. The aggressive, bustling commander said later that he started to feel like Napoleon – but not for long.

The Germans counter-attacked just before dawn. They appeared to catch the American infantry completely by surprise. They fled from Schmidt to the next village, Kommerscheidt. Here it became difficult for their officers to hold them. 'Kraut tanks!' they yelled in panic. 'Kraut tanks are coming.' Noncoms had to strike them. More than one officer threatened the men, telling them he would shoot if they did not hold their positions. But there was no holding the panicking battalion. As Staff-Sergeant Frank Ripperdam reported later: 'They were pretty goddam frantic and panicky.' It took two hours to assemble 200 men (a quarter of the battalion) to bolster the defences of the little village.

Cota threw in the dive-bombers. At the same moment German Panthers started to bear down. A P-47 fell out of the grey sky. At tree-height it went for the leading Panther. Shells slammed into it. The German tank reared up on its back bogies like a wild horse being put to the saddle for the first time. It came to an abrupt stop, thick white smoke pouring from its turret. Another tank was hit. Its crew fled, followed by machine-gun bullets stitching a vicious pattern at their flying feet. The steam went out of the German armoured assault. The remaining tanks retreated the way they had come.

Urgently Cota ordered Colonel Petersen to retake Schmidt. But Petersen felt he could do nothing without the support of Captain Hostrup's tanks, still stranded on the Kall trail. All night the engineers worked frantically to clear the way for them. By dawn on 5 November the tanks were on the move again. An hour later they strolled into Kommerscheidt to be welcomed by the hard-pressed defenders like the Seventh Cavalry by pioneers in a Hollywood western.

Now the Germans changed tactics. Instead of a frontal assault on the village, they filtered on to the Kall trail below. A lone jeep coming up with supplies spotted the infantry lurking in the trees. The jeep tried to escape – to no avail. The trail was too tight. The lieutenant in charge yelled, 'Shoot, man, shoot!', as the Germans opened up with their burp guns.

'I can't, Sir,' the driver answered miserably. 'I'm dying right here.' And he did.

Throughout that long, tense night, reports filtered back to Colonel Daley, in charge of the division's engineers. He ordered: 'Get every man you have into the line fighting.' The situation had to be desperate for skilled engineers to be used as riflemen.

By now the Germans seemed to be fighting in every part of Colonel Petersen's 112th's regimental front. One alarmist report after another flooded back to him. One said his men were 'crying like broken-hearted children'; another that the GIs were having to be *ordered* to eat their K rations. One battalion commander sat slumped in his cellar CP, his face buried in his hands, his shoulders heaving, sobbing his heart out.

Petersen's second battalion was hit. The men broke. Panic spread from company to company. Even the reserve company broke down. 'It was the saddest sight I have ever seen,' Lieutenant Condon of Company E reported later:

> Down the road from the east came men from F, G and E Companies, pushing, shoving, thowing away equipment, trying to outrace the artillery and each other, all in a frantic effort to escape. They were all scared and excited. Some were terror-stricken. Some were just helping the slightly wounded to run, and many of the badly wounded, probably hit by the artillery, were lying in the road where they fell, screaming for help. It was a heartbreaking, demoralizing scene.

So far, no one had seen a single German of the 116th Panzer Division assault group which was attacking. But it was no use pointing this out to the panicking fugitives. 'They ran as fast as they could,' the Battalion Personnel Officer, Captain James Nesbitt, remembered. 'Those we saw were completely shattered . . . There was no sense fooling ourselves about it. It was a disorderly retreat. The men were going back pell-mell.'

Some of the officers thought they had succeeded in forming a stop line. They built up a sketchy position running through the centre of the village. It was held by seventy men. But when the officers' backs were turned, half of these melted away to the rear as well.

At dawn on 7 November, with the rain pouring down in sheets, fifteen German tanks, supported by a battalion of infantry, attacked from the direction of Schmidt, heading for Kommerscheidt. The tank destroyers that had managed to make it up the Kall trail thundered into action. For once the Americans outgunned the Germans. One by one the TDs knocked out five Panthers.

But the American tankers were taking losses themselves. Slowly but decidedly the surviving TDs began to pull back. By noon the Germans had followed up. They were on the outskirts of Kommerscheidt, shooting up the '*Ami*' foxholes, using that terrible trick they had learned in Russia of swirling their tank round and round above some poor swine's foxhole, until he filled his pants, screaming in terror as the foxhole collapsed and buried him alive.

This time the men of the 'Bloody Bucket' did not break. But their courage ebbed away rapidly. A German tank stuck its long 75mm cannon right through the door of the house that served as a command post for the US battalions trapped in the village. This was the last straw. As Staff-Sergeant Ripperdam of L Company recalled:

> There was a hellish amount of noise and confusion and everybody was pretty nervous. I was feeling low. Then the first thing I knew, one of the boys outside said there was a big tank right on top of the battalion CP.

We took off to have a look. I saw the tank on the CP in a position to cover the entrance . . . There were American soldiers in front of it and they had their hands raised in surrender. There was a white flag showing . . . With this scene in our minds, we saw A and B Company men streaming back to the rear, running, but with most of them still carrying their weapons. We took off and joined them.

The events unfolding shocked Colonel Petersen beyond measure. He had seen his regiment run in panic – men he had known since childhood. And now, bitterly, he blamed General Cota. The divisional commander was the one who had issued an impossible order. Casting all logic and reason to one side, Peteresen handed what was left of his comand to a Colonel Ripple, telling him he was going to give 'Dutch' Cota 'a piece of my mind'. He would tell the 'little Napoleon' what was really happening in the Hürtgen.

Making his way alone down the steep heights of the rear, Petersen was wounded. Shortly afterwards he was wounded again, this time by German shellfire. When the engineers working on the Kall trail found him, he was babbling incoherently. The medics took him to the divisional aid station for treatment. Here he demanded to see Cota.

When the divisional commander arrived, he was appalled by the state Petersen was in – ashen, unshaven and red-eyed after four days without sleep. Tired and alarmed himself by the failure of his attack, Cota immediately jumped to the frightening conclusion that Petersen had abandoned his regiment. It was too much for Cota. The hero of the Normandy beaches (he had been awarded the USA's second highest medal for bravery there) fainted clean away.

He had good reason to do so, for the 'Bloody Bucket's' attack into the Hürtgen had proved one of the most costly American actions of the war in Europe. Petersen's 112th Infantry alone had lost *two-thirds* of its strength in the seven-day action. And the division had suffered a staggering 6,184 casualties out of a total strength of some 15,000 men. To all intents and purposes, the 28th Infantry Division was a spent force.

While the 28th Division almost bled to death, farther north the 'Rail Splitters' of the green US 84th Division prepared for their own baptism of blood in the Siegfried Line. Horrocks, who was to lead them into their first action at Geilenkirchen, was not happy with the 'Rail Splitters'. He found the rank and file excellent, if inexperienced. But he did not much care for the way the officers looked after their men.

To the American way of thinking, the British Army was very class-ridden – 'Permission to speak, Sir', etc. But as Horrocks saw it, the officers in the most democratic army in the world were little concerned with the welfare of their men, unlike upper- and middle-class British officers for *their* subordinates.

There was, for example, no attempt on the part of American officers to look after their men's feet – unlovely as they might be. In the British Army, officers were required to inspect their men's feet after a route march, or a couple of days when they could not take their boots off. It did not come as much of a surprise to Horrocks to find that, within a week of the 84th arriving in water-logged Holland, the Americans had suffered 500 cases of trenchfoot, the scourge of the US Army that winter in the Siegfried Line.

Nor did General Bolling, the 84th's commander, place much importance on ensuring that his soldiers had at least one warm meal a day in the line. British Army 'compo' rations were based on cheap cuts of beef and pork, but they did make quick, hot stews and satisfying corned beef fritters. There was even greasy Canadian bacon, that came in rolls covered by fat-smeared paper that could be used to fry the stuff in. (Unfortunately, the wag who invariably asked, when the compo ration boxes were opened, 'Which tin's got the cunt in, Sarge?' was always disappointed.) The Americans were forced to exist on 'C' and 'K' rations. When Horrocks learned this, he immediately ordered that 500 cans of self-heating soup be sent up to the front-line troops daily, increasing the number day by day. Bolling took the hint.

American security was very lax. They failed to evacuate the local German population, who might well betray details of coming attacks to their compatriots on the other side of the line. The British had no such compunction. They sent the locals streaming across the border into Holland, under the watchful eye of 'Redcaps' (military policemen), dragging with them whatever pathetic belongings Horrocks allowed them to take.

Relations between the veterans of the 43rd 'Wessex' Division and the 'new boys' of the 84th Infantry did not get off to a very good start, when the latter 'forgot' to clear a minefield they were all going to have to cross. Hastily, 'Butcher' Thomas of the 43rd sent his sappers in to do the job. In a single day, they collected 700 of the lethal little devices – but not all of them. When Brigadier Mole of the 43rd went to inspect his brigade at the start line, his vehicle ran over a cluster of mines. There was an appalling explosion in which the bloody remains of the dead Brigadier and fourteen of his soldiers disappeared.

At 1245 on 15 November, exactly on schedule, 1,200 Fortresses of the UK-based American 8th Air Force, flying in box-tight formations, and accompanied by an equal number from the RAF's Bomber Command, flew across Holland towards the Siegfried Line. As they approached the front, jeeps started to roll on the ground, guiding the pilots with ground-to-air radios. The flak started firing coloured anti-aircraft fire. Barrage balloons ascended to 1,500 feet. On the ground they were making sure that the 'flyboys' did not bomb their own people.

As formation after formation droned overhead, Anglo-American infantry on the alert at Geilenkirchen cheered. The power of the air force was on their side as they prepared for the little sideshow. Rapidly the guns – a thousand of them – of the two divisions, the 43rd and the 84th, thundered into action. The infantry waiting to go in would not have been too happy to know that only three percent of the aerial force had dropped their bombs on the bunkers of the West Wall. The rest, to be sure of avoiding the ground troops, had dumped their loads far to the rear.

The plan of attack was simple enough – it usually was on paper. The 84th would attack first. The 'Rail Splitters' would take the high ground a mile and a half away at a village called Prummen. With the right flank thus secure, the veterans of the 43rd would assault in a depth of two and a half miles, completely encircling Geilenkirchen. Here they would mop up. Then, to wipe up the German salient at Geilenkirchen totally, there would be a further advance of four miles' depth to capture the villages of Hoven, Wurm, Mullendorf and Beek.

Everything was timed to the minute, and depended on the two divisions keeping strictly to the timetable. If one failed to keep up, it would expose the other's flank to possible German counter-attack. But everyone, British and American, was confident that everyone else would keep up. Nothing could go wrong.

At dawn on the day of the attack, 'Monty's Moonlight'[53] threw its silver light over the battlefield. As the sky to the east started to reflect the ugly false dawn, two troops of 'Churchill's Funnies' rumbled up. These were special armoured vehicles, many proposed by the British Prime Minister, of the 79th Armoured Division, commanded by Montgomery's brother-in-law, until 1940 a humble lance-corporal in the Home Guard. They were 'flails', tanks fitted with a large steel drum on the front, to which steel chains were attached. When the drum rotated, the chains were thrown outwards to detonate mines without endangering the vehicle's crew. They now started their slow, hazardous work of clearing two paths through the minefields, so that the infantry could advance.

Behind them the British gunners waited. By now, after five years of war, they had got their 'shoots' down to a fine art, superior not only to the American artillerymen, but to the German enemy as well. They were so good that they could bring down the fire of 300 guns within thirty seconds on any given spot. Now they were 'victored'. After a brief, five-minute bombardment, two battalions of the 84th's infantry rose from their holes and started to advance. They were going into action for the first time at the most dangerous place in Western Europe – the Siegfried Line. In front of them rumbled the British Shermans.

To Horrocks' relief everything went surprisingly well. The 'new boys' made no serious mistakes, and by midday they were still advancing. That

'We're gonna hang out our washing on the Siegfried Line . . .'

Goering views the completed West Wall in 1940.

Surrender. German troops take over the Maginot Line, 1 July 1940.
The next time Fort Hochwald would see action it would be defended
by Germans against Americans.

As always, civilians suffer. German refugees from the American
advance along the northern border of Alsace found refuge in caves,
where they tended the goats and cows that provided milk and cheese.

Waiting for the attack. Dragon's teeth near Brandscheid.
The wooded section at upper left is the edge of the Schnee Eifel.

The dragon's teeth as they are today.

Soliders of Headquaters Battery, 903rd Field Artillery Battalion try to push a service truck out of deep snow in the Hürtgen Forest.

US Army engineers use sheet metal captured from the Germans to roof log huts in the Hürtgen Forest.

White-caped US Infantry moving out in December 1944.

Soldiers of a US field artillery battery practise demolishing a German pillbox with a bazooka in the snow-covered Hürtgen Forest.

The defenders of the West Wall. The German Infantry
veterans referred to themselves as 'stubble-hoppers'.

Two Canadian Privates stroll in the grounds of the historic Rhine
castle of Moyland after its capture by Canadian troops. They wear
'captured' silk hats and carry walking sticks. The dead horse
in the foreground highlights the incongruity of the scene.

A great screen of smoke rose up before Eisenhower's
forces when they stormed the Rhine.

The 'Ultimate Weapon'.
A Crocodile flame-thrower of 'Churchill's Funnies' in operation.

Just one of the 4,000 casualties suffered by
the 4th Division in the Hürtgen Forest.

The price of victory in the attack on the West Wall.
American dead at the Margraaten Military Cemetery.

was enough for the British general. The guns opened up again briefly. This time two battalions of British infantry from the 43rd began their advance.

For the most part they were stocky farm boys from the West Country. Ruddy-cheeked and heavy-legged, they moved forward with the inevitable tea mugs hanging from their 'small packs', plodding slowly and warily through the mud.

The Shermans with their narrow tracks started to lag behind. The mud was too much for them. (It took the American armaments industry a long time to realise that tanks need broad tracks for mud; something the Germans had known since Russia.) Doggedly the infantry plodded on. Their trucks, laden with supplies, started to sink up to their axles in the goo. Still they went on. Then the Germans hit them. Self-propelled guns came out of the woods firing. The mud was not stopping *them*. In a matter of minutes, thirty or so infantrymen went down killed or wounded, together with the commanding officer, writhing in agony in the mud.

All that day and through the night, the British and Americans fought their way forward, capturing objective after objective, until finally by the following day they had surrounded the West Wall bastion of Geilenkirchen. 'Splendid job of work,' the senior British officers chortled. 'Jolly good show!' This first joint Anglo-American operation against the Great Wall of Germany 'was going splendidly'.

In reality the operation had only just begun. That night the heavens opened. The rain fell in sheets. The infantrymen, up to their waists in their water-logged pits, were drenched. The fields turned into quagmires. To their front, the German guns opened up on the 'new boys' of the 84th. But, next day they were on their feet again, advancing against the pillboxes and bunkers. They did not get far. Just after first light tanks of the veteran German 15th Panzer Division rumbled towards them, their long, overhanging 75mm cannon seeking out their victims. Watching them, the veteran infantryman, Brigadier Essame of the 43rd Division, thought: 'It was galling to see their tanks with their broad tracks manoeuvring over muddy fields impassable to our own.' Predictably, the green infantrymen of the 84th went to ground.

The men of the 43rd kept going. They had seen it all before – in Normandy and at Arnhem. But even the veterans were feeling the strain as it rained and rained, almost as if some god on high was determined to blot out this man-made abomination below. The historian of the Duke of Cornwall's Light Infantry wrote later:

Years after the event, those who survived recalled the intensity of the enemy fire and the sloppy ground on which they had to move to reach their objective. What is difficult to describe is the physical agony of the infantryman ... The November rain seemed piercingly cold. After exertion, when the body warmed, the cold air and the wet seemed to penetrate the very marrow of every bone in the body so that the whole shook as with ague, and then after shaking would come the numbness of the hand and leg and mind and a feeling of surrender to forces of nature far greater in strength than any enemy could impose.

It could only be overcome, as the historian added, 'by the inherent claim of self-preservation and the determination to do one's duty'.

After a hard, four-day slog under terrible conditions, the two allied divisions were just about at the end of their tether. As Brigadier Essame later wrote: 'Only those with actual experience of such circumstances know the moral struggle over their own emotions which battalion and brigade commanders had to endure and overcome. It is not easy to order rain-soaked soldiers once more into action in the dripping woods.'

But Essame was forced to overcome his own emotions. That day he ordered the Duke of Cornwall's Light Infantry, which had already lost its battalion commander, and would lose another before the campaign was over, to capture the woods around the village of Hoven.

Unfortunately, General Harmel's 10th SS Panzer Division, victors of Arnhem, were waiting for the Cornwalls. The SS Grenadier met the British with a murderous hail of fire. They went down on all sides. The muddy fields were littered with crumpled, khaki-clad dead. The SS advanced. They tried to cut off survivors as the pitiful cry went up: 'Stretcher-bearer . . . stretcher-bearer . . . over here!'

As the medics braved the fire, they avoided the upturned rifles with their muzzles stuck into the mud. For these indicated the positions of those with no further need for medical attention – they were dead. The Cornwalls made it to the outskirts of the little German village.

Now a nightmare began. The slightest movement, even though it was dark, resulted in the whine of the sniper's bullet or the high-pitched, hysterical burr of a German MG 42. The enemy were everywhere in the brick rubble, that was all that remained of the ruined village. Still the DCLI did not waver. They dug in and waited.

Now everything hung on the 'Rail Splitters' of the 84th reaching them before dawn broke. If they failed, the DCLI would be cut off and at the mercy of the SS. The 10th SS Panzer had thrown a wedge in their rear.

But the American drive had stalled. It had been totally unable to get through a line of bunkers on the heights of the village of Suggerath on the right flank. Here the SS were holding the West Wall in strength.

What was Essame to do? He knew if he was going to save his own men, he would have to pull them out under the cover of darkness. But that might be letting the Yanks down, should they succeed in breaking through the Wall. He was between the devil and the deep blue sea.

It was about that time that Horrocks, the corps commander, appeared out of the wet darkness, muffled in a rain-soaked 'mac'. Essame explained the situation. He finished with a warning that the SS would attack at dawn. He was certain of that.

Horrocks, who was a strong believer in the 'Yanks', thought the 84th would manage to link up with the trapped Cornwalls, but he would leave the decision about what had to be done in Essame's hands. As Essame wrote: If the Brigadier [Essame himself] wished to withdraw the DCLI now, while there was still time, he could do so. If he chose to stay and gamble on the Americans resuming their attack at dawn, whatever happened, he would have Horrocks' backing.'

It was a tough decision for Essame, as he sat there on a ration box in his gloomy farmhouse headquarters, with the guns thundering outside, the sky split by their angry, red flashes, and the rain beating furiously against the blacked-out windows. Could he risk the lives of some 500-600 British soldiers, gamble them on the inexperienced, unpredictable Yanks? Since June, when they had entered the battle, the DCLI had suffered one hundred percent casualties. Dare he risk the lives of their youthful replacements? As he wrote: 'The DCLI had never fought, since the early days of Normandy, otherwise than to the bitter end.' But could he subject them to yet another terrible blood-letting?

As the rain pelted noisily down, Horrocks waited patiently, watching Essame's face in the flickering, yellow light of a petroleum lantern. Finally the Brigadier nodded. He would stay and take his chance of a bloody tragedy.

Horrocks hedged his bets. He sped away into the night, his command Humber chased by angry tracer, and reported to General Bolling's HQ. He promised the American, who would soon lose his son as a German POW in the Siegfried Line, that some of his 'Funnies' would attack at first light, covering the one and a half miles that separated the lead US infantry from the trapped British – if the former would attack. Bolling agreed his men would.

But the Americans did not make it. Predictably the SS attacked at dawn. They came with their characteristic daring elan. D Company's commander, Major Spencer, was severely wounded trying single-handedly to stop a German tank. Another DCLI company was cut off. House-to-house fighting broke out. Those who could crowded into the cellars and fought from there. A German doctor was captured. When asked why he was fighting, he truculently told his captors: 'I'm fighting for my country, the same as you.'

Now most of the village was on fire. The Cornwalls' ammunition ran out. They fought on with the ammo taken from the German dead. Two more company commanders were severely wounded. Still the 'Yanks' were nowhere in sight.

That afternoon, under a lowering sky, the SS pushed home their attack, applying more and more pressure. The DCLI, virtually out of ammunition, and with no anti-tank weapons to counter the 10th SS's lumbering, armoured giants, began to pull back. Its D Company up front had been reduced to fifteen men out of the original 120. A Company was under heavy attack by tanks and men of the SS. In the event, the DCLI's survivors counter-attacked and drove the enemy back fifty yards. How no one ever knew. But the gain did not help much. The two surviving majors, both wounded, made Brigadier Essame's decision for him. With the Americans still not arrived, they began to pull their survivors back.

Shortly afterwards news came in that the 84th had finally broken through. But by now it no longer mattered. The seventeen-division attack, which 1st Army Commander, General Hodges, had maintained was 'the last offensive necessary to bring Germany down to her knees' had failed. Essame later felt the reason was that General Bradley, the US Army Group Commander, had chosen to attack 'where the Germans were numerically stronger and where they had every advantage in the form of concrete defences and thick forests – a military problem new to his troops and for which they had not been trained . . . Condemned to a battle of attrition, the infantry sustained such losses that divisions were quickly exhausted in battle.'

The Siegfried Line had beaten the Allies yet again.

NOTES

53 Searchlights fixed so that their beams reflected downwards to light up the battlefield.

6

The Death Factory

I was the only one still able to walk out of those awful woods. I might also have been crying.

Lieutenant George Wilson, 22nd US Infantry Regiment

This was the first time I ever saw a German dog eating a roasted German Kraut.

Ernest Hemingway, *Across the River and into the Trees,* 1950

Late on the afternoon of Wednesday 15 November 1944, Lieutenant Colonel Tom Kenan, Second Battalion of Colonel Lanham's 22nd Infantry Regiment, was looking out of the muddy hole that was his CP in the Hürtgen Forest. In front of him he saw a stranger wearing a helmet, GI pants, and carrying a small pack. Kenan could not conceal his surprise at this sudden presence in the midst of his dug in battalion.

He must have asked himself what this 'civvy' was doing up here in the firing line. He was obviously too old to be a soldier – 'He looked at least sixty' – and was peering through steel-rimmed spectacles; not the sort one would expect to find in the front line with the teenagers of the 'PBI' (Poor Bloody Infantry).

So far Kenan had not recognised the stranger, but he was impressed by the man's bulk, which was accentuated by a white, sheepskin-lined jacket worn against the biting cold. In contrast, Kenan thought the glasses perched on the end of the stranger's red, alcohol-swollen nose were 'pitifully small and inadequate'.

The stranger, who was of course Ernest Hemingway, introduced himself as if it was perfectly natural for him to turn up like this in the remote, embattled Hürtgen Forest. He explained to Kenan that he had just come up from General 'Tubby' Barton's HQ in the schoolhouse at Zweifall. The Divisional Commander had sent him up to be briefed by 'Buck' Lanham. If Kenan wondered how a civilian war correspondent had got hold of the top secret information that a major offensive was scheduled to start the next day, he kept his thoughts to himself. After all, this was *the* Ernest Hemingway, the movie of whose novella, *To Have and Have Not*, had just been premiered in Hollywood, starring Humphrey Bogart and his new, 18-year-old lover, Lauren Bacall.

Without demur, Colonel Kenan led Hemingway to Lanham's caravan. Once such accommodation had been the prerogative of senior army commanders. Now, even lowly colonels had them towed all over Europe. It was the ultimate military status symbol of late 1944.

Together with another correspondent, Bill Walton (an American journalist who had wanted to become a paratrooper) they settled down over drinks in the Colonel's caravan, which featured a painted German steel helmet, used by Lanham as a chamberpot.

'Buck' Lanham was not a happy man. He told Hemingway that he had had a premonition that he would not survive the coming battle, the US Army's third major attempt to break through the West Wall, the Hürtgen Forest and out into the Rhenish plain. Hemingway exploded. He told Lanham hotly that he was sick and tired of 'all this shit' about premonitions. His bête noire, his famous rival, US war correspondent Ernie Pyle, was always having the damned things. But *he* was still alive.[54] Getting carried away, Hemingway launched an attack on Pyle who had been on all the American fronts since 1942, while Hemingway had been dodging the war in neutral Cuba. But even as he ranted, Hemingway 'knocked on wood' on Lanham's table – he was as superstitious as any man.

Next morning, while Hemingway was having his first drink of the day, the three-division attack into the Hürtgen got under way. He wrote that the assault had 'jumped off' after first light. But there was little dash about the initial assault; the terrain was too rugged, there were German bunkers everywhere, and the trees were too dense.

One of Lanham's staff told Sergeant Mack Morriss, correspondent for *Yank* magazine: '[the advance] is like wading through an ocean. You walk in it all right, but water is all around you'. The result was that the battalions soon broke up into little groups of men, under the command of junior officers and noncoms, and isolated from each other in the green hell they called 'the Death Factory'.

For once the weather was on the side of the attackers in the 'Awful Eifel'. Lieutenant George Wilson of the 22nd, shortly to be the only surviving front-line officer of the outfit that had landed on Utah Beach on 6 June, recalled: '[There were] two inches of new snow . . . Our world was suddenly clean, fresh and uncorrupted, and it seemed senseless that we were not deerhunting back home in Michigan, but at war with people on the next ridge.'

The 'clean, fresh and uncorrupted' world described by Lieutenant Wilson, was not to last for long. As he put it: 'Second Battalion immediately ran into a tough German defense . . . From dug-in positions they put down brutally accurate mortars and artillery on our men out in the open, and chewed us up with direct machine-gun and rifle fire. Our casualties were dreadful.'

By five o'clock it was pitch black and the battle effectively stopped. The men knew they had to get under cover quickly, or else. Colonel Lanham gave the order to dig in for the night. But where and how? An officer of Lanham's 1st Battalion stated grimly: 'A man would throw away his rifle before he would give up his ax.' He explained: 'With an ax he could chop wood [for fuel and shelter] and also kill Heinies.'

Many had difficulty locating their parent companies to dig in with for mutual protection. Wilson recalls taking his men back through the heavy, freezing darkness.

The only way we could get back was to trail one hand on the field telephone wire. We stumbled along over roots and small depressions, and slashed through the undergrowth, and then we piled up against some barbed wire. It took some time to cut through the wire and bend it back in the darkness.

Finally the lost men reached their company positions, were ordered to dig in, and were told by the company commander, 'Let's hope for a good night.' His wish was seemingly granted until next day's grey dawn when Wilson discovered he had been occupying a foxhole right above the entrance to a dugout in which 'there were four terribly frightened German soldiers'. This was typical of the confused situation in the Hürtgen Forest. The Germans 'could not surrender fast enough' – they thought the surprised '*Amis*' might toss a grenade into their hiding place and wipe them out. Lieutenant Wilson, for his part, reflected that they could have 'finished him off' at will, any time during that long, cold night.

Next morning Hemingway, who of course had not spent the night in a freezing foxhole, accompanied Lanham on his rounds of his three battalions. Their jeep stopped at the CP of the acting commander of the 1st Battalion, who was scheduled to kick off the day's attack. He was 'a little gray man', Major Drake, in whom Lanham did not have much faith. Afterwards Lanham confided his doubts to Hemingway, suggesting that he might have to relieve Drake in a day or two if he did not 'shape up better'.

Hemingway broke his pensive silence and said solemnly, 'Buck, you won't ever have to relieve him.'

'Why?' Lanham snapped.

'He won't make it,' Hemingway replied, 'He *stinks* of death.'

Their jeep had just reached the 22nd Regimental Command Post when Lanham's executive officer, Colonel Ruggles, came up and saluted. 'Major Drake has just been killed, Sir. Who takes the First Battalion?'

Hemingway did not comment. Instead he walked on alone to Lanham's prized caravan. When he had gone, Lanham summoned another officer, a Major Goforth, to take over the First. He gave him just one order. 'On arrival I should not get into the same hole as Colonel Henley. We've lost too many officers already.' Lanham did not want to lose two key officers to the same shell. But before it was all over, Lanham would lose many more, and his 'beautiful regiment', as he called it, would have virtually vanished in the 'Death Factory'.

That same day, Wilson experienced the loss of his whole battalion command, his commander, Colonel Walker, 'and his entire staff being casualties'. Then he lost his company commander. He was replaced immediately by a new man, who did not last long either. After many of his new company had been hit by German shellfire, having been ordered to an untenable position by the major, 'our new commander broke down in tears, blubbering about how it was all his fault. He kept at it, and when I realized he was completely out of control, I called battalion . . . and was told to send him back to the aid station'.

A few hours later the company commander was replaced by yet another – this one had been wounded some time earlier. Despite the November cold, he had 'beads of sweat plastered to his forehead; his fingers trembled so much he couldn't manage to light his cigarette'. He went back to battalion the next day. And so it went on.

Hemingway stuck it out for eighteen days while the 22nd Regiment was shot to pieces. He never did report what he had seen for his employers at *Collier's*. (He said he did not want to waste the 'good stuff' on a weekly magazine.) All he ever wrote about the Hürtgen that November were a few snippets for his 1950 novel, *Across the River and into the Trees*, in the slick, unfeeling, grand guignol style he had adopted in that period of his life, when he was the tough soldier back from the war. But 'Buck' Lanham, the would-be writer, did express his feelings. He moaned at the end of that terrible time: 'My mental anguish was beyond description. My magnificent command had virtually ceased to exist.'

In the sleet, rain and snow, and the terrible violence that followed the first, and only good, day of the 22nd's attack on the Hürtgen fortifications, the suffering and losses were appalling. On the second day, after Colonel Walker of the Second Battalion had been killed, the now Major 'Wild Man' Blizzard, who as a lieutenant had taken the first patrol across the Our river back in September, took over the Second. By the time he reached the Battalion Command Post, not a single member of the staff remained on his feet. Blizzard had to fight his battle unaided, save for the services of a lone runner.

The 22nd's casualties mounted daily, as did those of all the other formations engaged. One hundred . . . two hundred . . . three; on one terrible day there were nearly *five hundred*. Even Lieutenant George

Wilson was hit. 'My right arm stung. I looked down. A sliver of shrapnel was sticking out of my right forearm.' He carried on, but as he remarked later: 'I just have been pretty stupid because it simply never occurred to me to go back to the aid station about five hundred yards to the rear.'

But others did – by the whole company! They were hauled down the slopes where they had been hit by cursing, sweating, frightened litter parties, lugged through the Weisse Weihe beck, which was flooded and neck deep, and deposited in the regimental aid post – a roofless farmhouse. Here they were worked on by weary, harassed, bloodstained, chain-smoking doctors, who cleared away those capable of fighting again and the lightly wounded. The more seriously wounded – with the sucking wounds of the lungs, hits in the guts, severed legs and the like – came last. And all the while, the piles of 'stiffs' outside, freezing in the cold, grew larger. Severed limbs crackled merrily, like sizzling bacon, in the pot-bellied stoves.

There were other casualties too. They could not be repaired with the surgeon's needle, scalpel, and sulpha drugs. Their filthy, faeces-soiled uniforms bore wound tags with a single word scrawled in endelible pencil – EXHAUSTION.

At first they had come in a trickle, sobbing, screaming, stupefied with shock, limbs trembling like leaves, jumping at any sudden noise, eyes wild, wide and staring as if they had witnessed an unspeakable horror. Then, as the fighting in the 'Death Factory' intensified, they had arrived at the aid posts, and later at the dressing stations, in their scores, then hundreds, and finally in their thousands. Their condition did not acknowledge rank. It afflicted soldiers from 18-year-old GIs, who had hardly begun to shave, to company commanders, even colonels in charge of whole battalions. The literature of the time is full of such cases of what had been called 'shell-shocked' or 'bomb-happy' men; now they were given the more prosaic designation, 'combat fatigue'. (The victim's fellow soldiers were known to use a more down-to-earth description, 'No good, yellow-bellied son-of-a-bitch', for example.)

Lieutenant Wilson, recuperating after picking up the pieces of a dead officer and finding underneath him the shattered body of a badly wounded, but cheerful, NCO, was suddenly confronted by a new radio man. 'He was shaking violently and tears streamed down his face. His whole body quivered with spasms, and he was barely able to tell me between sobs that he couldn't take it "up here" . . . He sobbed like a baby throughout the whole outburst and beat his head on the ground.'

Wilson, the veteran, tried to reason with the 'new boy'. When that failed, he threatened him. He would be shot as a deserter. 'Then I told him how ashamed his parents would be and he still didn't care. Nothing seemed to work, although somehow he became a little calmer and then he shocked me with his remark: "I'm just a dirty, no-good, yellow Jewish

SOB." All this was enough for me and I sat back completely stumped.'

In fact, the radio man was faking. He was a 'gold-bricker'[55], as the GIs called such individuals. But there were plenty who were not 'gold-brickers'. At Eupen in Belgium, the nearest large town to the Hürtgen, the authorities set up the 622nd Exhaustion Center to deal with these unfortunate men. They were kept separate from the rest of the Fourth Division wounded. They were injected with enough sodium amytal to keep them asleep for three days, being woken only to eat and carry out their bodily functions. At regular intervals they were administered intravenous saline solution until, hollow-cheeked, bog-eyed, and still shaking, they were woken to be put under scalding showers and to be shaved.

After that, the medics asked them some questions, and there was some elementary psycho-analysis, but not much. The front was crying out for riflemen. So most were shipped back into the line where, predictably, some fifty percent broke down again.

The 22nd's regimental chaplain, Dr Boice, thought there were too many 'gold-brickers' among the combat fatigue cases. 'Having once found that he could be evacuated with combat fatigue,' he later wrote, 'the soldier knew instinctively that the medical tag reading "Combat Fatigue" represented for him safety and surcease. Frequently some soldiers made the circuit from the rest center to the front lines three or four times. It was another one of the hells of war. The psychiatrists had no choice, for there was no other place to send the man unless he was physically disqualified or mentally unstable.'[56]

Hemingway, who kept drifting in and out of battalion and regimental headquarters during the battle, did not believe in combat fatigue. A soldier who ran away or 'chickened out' and refused to fight was 'yellow'. And of course he did not like the psychiatrists – the 'trick cyclists' – who sent these shirkers to the rear, while their comrades stuck it out in the snow and the mud.

But although Hemingway undoubtedly shared the views of senior officers, who would die nice and warm in their snug beds, he was brave. All of the 22nd's officers admired him because he had come to the 'Death Factory' of his own free will. Colonel 'Swede' Henley, one of the battalion commanders, thought highly of a civilian who was twice his age. He later recalled:

He stayed with me in my command post in the front lines in the rain, sleet and snow. He was always right in the thick of the heaviest part of the fighting, looking for something to write about. He carried two canteens – one of schnapps, the German equivalent of southern corn whiskey, and the other of cognac. He always offered you a drink, and he never turned one down.

To 'Swede' Hemingway stated, 'There's nothing to be scared of in combat. Either you're killed or you aren't.' If you were killed in battle, that was it. You knew no more. If you weren't killed, you had won. What Hemingway overlooked in his simplistic philosophy, was the constant, permanent, twenty-four-hours-a-day misery of the poor infantryman, slogging through the ankle-deep mud, spending his nights, usually scared out of his wits, in waterlogged foxholes, living out of mostly cold cans. There were no canteens of strong drink for him, no classy chats about the cosmos, no philosophising about the nature of combat.

It was not the prospect of being killed that broke men in the 'Death Factory', but the unrelenting misery and ever-present danger. This was something that Hemingway could never have understood. Even when, in due course, he came to blow his brains out with a shotgun, he probably never appreciated what made men break down. Perhaps he thought suicide an act of bravery.

During the night of 26 November, a patrol from Lanham's 22nd Infantry reached Grosshau, a village on the ridgeline road to the ruined Rhenish city of Dueren. If they could capture Dueren, they would be practically out of the Siegfried Line and on their way to the Rhine, the last natural obstacle in the way of the Allied drive to the heart of the Reich.

At 0900 next morning 105 men of Lanham's Company B attacked the high ground outside Grosshau. The leading platoon was decimated within ten minutes. Every man was either killed or wounded. The Germans had been waiting for them. Another platoon went into the assault. The German machine-guns were waiting for them too, and they were reduced to ten men, pinned down by merciless fire.

The men were desperate. A GI volunteered to knock out the main German machine-gun. He was ripped apart before he had gone a dozen paces. A sergeant now took up the challenge. He suggested he would outflank the machine-gun. He never made it.

Now it was the turn of PFC Macario Garcia, who had become an American citizen only the year before. He disappeared alone into the woods. Grenades explosions were heard. A short while later Garcia reappeared. He was wounded but he brought with him four German POWs. 'Goddam,' he exclaimed in his fractured English, 'I kill three Germans and knock out the machine-gun.' He was evacuated to the rear before any of his companions even found out his first name. 'That man is going to get the best medal I can give him,' Lanham declared when he heard about Garcia's bravery. And in due course, the 'Tex-Mex', as people of Garcia's origins were contemptuously called, received his new country's highest award – the Congressional Medal of Honor. He was one of the few who won it in the battle for the Siegfried Line and who survived to receive it in person.

Still the killing went on. General 'Tubby' Barton, Fourth Division's commander, was irritated by what he saw as the 22nd Regiment's slow progress. He ordered Lanham to take Grosshau that day 'regardless of cost'. Lanham tried a ruse. Under a flag of truce he had invited the defenders of the place to surrender. They declined. Lanham threw in his entire Second Battalion. In two hours they advanced no more than seventy-five yards down the street through the destroyed village. The Germans launched a counter-attack, Lanham replied with tanks. They ran into a minefield. Tracks snapped in the explosions and furled out behind the abruptly stalled Shermans like shattered limbs. By nightfall the Second had suffered 162 casualties, about a fifth of his strength.

Naturally Hemingway burned with desire to visit the 22nd's main objective. Although Grosshau was still under fire from a huge railway gun located in Dueren's principal station five miles away, Lanham let him go, accompanied by the would-be paratrooper-correspondent, Bill Walton.

A picture taken that day of Grosshau[57] (Hemingway called it 'Potato Village') shows it to be a mass of shattered ruins in the slanting November sunlight, its single street a morass of churned mud. Even the small church, St Apollonia, had been hit repeatedly by shells. Most of its belfry had been destroyed, but one solitary bell remained intact (it is still there today).

From this last visit to Grosshau, on the day after it had fallen, came one Hemingway dispatch for *Collier's*. It was rather prosaic, but it did do justice to the tragic, pointless battle for the whole of the Hürtgen. He wrote:

> No one remembered the separate days any more, and history being made every day was never noticed, but only merged into a great blur of tiredness and dust, of the smell of dead cattle, the smell of earth new-broken by TNT, the grinding sound of tanks and bulldozers, the sound of automatic rifle and machine-gun fire, the interceptive dry rattle of German machine-pistol fire, dry as a rattler rattling, and the quick spurting tap of the German light machine-guns – and always for others to come . . .

For Hemingway, 'History was now old K-ration boxes, empty foxholes, the drying leaves on the branches that were cut for camouflage . . . But mostly history was getting there when we were to get on time and waiting for others to come up.' But there was no *feeling* for the men of the 22nd Regiment, now coming out of the line at last – men like George Wilson, one of the two surviving officers of his battalion:

> I was in a daze probably from delayed shock. I was thinking of all the men who had started out with me in the F Company attack a few weeks back. I was the only one still able to walk out of those awful woods. I might also have been crying. At any rate my vision was misty and I

didn't see my old friend from E Company, Supply Sergeant O'Malley when he came up to me as I shuffled along the trail.

O'Malley threw his arms around me in welcome and then insisted on taking all my gear . . . and carrying them the rest of the way. I tried to say something to him, but I became all choked up and couldn't.

It was not surprising that the poor young officer became 'all choked up'. In the eighteen days that Colonel Lanham's 22nd Infantry had spent in the battle, the Regiment had lost 3,000 men. Wilson summed it up: 'This came to about 100 percent loss for the three battalions in the regiment. It was an awful beating – a terrible price for that damned patch of woods, a total of about five miles.'

Five years later, when Hemingway came to write about his experiences in fictional form in *Across the River and into the Trees*, and gave his paying readers 'the good stuff' he had denied *Collier's* in 1944, he described how his protagonist, Colonel Cantwell, is met by a grey-faced GI in Grosshau. The GI says, 'Sir, there is a dead GI in the middle of the road up ahead, and every time a vehicle goes through, they have to run over him and I'm afraid it is making a bad impression on the troops.'

One wonders if a GI would have spoken in those terms during that terrible time. At all events Cantwell/Hemingway goes to look at the dead GI, decides he has to be removed from the road and helps to lift him, '. . . and I can remember just how he felt, lifting him and how he had been flattened and the strangeness of his flatness'. Later, Cantwell goes farther down the muddy road through Grosshau and, for the benefit of his 19-year-old Italian girlfriend, who is supposedly enthralled by his descriptive powers, recalls: 'We had put an awful lot of white phosphorous on the town before we got in for good or, whatever you call it. This was the first time I ever saw a German dog eating a roasted German Kraut. Later on, I saw a cat working on him, too. It was a hungry cat, quite nice-looking basically. You wouldn't think a good German cat would eat a good German soldier, would you? Or a good German dog eat a good German soldier's ass which had been roasted by white phosphorous?'

Of course, Hemingway's description was intended to give his 'paying' readers a cheap frisson of horror. But what understanding, respect or honour did it pay all those young soldiers, dead and crippled, who had fought with 'Papa Hemingway' in their midst?

For Hemingway, the 'Death Factory' had simply been 'material', the stuff from which he would fashion his 'great trilogy' of World War Two novels (he never wrote them). Now with this knowledge, gained at the price of so many pointless deaths, he left for his 'HQ at the Ritz' in Paris to find out if 'Mr Scrooby' would finally work with his new mistress. He was never to return to the fighting front.[58]

In the event, there was no good reason for Hemingway to return to the northern part of the West Wall. All the way, from Patton's Army in the south in the French Saar, up through Eifel-Ardennes, on to the Anglo-American positions in southern Holland, the Allied attack had ground to a miserable, beaten halt.

It was not just a lack of supplies, with which the American top brass had excused their lack of progress back in September-October, nor the terrible climatic conditions which were a convenient new excuse in November-December. Even Eisenhower's 'broad front strategy' , that is, attacking all along the Siegfried Line simultaneously, could not be offered as an explanation of the Allies' failure.

The reason for Eisenhower's failure to crack Hitler's West Wall was to be found elsewhere. It was really very simple. The German soldier, defending his homeland for the first time, was exhibiting more determination and stamina than the Allied soldiers attacking him. The battered German formations, who had fled France in September 1944, fought off mainly American divisions which outnumbered them three or four to one. With their backs to the wall, the Germans were fighting *'bis zum bittern Ende'*.

In that last week of November 1944, it must have seemed to the new Land Commander, General Eisenhower, that, unless the enemy made some grave tactical error, such as leaving their Siegfried Line defences, the 'Krauts' would be holding the West Wall against all-comers for eternity.

NOTES

54 Hemingway always called himself 'Ernie Haemorrhoid, the poor man's Ernie Pyle'. In fact Pyle, who was greatly admired by the average GI, was killed in action in the Pacific in 1945.

55 The term for a conman who sold people gold-painted bricks as genuine bullion.

56 In recent years a secret US Medical Corps film of such men has been released. It is a horrifying record in celluloid. Indeed, one of the doctors who presented it later refused to send 'healed' combat fatigue cases back into the line.

57 Even now, more than fifty years later, there are outhouses with roofs made from beaten shell cases from US 75mm shells. Five years ago, when the local school was being renovated, a complete, intact US aid station was found in the cellar, just as it had been left in 1944. The stretchers were stained a rusty brown with dried blood.

58 In December 1944 he left the Ritz to return to the 22nd Regiment in Luxembourg at the time of the 'Battle of the Bulge'. But he spent most of his time drunk or sick in bed, drinking looted wine in a priest's house several miles behind the line. Today, courtesy of the author, there is a plaque to Hemingway. But then there are plaques all over the place commemorating World War Two in 'Little Luxembourg'.

BOOK 2

November to December 1944

But if Intelligence was not to blame, who was?

Major-General Ken Strong, Eisenhower's Chief of Intelligence, 1968

1

The Rhine is Reached

There we were on this hill about a thousand yards from the fort and we see these eight-inch shells bounce right off the walls. Honest to God, eight-inch shells – the heaviest stuff we've got and they didn't even make a dent . . . I guess we were all thinking, 'How in the hell are we going to take that place?'

Harry Garman, Infantryman, November 1944

At dawn the little French general, who was under sentence of death by his own '*grande nation*', disobeyed orders yet again. But that was nothing new. General Leclerc, commander of the 2nd French Armoured Division, had been accustomed to disobeying any order that did not suit him since 1940. After all, '*la gloire*' was at stake. The upholding of France's honour and prestige came before the petty wishes of those turncoats and renegades who had sided with their Nazi conquerors, or had joined the 'collabos' of the pro-German Vichy government. It even took priority over the wishes of the British Army authorities under whom he had once served, and the Americans, who were now his military masters.[59]

Now the stubborn armoured commander, who had captured Paris in August 1944, ordered his division to take Strasbourg, that other French icon, in a surprise attack to be launched on the morning of 23 November.

Lieutenant Triumpho, a member of a three-man jeep team liaising with the 2nd French Armoured Division, set off at dawn with his jeep at point. A French-speaking American, he knew the dangers. The Germans had a garrison of 15,000 men in the capital of Alsace, and a sizeable proportion of the German-speaking population were pro-Nazi (they had, after all, been '*Reichsdeutsche*', that is ethnic Germans, since 1940). So Leclerc's flying columns, coming out of the Vosges mountains and heading for the Rhine below, faced not only the prospect of having to fight the German garrison, but the possibility that they might be betrayed by pro-German Alsatians before they ever reached Strasbourg.

But, as the young artillery officer recorded, luck was on Leclerc's side. 'We went roaring across the plain in our jeep, along with four or five light tanks and a few halftracks of infantry. We passed working parties and groups of German troops and they just stood open-mouthed. When they saw we were French troops, they were scared to death, for they had heard the French didn't take prisoners.' Leclerc's surprise attack was obviously paying off.

On and on the flying columns roared. At the front the French officers strained to catch a first glimpse of Strasbourg's famous cathedral. Just behind the point, Leclerc saw the church, ordered a stop and commanded an officer who spoke German to call the nearest German garrison over the public telephone. The French officer cried over the intact line, just as if he was in extreme difficulties, 'We need help here, *urgently*. Send up a battalion!'

Obligingly the Germans dispatched the duty battalion, which went straight into the bag. Leclerc did not hesitate. The one combat-ready battalion was out of the way. He ordered the drive into Strasbourg to continue. As Leclerc's corps commander, US General Haislip recalled, long after Leclerc had died in mysterious circumstances: 'Leclerc told me about it with the greatest glee. He simply loved that sort of stuff.'

Civilian Dennis Woodcock, an English Quaker driving an ambulance for the French, remembered how it was when Leclerc entered the Alsatian capital: 'The Germans hadn't the faintest idea of what was happening . . . They were absolutely flabbergasted. Thousands were not fighting men at all.[60] They were civilians, admin. people, going around carrying briefcases, shopping or out with their wives. We landed right in the middle of them, and the battle-stained French soldiers looked quite out of place.'

Here and there fighting broke out. It did not worry Leclerc. He was eager to savour his own triumph – first Paris, now Strasbourg. The coded message, 'cloth in iodine', was flashed back to his advance CP. The Frenchman did not hesitate. With his escort, he made a dash for the heart of the newly captured city, right on the banks of the German Rhine. Behind him his aide, Captain Chatel, recorded that triumphant entry:

> There were some fantastic things happening. As we passed a barber's, I saw a German officer shot as he was coming out to a staff car waiting at the kerb. The streetcars were still running and many of the Germans, mainly non-combat troops, were going about their duties quite oblivious to us. Then I saw the most moving thing. As the townfolk realised that we were French, many of them fell on their knees, crying with joy and uttering prayers of thanksgiving. We drove straight for the *Kaiserpalast*, where the German High Command and Gestapo HQ were. When we arrived cups of coffee, poured out for the German staff, now under guard, were still hot. That is how great the surprise was.

While this was going on, Lieutenant Tony Triumpho decided to cross the great Rhine river, Germany's last natural barrier of any importance. 'We raced right across Strasbourg and crossed the Rhine to Kehl on the German side,' he recalled. 'There seemed nobody about. We made a reconnaissance to find out what we could, and all we heard was the chirping of the birds. It was most eerie and deserted.'

Not far away, a BBC war correspondent recorded the event for his listeners on the 'Home Service'. 'There it is, set against the rain-dark sky to the east, a looming outline of distant hills – the Black Forest, the western barrier to Hitler's Reich. We felt we'd come to the end of a long journey . . . *We'd got to the Rhine at last!'*

When the Supreme Commander heard the news at his palatial HQ at Versailles, he was not pleased. Leclerc had gone against orders to advance to the Rhine. This was given as the main reason for his displeasure – afterwards. Nor was 'Ike' too overjoyed by the manner in which Leclerc was already beginning to rule the Alsatian capital. He had proclaimed he would have five German hostages shot for any one of his men cut down by remaining snipers.[61]

Everywhere Leclerc's soldiers were arresting French officials, business-men and civilians suspected of having worked with the Germans – and there were a lot of them.[62] Indeed, Eisenhower was so incensed that he ordered Leclerc to restore the original, German-language street signs throughout Strasbourg. This was, he stated, to avoid 'administrative chaos', though the Supreme Commander did stop short of having the blue and white sign, *Adolf Hitler Platz*, put back.

All things considered, Eisenhower concluded in that last week of November that it was time he visited the command to which Leclerc's 2nd Armoured Division belonged – US General 'Jake' Devers' Sixth Army Group. Devers would have to be reminded to obey the Supreme Commander's orders, or else . . .

On 24 November Eisenhower and Bradley left Patton's Third Army and rolled south into Devers' area. They were driven by Eisenhower's secretary-cum-mistress, Kay Summersby. Although she was British, she sported the single gold bar of a US second-lieutenant in the WACs. Usually Eisenhower was happy when he was on the road with the green-eyed ex-model; there they could get away from the prying eyes and protocol of Supreme HQ, but not here.

That Friday the weather was terrible, his wife, Mamie, was sending him jealous, nagging letters from Washington, Devers was proving too big for his boots, and, yet again, Montgomery was trying to damage his reputation in London. But there was worse to come.

They had just rolled into Corps Commander Haislip's HQ to discuss the continuation of his offensive in Alsace, when Haislip ran out into the rain and mud crying, 'For God's sake, Sir, I was just on my way down to tell you not to come. Please go on. We don't want you. There's a report of an armoured breakthrough on the front held by our cavalry.'

Summersby looked round at her fellow drivers. Their faces betrayed their thoughts at that moment, as they noted that the Corps HQ staff were preparing to defend themselves. They reckoned: 'When headquarters had to fight, it was time for generals to get out.'

Eisenhower laughed off the warning. He snorted, despite his evil humour, 'Dammit Ham[63], you invited me for lunch and I'm not going to leave until I get it.'

But the commander's obvious near-panic reinforced Eisenhower's grim mood. He decided that he liked Devers and his plans even less than he did when they worked together briefly in London before the invasion. Bradley was not too fond of his opposite number in Alsace either. He later wrote: 'I studied Devers closely and formed my own independent opinion of the man. I found him overly garrulous, saying little of importance, egotistical, intolerant, not very smart and much too inclined to rush off half-cocked.'

This was a damning indictment of a fellow American senior commander, but one that Eisenhower shared. Eisenhower called Devers a '22 caliber general', not a very flattering assessment of a lieutenant-general and US Army group commander. But was it Bradley's and Eisenhower's real reason for what was about to happen?

During lunch, which Haislip had not wanted his high-ranking visitor to eat, Eisenhower discovered that, despite the emergency, Haislip and his fellow corps commander, General Brooks, were still making plans to cross the Rhine and attack the Siegfried Line. Both commanders were already drawing up plans for an assault crossing of the mighty river between Strasbourg and the German city of Rastatt. They had sent company-size patrols over the Rhine.

The men of the US 3rd Infantry Division, 'The Rock of the Marne'[64], had met little opposition as they pushed into Germany from the river. They had come across Siegfried Line bunkers, and (in view of what they had read in *The Stars and Stripes* about attacks on the Line in the north) had approached the fortifications cautiously. Their caution had been unnecessary. The bunkers were unoccupied and seemed to have been long abandoned. A major attack across the Rhine began to look like a bit of a 'walkover'.

Haislip and Brooks certainly thought so. They had signalled their opinion to Devers, 6th Army Group Commander, and he gave them the green light for a major crossing. The US Seventh Army, the major component of Devers' group, had won woefully little publicity since it had invaded the South of France the previous August. Now the time had come, Devers obviously thought, to upstage the 'gentlemen up north'. Top American generals thought that way during World War Two – PR had invaded the battlefield.

Once a firm bridgehead had been established over the Rhine, Haislip and Brooks were convinced that Devers would give them the go-ahead for an advance along the German side to link up with Patton's Third Army in the Saar. Normally that notorious publicity-seeker would not have agreed; he tended to keep all kudos for himself. But this time, it was later discovered, he did. 'Ole Blood and Guts' confided to his dairy that if he were in Eisenhower's place, he would send at least Brooks' VI Corps across the Rhine to carry out such an operation.

Eisenhower thought differently. After lunch with Haislip, the little cavalcade drove to Brooks' HQ. Here Eisenhower discovered – to his apparent alarm – that plans for a Rhine crossing were even further advanced. Without any prior consultation with Ike's HQ back in Versailles, Brooks and his staff had been busy drawing up plans for a crossing between Strasbourg and Rastatt. From there, if they got the green light, the planners hoped to reach the southern German *Autobahn* network, which would lead them into Franconia, Bavaria, and across the old, pre-1938 border into Austria, now known as the '*Ostmark*' and part of the greater German Reich. This was, in fact, the axis of the advance the Seventh Army would eventually take on its road to victory. But that would be almost six months later, and by then the whole military situation in the west would have changed dramatically.

Eisenhower, angry beyond measure (for reasons not explained at the time[65]), flew off the handle. He did not wait for his staff to work on the situation. He issued verbal orders – on the spot, an unprecedented act for such a senior commander – to halt all plans for a Rhine crossing immediately. Instead the Seventh Army was to turn north on the Allied side of the Rhine and link up with Patton. In other words, Devers' Seventh Army would once more be reduced to the role of flank guard to Bradley's 12th Army Group to the north.

When Jake Devers heard of Eisenhower's proposal, he could not believe his ears. After three months of battering at the Siegfried Line, at a cost of well over 100,000 battle and non-battle casualties, Bradley's 12th Army Group had forced a shallow gap, which they had been unable to break out of, between Geilenkirchen and Aachen. The only impact those bitter, bloody weeks of fighting seemed to have made on the Germans was to have concentrated their reserves in the area between Cologne and Aachen to stop the Allies making their dash for the Rhine fifty miles away.

Now here Devers was on the banks of the Rhine, with perhaps no more than a hundred yards of unguarded water to cross (in fact, they had already been crossed by the Third Division's patrols) and Ike was determined to stop him. Why? Was it because Ike disliked him? It was common gossip at Supreme Headquarters that Eisenhower had refrained from sacking Devers because the Supreme Commander could not bring himself to bust a lieutenant-general.

Returning to his own HQ, after hearing about Eisenhower's sudden and surprising decision, Devers resolved to fight back. After all, he had the ear of the most powerful general in the American Army, the Chief-of-Staff,

General Marshall. Although Marshall was Eisenhower's mentor, and had promoted Ike over the heads of 366 other US officers of equal rank, the stern head of the Army in Washington took no nonsense from the Supreme Commander, who was afraid of him.

At his headquarters, the Hotel Hermitage at Vittel, which is still there, Devers collected his thoughts. He knew that Eisenhower would have to come across for a formal dinner – a matter of common courtesy – and he wanted to be ready for him and Bradley.

His exact thoughts are not known. Normally loud-mouthed and disinclined to hide his light under a bushel – it was said of him by Eisenhower: '[Devers] was often inaccurate in statements and evaluations . . . [so far] he has not produced among seniors of the American organization here a feeling of trust and confidence' – Devers does not seem to have made any overt comment about Eisenhower's decision. His staff, however, felt that Eisenhower was again attempting to play down any real contribution Devers' Seventh Army was making to the war effort. Once more, the attention-grabbing headlines were being reserved for Patton and Bradley. This time, their boss was going to give the 'gentlemen from the north' a run for their money.

So it was that, after a formal dinner in the Hotel Hermitage, the three high-ranking officers returned to Devers' private office to discuss the proposed Rhine crossing.

Eisenhower opened the discussion with the statement that, before any crossing was to be undertaken, all remaining troops of the German 19th Army, still on the Allied side of the river, should be dealt with. According to Eisenhower's account, Devers retorted that the French First Army, under the command of his Army Group, 'could easily take care of them.'

Devers might have been a little optimistic in his assessment of the French First Army. It had suffered severe losses, and was strapped for reinforcements from central France. Indeed, its commander, General de Lattre de Tassigny, who had once volunteered to help the Germans invade Britain, complained to de Gaulle that France, as a whole, seemed to have forgotten his army fighting in Alsace.

Eisenhower suggested that Devers' estimation of the French's fighting power was 'over optimistic', and that he 'probably overrated the defensive power of German units when they set themselves stubbornly to hold a strong position' (he was obviously thinking of the three-month battle for the West Wall). The discussion grew more heated.

Eisenhower drew on all his authority and prestige to make Devers toe the line. He virtually ordered Devers to turn his Seventh Army north to join Patton in the Saar – this despite his current Supreme Headquarters directive, providing for any opportunistic crossing of the Rhine by any commander during the November offensive, which was coming to an unhappy end in the Hürtgen.

The Supreme Commander applied more pressure. If Devers would not follow his 'suggestions', Ike might be forced to take away two divisions from Devers' Army Group, and arrange for Haislip's corps to take on a larger area of territory to the north-west, thus weakening the effectiveness of that corps.

Devers objected fiercely. He snorted that it was his Seventh Army that should be reinforced, not Patton's Third, currently bogged down in the mud of Lorraine. Here, the so-called 'GI General'[66], the plodding General Bradley, once Patton's subordinate and now patron, stepped in. He said that any attempt to force the Rhine and the Siegfried Line defences beyond would be foolhardy. Bradley, who did not know about the Third Division patrols, was taken aback when Devers replied that *his* troops had already been through the West Wall south of Rastatt and had found the bunkers empty and abandoned.

This left Eisenhower absolutely cold. With his normal ear-to-ear grin, with which he had charmed cinema audiences on both sides of the Atlantic, noticeably absent, he ordered Devers to get on with the job as outlined – clean up the Allied bank of the Rhine in his area. There would be no full-scale breakthrough of the Wall positions. If Devers accepted this without further objections, he would be allowed to keep his two divisions. Indeed, a grateful Supreme Commander would give him one of the new US armoured divisions currently arriving in the European theatre of operations from the UK.

It was blackmail, pure and simple. But Devers knew when he was beaten. By now it was the wee small hours of that November morning. He gave in and let Eisenhower have his way. As well as being tired, all three generals were still very angry. It is on record that Eisenhower emerged from the meeting 'as mad as hell'. For his part, Devers flung himself into his bed wondering, as he wrote in his diary, whether or not he was 'a member of the same team'.

Before the meeting in the Hotel Hermitage, Devers and his two corps commanders had been convinced they would have no difficulty getting across the Rhine in force and breaking through the Siegfried Line. Brooks' VI Corps could then have headed north-east in the direction of Karlsruhe, outflanking the whole of the West Wall running parallel to the Rhine.[67]

It has since been argued that the terrain on the other side of the Rhine between Strasbourg and Rastatt was not right for a massive breakout. Yet, four months later, when the US 1st Army captured 'the most famous bridge in the world' at Remagen, Eisenhower had no hesitation in ordering his subordinates to 'shoot the works'. The Supreme Commander tossed aside Montgomery's grand strategic plan for a mass crossing of the great river. Two and a half weeks before Monty was due to cross, Eisenhower allowed his generals to push four whole divisions across at Remagen into the most unlikely spot in the entire front – a thickly wooded, hilly area with a road network made up of second-class country roads and lanes. Why then had he turned Devers down in November '44? It could not just have been on account of the terrain.

On the face of it, we do not know. The exact content of that late-night meeting in the Hotel Hermitage is virtually a closed book to students of World War Two. Eisenhower does not refer to it directly in his account of the campaign, *Crusade in the West*. Nor does Bradley in two volumes of memoirs. Despite its crucial importance, we only know that it took place at all because Devers mentions it in his diary, as does Major 'Chet' Hansen, Bradley's aide, in his journal. It seems that neither Eisenhower nor Bradley wanted the world to know that they could have crossed the Rhine and breached the Siegfried Line in November 1944, rather than in March 1945.

Three decades after the event, General Garrison Davidson, the Seventh Army engineer who would have been responsible for moving his command's two assault divisions across the Rhine in November, wrote:

> It is interesting to conjecture what might have been the effect of the exploitation of an unexpected crossing of the Rhine in late November ... I have often wondered what might have happened if [Eisenhower] had had the audacity to take the calculated risk as General Patton would have, instead of playing it safe. Perhaps success would have eliminated any possibility of the Battle of the Bulge. 40,000 casualties[68] could have been avoided and the war shortened by a number of months at the saving of thousands of lives.

But perhaps General Davidson, when considering what might have happened if the Supreme Commander *had* taken that 'calculated risk', failed to explore the possibility that Eisenhower wanted the Battle of the Bulge to take place; that he knew the Germans were going to attack in the Eifel-Ardennes out of their West Wall positions; and that Eisenhower *actively encouraged the enemy to do so*.

One year after the Battle of the Bulge began, the victorious General Eisenhower wrote to the then US Secretary of War, Robert Pattison: 'I am unalterably opposed to making any effort to publicize at this time any story concerning the Ardennes Battle or even of allowing any written explanation to go outside the War Department.'

Pattison, clearly unaware of just how powerful the military lobby in Washington had become, wrote back[69]: 'I believe the main feature of this operation [the Ardennes Battle] – the events leading up to it, the incidents of the fighting and the outcome – should be made known to the American people. Otherwise they will hearing nothing but fault-finding and many of them will think the Army is covering up.'

It was not 'the incidents of the fighting and the outcome' that worried

Eisenhower. They were clear. The troops had fought well in what came to be known as 'America's Gettysburg of the 20th century' and the outcome was clear. It had been a splendid, if costly, victory. It was 'the events leading up to it' that worried Eisenhower. But in true Washington fashion, the traditional wheeling and dealing that takes place on Capitol Hill ensured that the Great American Public never did find out what happened before the German 'surprise' attack was launched on the 'Ghost Front' that Eisenhower and Bradley had created in the Eifel-Ardennes.[70]

There are three aspects to the conventional explanation of why the American top brass did not discover, until it was too late, that the Germans were missing three armies, totalling perhaps some 600,000 men, in the Siegfried Line positions between Monschau and Echternach: in reality they were a failure on the part of Allied Intelligence; an inability to carry out aerial reconnaissance of the front because of bad weather; and, most importantly, the fact that the Ultra decoding operation went dead on the Allies because the Germans were now using their own land lines instead of their Enigma coding device.

Until 1973, when the secret of Enigma was first revealed, military historians, examining the run up to the great 'surprise' attack, concentrated on Intelligence and air-to-ground reconnaissance. Most concluded that those engaged in reconnaissance did bring back evidence that something was in the wind in the last weeks of November and the first week of December, but that the information was not interpreted accurately. In the end, they maintained, over-optimism among High Command and Intelligence failure combined to lead Eisenhower to believe that a German attack was not to be expected.

Then came Group Commander Fred Winterbotham's[71] *The Ultra Secret,* which revealed that Allied code experts had been able to read Hitler's orders to his commanders almost as soon as their addressees could. This revelation changed everything. But those who were protecting Eisenhower's reputation quickly came up with an explanation that staggered those who maintained that Eisenhower must have known what was to come – thanks to Ultra. His apologists pointed out that the Germans had stopped using Enigma during the run up to the Battle of the Bulge. But they seemed to overlook something suspicious – why did the enemy stop using their normal means of communication. Were they trying to hide something?

It does not matter now. Ten years after the Ultra debate had died down, it started to become clear, from the declassification of certain documents in Washington, that Eisenhower had had another top source of intelligence all the time. Without Ultra and all the conventional sources of information about the enemy's intentions, Eisenhower *had* known that winter of 1944 what had been going on on the other side of Hitler's West Wall. His apologists could have saved themselves the trouble. MAGIC made its debut.[72]

NOTES

59　Captain Viscomte de Hautecloque had changed his name to Leclerc and had fled France in 1940 to join de Gaulle. The Vichy government had sentenced him to death in absentia. Thereafter, General Leclerc had steadfastly refused to have anything to do with those who had served Vichy, including Marshal de Lattre, commander of 1st French Army, currently serving under the Americans. (De Lattre had supposedly offered to help the Germans invade Britain in 1940, and had only fled France, in a submarine, in 1942.)

60　Under the Germans there had been very active cooperation between the French heavy industry of Alsace-Lorraine and the Reich. That same cooperation was rekindled just a few years after Nazi Germany had been defeated. It came as no surprise when Strasbourg was named the first home of what later developed into the EEC.

61　When de Gaulle came to Strasbourg a few days later to celebrate a thanksgiving Mass, the windows of the cathedral had to be covered with blankets to deflect sniper fire.

62　A month before Leclerc took Strasbourg, German and French industrialists held a top secret conference in the Maison Rouge hotel (it is still there in the city). The 'Friends of Reichsführer SS Himmler' industrialist group made their decisions about how Germany's financial capital should be invested in plants abroad in order to finance a future 'Fourth Reich'. Most of the non-German participants and their decisions remain unknown to this day. This may explain why Strasbourg 'happened' to become the home of the 'Common Market' – based on the one the Nazis had been running for four years.

63　Wade Hamilton Haislip

64　A nickname gained from the Division's stand on the Marne river in World War One.

65　There was a minor German threat to Haislip's flank, but nothing of great importance.

66　In the middle years of the war, the Army's PR men gave bold nicknames to most of the American generals – 'Wild Bill', 'Hairless Harry', 'Iron Mike', etc. They tried to do the same for the colourless Bradley, but all they could come up with, on Eisenhower's specific orders, was 'GI General'. It never caught on. GIs did not have 'GI generals'.

67　In a similar move four or more months later, Pattons forced the Germans to withdraw from the West Wall or be trapped. Rapidly the defenders abandoned their positions before it came to that.

68　The official US figure is 80,000 plus 2,500 British casualties (never mentioned by American historians). A further 100,000 or so were incurred in the four months of 1945 after the Battle of the Bulge was officially declared to be over.

69　On 19 December 1945.

70　Even today some of the relevant documents are still 'classified', even down to the relatively harmless US Army Inspector General's reports on individual units.

71　Winterbotham was not really a Group Commander. But because of his job, as he told the author at the time, he used any rank he chose: 'I could have been a bloody Admiral if I had wanted to'.

72　The thousands of MAGIC documents that were finally declassified were so mixed and scrambled that it might have been assumed there had been a deliberate attempt to make it impossible for the researcher to find the relevant bits and pieces of the jigsaw.

2

Dark December

*It is plain that the enemy's strategy in defense of the Reich is based
on the exhaustion of our offensive to be followed up by an all-out
counterattack with armor between Roer and the Erft supported by
every weapon he can bring up.*

1st Army's Intelligence Estimate No. 37, 10 December 1944

About a month before Eisenhower angrily ordered Devers not to cross the
Rhine in strength and attack the Siegfried Line, far away in Washington,
Ike's mentor, General George Catlett Marshall was faced with an
agonising decision.

By nature, the stern, old-fashioned general, who would not allow even
the President to call him by his first name, did not like politicians. They
were always interfering in matters they knew nothing about, especially
his beloved US Army. Now a handsome, up-and-coming politico,
Governor Tom Dewey, who was running for President in the 1944
election, was threatening to reveal all he had been able to find out (from
what source is not known) about the American armed forces' most secret
decoding operation, 'MAGIC'.

For the past four years, perhaps longer, the top secret MAGIC decoders
had been cracking key Japanese communications at nearby Arlington
Hall, Virginia. Now Governor Dewey, a very high-profile public figure,
was preparing to make public that his Presidential opponent, Roosevelt,
had known all about the 'surprise' Japanese attack on the US Fleet at Pearl
Harbor in 1941. In other words, Dewey was going to use a top military
secret to discredit Roosevelt and win the election. This was gambling for
very high stakes – just how high only a deeply worried Marshall knew.

For there was more to it than simply the question of what really
happened at Pearl Harbor on 7 December '41. Dewey did not know that
the same MAGIC coding operation was still being used by the Japanese. If
he made public what he knew, he could destroy a potentially war-
winning Intelligence operation, as vitally important as Ultra at Bletchley
Park. What was Marshall to do?

In the end, without the knowledge of President Roosevelt, Marshall sent an emissary to Dewey. But Dewey did not believe what the US Chief-of-Staff was telling him. He thought it was a whitewash to cover up Roosevelt's double-dealing. In 1940-41 the President had tried every trick in the book to get the US into the war against the Axis powers. Pearl Harbor, which (in Dewey's view) he could have prevented, did the trick for him.

Marshall tried again. On 27 September he wrote a long letter to Dewey, explaining his position. In it he wrote:

> Now the point to the present dilemma is that we have gone ahead with this business of deciphering their [the Japanese's] codes until we possess other codes, German as well as Japanese, but our main basis of information regarding Hitler's intentions in Europe is obtained from Baron Oshima's messages from Berlin reporting his interviews with Hitler and other officials to the Japanese Government. These are still in the codes involved in the Pearl Harbor events.

Marshall went on to state (giving away a major secret, and one that remained secret long after the Ultra revelations):

> The conduct of General Eisenhower's campaign and of all the operations in the Pacific are closely related in conception and timing to the information we secretly obtain through these intercepted codes. They contribute greatly to the victory and tremendously to the saving of American lives.

Even before he had finished reading the long letter, the ambitious Dewey exclaimed: 'Well, I'll be damned if I believe the Japs are still using those two codes', by which he meant those used prior to the 'Day of Infamy' at Pearl Harbor.

Marshall's courier, who had taken the letter to Dewey, assured the former New York 'gang-buster' that this *was* the case, and that one of the two codes 'was our life blood in intelligence'. Indeed, Churchill regarded this 'secret weapon' – the Ultra/MAGIC operation – as having saved the United Kingdom in the dark middle years of the war.

Dewey grunted and said, 'There is little in this letter I don't already know. There is one point though. What in hell do Jap codes have to do with Eisenhower?'

The courier, Colonel Clarke, filled him in discreetly about the Bletchley operation and its value as a primary source of information for the Supreme Commander about the Germans. He added that by 1944 the decoding of the Japanese diplomatic cipher had, for Eisenhower, become just as important. Indeed, Eisenhower was one of a handful of recipients in Europe of what was called 'Black Book Ultra'.[73] This 'Ultra within Ultra' was strictly limited to top Americans, such as McArthur in the Pacific and the President himself.

Finally Dewey was convinced. He went to another room to have a brief discussion with an adviser, before returning and saying to Clarke: 'Colonel, I do not believe there are any questions I want to ask you, nor do I care to have any discussions about the contents of this letter.' Upon which they shook hands and, in parting, Governor Dewey said: 'Well, I hope we meet again under more auspicious circumstances.'

They never did, and that letter dated 27 September 1944, written at the time when US V Corps' first attack on the Siegfried Line finally failed, disappeared into the top secret files for three or four decades.

But who was the Japanese diplomat, Oshima? And why was he so important to Eisenhower, who played no part in the battle against the Japanese in the Pacific? More importantly, what role did he play in the events of that 'Black Christmas' of 1944?

In December 1940, one year before Pearl Harbor, Baron Hiroshi Oshima, a soldier-aristocrat and career diplomat, returned to Berlin. The 54-year-old had first served in the Nazi capital as military attaché of the Tokyo government in 1934. In that period he had become a fervent admirer of Hitler and had made excellent contacts with leading German generals and National Socialists. Now Oshima was returning as the Japanese ambassador, who had the ear of the Führer. For Hitler admired the Japanese for their series of victories in China and would soon admire them even more as they sent the Anglo-Americans scuttling in fear throughout the Far East. It was not long before the small, plump, bespectacled 'honorary Aryan' became Hitler's confidant . . . which was to prove very helpful to the Allies.

The US Intelligence Signals Service had broken the Japanese diplomatic code a few months before Baron Oshima returned to Berlin. As a result, Oshima would prove to be a key source on Hitler's thinking and planning right up to April 1945. Indeed, the little Japanese, as representative of Germany's most powerful ally in the 'Pact of Steel' or 'Axis' (Germany, Italy and Japan), was probably closer to the Führer than many of Hitler's intimates.

Over the years Oshima unwittingly revealed to the Allies in 1941 that Germany intended to invade Russia; two years later he reported to his masters in Tokyo that, although the Allied 'Bomber Barons' were inflicting heavy damage on German cities, it was not affecting Germany's war production. Indeed, he signalled to the Japanese capital in January 1944 that German output of essential heavy weapons, such as tanks and aircraft, was actually increasing, something which the German Minister of War Production, Speer, later confirmed.[74]

As D-Day approached, Oshima was invaluable for the information he was sending on the fortifications of the 'Atlantic Wall'. He signalled details of the German defences at Dieppe, Boulogne, Le Havre, etc., right down to where individual machine-guns were sited. He was even able to tell Tokyo – and so also the Allied code-breakers in Arlington and Bletchley – that Hitler did not believe the Allies were going to land in Normandy. That must have made the supposedly agonising decision to send in the invading force on 6 June 1944 a lot easier for Eisenhower.

During the summer of 1944 Oshima was silent. His eavesdroppers waited on tenterhooks. Finally, on 4 September Oshima told Tokyo that he was to meet Hitler the following day. By now the *Wehrmacht* had been defeated in France and was scuttling east in some disorder for the sanctuary of the Siegfried Line. Naturally the backroom boffins in Britain and the United States could not wait to get to work on Oshima's messages.

At first the decodes reflected the customary Hitlerian ramblings. The Führer could be as long-winded as the average pot-bellied German burgher pontificating at his local *Stammtisch* (local regular's table) over beer and pretzels. But then the boffins must have sat up in shock at what was coming through. Hitler told Oshima that, now that his divisions were reaching the security of the West Wall, he planned a counter-attack with forces being massed south-east of Nancy, soon to be Patton's Third Army HQ.

The news that Nazi Germany could be considering a counter-attack at this stage of the war in the west, with the German Army in France apparently shattered, must have made those interpreting Oshima's dispatches spill their tea. But as they ploughed through the decodes, they were in for more surprises. Oshima summarised what Hitler had said to him: 'It was his intention, as soon as the new army of more than a million men, now being organised was ready, to combine them with units to be withdrawn from the front in every area and, waiting upon the replenishment of the air forces, which is now in progress, to take the offensive in the west on a large scale.'

According to Oshima, Hitler expected this build-up to take place under the cover of the overcast, rainy weather usual in the Siegfried Line in September-October. The Allies would be unable to make full use of their overwhelming air superiority. Oshima reasoned that Hitler would attack in the west with this new, million-strong army 'after the beginning of November'.

That was the last interview Hitler granted the Japanese ambassador, though their relationship continued to function, even at atomic bomb level.[75] But could Allied Intelligence believe what Oshima, albeit unwittingly, was telling them? Was Hitler spinning the Japanese some kind of line? Surely it was clear that Hitler's Germany was on the brink of defeat. There was only one way to find out.

The attack that Oshima predicted would come in Lorraine in mid-September. On 18 September von Manteuffel's 5th Panzer Army (soon to play a key role in the Battle of the Bulge) launched an attack on Patton's Third Army at Luneville in the Nancy region. The German counter-attack lasted for eleven days but ended in failure. However, it did stop Patton's drive for the Siegfried Line. He would not be going through it 'like shit through a goose' this year.

Now Bletchley and Arlington concentrated their efforts on the MAGIC operation. During the period in question, Oshima sent twenty-eight signals to Tokyo dealing with the coming German offensive. On 16 November he met Germany's Foreign Minister, von Ribbentrop, formerly German ambassador to Great Britain.[76] Oshima reminded the vain '*England-Experte*' what the Führer had said about the great counter-attack in the west.

Von Ribbentrop was evasive. He would not reveal details of Hitler's timing. He said Germany *might* attack in the west. On the other hand, she might go in against the Red Army in the east.

Oshima mentioned the great Ludendorff offensive of March 1918, which had sent the British 5th Army in France reeling back towards the Channel. However, the ambassador suggested, some historians took the view that the offensive had in reality hastened Germany's defeat. Would it not be better and wiser 'for Germany to fight a war of attrition', as she had been doing for the last three months in the West Wall?

'Absolutely not,' von Ribbentrop snorted. 'The Chancellor believes we cannot win the war by defence alone and has reiterated his intention of taking the offensive to the bitter end.'

Oshima came away from his meeting with von Ribbentrop unconvinced. He signalled Tokyo that the German Foreign Minister's remark was 'one of those instances in which truth from the mouth of a liar reaches the highest pinnacle of deceptiveness'. However, later that same day, he changed his mind. He had a message transmitted to Japan stating that 'we may take at face value' the intention of the German leadership to attack, for 'a Germany whose battle lines have contracted virtually to the old territory of Germany[77] . . . will have no choice but to open a road of blood in one direction or another'. In his opinion, the 'road of blood' would lead westwards.

Of the twenty-eight messages Oshima sent to Tokyo between 16 August and 15 December 1944, eighteen stated that Germany intended to resume the offensive as soon as possible. In eight of them, the Japanese ambassador went on record, stating confidently that a large-scale attack would begin soon, and he singled out the Aachen area as its most likely objective. This, of course, was the 'small solution', advocated by Model.

The question now arises, why did Eisenhower not act on this information before the 'surprise' attack that was to have such disastrous results in the loss of young lives and territory? We know from the Marshall-Dewey correspondence that the American Chief-of-Staff believed that the Oshima decodes played a key part in Eisenhower's decision-making in Europe. Indeed, one of the earliest official visits Eisenhower made back home after Germany's defeat in 1945 was to Arlington. Through his Assistant Chief-of-Staff, General Vanderberg, he told the decoders that the information they had produced on the German fortifications 'was vital to the success of the Allied invasion of June 1944', and that he wanted to express 'his gratitude for the information from the Japanese diplomatic intercepts which had been provided to him'.

If then the Supreme Commander had always based his strategic decisions on Intelligence's assessments of German intentions gained from Ultra and MAGIC, why had the deciphered messages between Berlin and Tokyo not alerted him to the impending danger – even if Ultra was not now functioning one hundred percent? Oshima had always proved reliable in the past. Now in September 1944 the German counter-attack at Luneville, as predicted by Oshima, had shown he could still be relied on.

Was it gross carelessness on Eisenhower's part? Other indications were that, if the Germans were to attack, they would do so from their Siegfried Line positions along the Our-Sauer rivers line. The area was ideal for cover. The German positions were, in some cases, only yards from those of the Americans. The front could be well supplied across the Rhine through the half dozen railheads built in the Eifel in the Kaiser's time for military purposes.[78] Most importantly of all, this was the American 'Ghost Front', held by four US divisions along a sixty-mile front (two of them green, and the other two, the 4th and 28th Infantry Divisions, badly battered by the recent fighting in the Hürtgen).

In his confidential memo to Secretary of State for War, Pattison, in December 1945, Eisenhower confessed that he knew the Germans were about to attack. His problem had been that he did not know *where*. The facts tell that he was lying. He knew it was going to be in the weak 'Ghost Front'. Others in the Allied camp knew as well.

On 12 December, four days before the Germans attacked and seven days before he was called on by Eisenhower to do anything about the 'surprise' attack, Patton ordered his staff to 'be in a position to meet whatever happens. [Make] a study of what the Third Army would do if called upon to counter-attack such a breakthrough [in the north].' How did Patton know? Was it just clever guesswork on his part? Or had he known in advance that the Germans were going to drive out of the West Wall positions and attack over the Our-Sauer rivers line? And if he did know, who had told him?

Even the British, who had little close liaison with Eisenhower ever since Monty and Ike had begun to fall out over the question of command, knew in advance that something was afoot. As General David Belchem, Montgomery's Chief of Operations, stated a quarter of a century after these events: 'I do recall that in the British sector of the front we received

Soldiers of the US 87th Infantry Divison clear Coblenz.

Although under open arrest, Lt-Col. Richardson of the 10th US Armored Division risked his life to place explosive charges under Trier Bridge. He was killed in action a few days later. Patton called him 'a plucky little son-of-a-bitch'.

'Heartbreak Corner' – the last position in the Siegfried Line captured by the US Army before the Battle of the Bulge.

Traffic passes a bogged down tank-dozer during the 42nd Infantry Divison, Seventh US Army drive on Germany. The pillbox on the right is an outpost fortification of the Maginot Line.

The town of Cleve, captured by the Somerset Light
Infantry during the Battle of the Reichswald.

Lt General Jacob L Devers (left) talks to Brigadier General Peter P
Rodes; Maj. General Allison J Barnett (right) talks to Maj. General
Wade H Haislip in St Jean Rohrbach, France in February 1945.

The Germans were reduced to using young boys to boost their strength. These two prisoners, members of the 6th SS Mountain Division, were capturned by US Seventh Army soldiers in the Wimmenau area of France.

Twelve hundred men, mostly Serbs, Yogoslavs and Russians, escaped en masse from a German prisoner of war hospital in St Wendel, France. Here they wait in a Maginot Line bunker for transportation to the rear of the US Seventh Army sector.

The 20-strand copper wire glistens in the sunlight as men
of the 257th Signal Construction Company, 7th Army Group
follow close behind advancing troops.

The last barrier – the Rhine is crossed.
US troops use a captured German 75mm anti-tank gun to blast
the enemy at the Rhine Herne Canal near Recklinghausen.

'The most famous bridge in the world' – for a week.
The Remagen Bridge before its collapse.

Patton's victory at the Rhine. Truckloads of German troops
were captured during the Third Army's drive to the Rhine.

They passed this way.
The author points
out tank tracks still
visible in the forest
fifty years later.

The 'Cat's Head' bunker today.

The 'Cats Head' bunker, restored in 1999 and now open to the public.

The 'Cat's Head' today, looking over the Sauer river where the US 76th Division made its assault crossing from Luxembourg in 1945.

some slender indication of a possible enemy action of some kind in the Ardennes during early December. But the information was so vague, and our US Allies so sure of continued inactivity there, that we disregarded them.'

'Vague' they may have been, but within thirty-six hours of the German attack, before even Eisenhower's subordinates were aware of what had hit them, Montgomery was already (unofficially) taking over command of Hodges' First Army together with the US 9th Army. He had alerted his five-division strong XXX Corps to move into the Ardennes, and was already moving SAS troops plus armoured cavalry to the stopline of the Meuse river[79] in the Ardennes – all without Eisenhower's permission. How had Montgomery been so well prepared? Intuition . . . foresight . . . *or concrete knowledge of what was to come*?

By December 1944 Eisenhower's armies had been battering themselves against the Siegfried Line for three long months, and were getting nowhere. Losses were very high, and by the start of the month, Eisenhower's infantry divisions, which were doing most of the fighting, were down to eighty percent of their official strength. In the Hürtgen alone, the 1st Army was sending in an infantry division virtually every two weeks, and withdrawing it at the end of that time, decimated, with losses amounting to as much as fifty percent of its riflemen.

Bolder, if blinkered, spirits at Eisenhower's HQ were maintaining that the Allies were winning this bloody battle of attrition. In fact, the opposite was true. The Germans raised a dozen new, if smaller, divisions equipped with the latest weapons, at a time when Germany's arms production was the highest it had been throughout the entire war. In contrast, the Allies were finding it exceedingly difficult to fill the gaps in their decimated infantry.

Britain was forced to cannibalise two infantry divisions, the 50th and the 59th, to find replacements, and Churchill ordered the call-up of another quarter of a million men for the infantry, although most of them were in 'reserved' occupations and aged up to 45. For his part, Bradley ordered a five percent levy on the US Army's rear echelon personnel, and even called for volunteers among blacks in a hitherto strictly segregated army.

How then was Eisenhower to break the impasse on the German frontier and crack the Siegfried Line at last? That running sore had to be dealt with sooner or later, or his job would be on the line. Marshall did not tolerate failure for very long.

In that autumn of 1944 it must have seemed to a sorely tried Eisenhower that there could be only one way to lure the Germans out of their Siegfried Line and make them do battle on ground of his choosing – where he would be able to exploit Allied air and armoured superiority. That was to bait a trap for them, to offer a tempting target, that Hitler would know he could take easily with his massive new build-up in the west. And that target had to be the 'Ghost Front'.

The Germans had had weeks in which to assess the strength of the American units holding the sixty-mile front. Each US division was manning twice the length of line normal when facing top-rate troops – on average five miles. German spies – 'sleepers', long-serving agents left behind in Allied territory in September, and special reconnaisance parties which (as was ascertained later) had penetrated as far behind the Allied front as Bastogne – had long ago spotted the weaknesses of Middleton's US VIII Corps in the Ardennes. Even Colonel-General von Manteuffel, commander of the German Fifth Panzer Army, had spied on the American 106th, 28th and 4th Infantry Divisions from the German front-line positions.

Eisenhower had done nothing to rectify these weaknesses in the 'Ghost Front'. By December major offensive operations had come to a virtual standstill on Bradley's 12th Army Group front. Nowhere along the whole Siegfried Line was there a single Allied armoured division engaged in the fighting. All fourteen were in reserve of one kind or another. Why? Because it would be the armoured divisions to left and right of the US corps on the 'Ghost Front' that Eisenhower would need to respond rapidly, once the Germans had launched their 'surprise' assault out of the West Wall.

Eisenhower, as has been suggested, *knew* the Germans were coming. He *wanted* them to come. He was prepared to sacrifice those green youngsters, disguised as infantrymen, holding the line of the Our-Sauer rivers, if it would get the enemy out into the open. He knew he would not survive another Normandy, where it had taken the Allies from June to August to break out of the beachheads. The cost in lives had been horrendous.

Montgomery, as overall ground commander, had taken the flak. Normandy had marked the beginning of his decline in the public eye as the Allies' most famous battle commander.

Now Eisenhower had been head of all Allied ground forces, his first ever field command, since the end of September. He had been foiled on the Siegfried Line time and time again. Sooner or later the Great American Public would become aware of what was happening on the German border, and of how many lives that damned West Wall was costing.[80] Then heads would roll, and Eisenhower knew that Churchill still constituted a powerful force, and would support any move to have 'Monty' take over again.

In short, the Siegfried Line had held him up for too long. It was time the 'Krauts' came out of their damned bunkers and from behind their 'dragon's teeth' and fought in the open.

Opposite Middleton's four divisions on the 'Ghost Front', the Germans were ready to do just that, confident that the enemy was not aware they were coming. This was 'five minutes to midnight' as the Germans called it (in English, 'the eleventh hour'). Nearly three million German soldiers had already died. Now the surviving best and the bold, the fiercest and the most fanatical were going to make one last desperate effort to alter the fate of the Reich. Hasso von Manteuffel, Otto Skorzeny, Heilmann of the legendary 'Green Devils' . . . and all the other doomed, desperate heroes of the 'Thousand-Year Reich' knew it was now or never.

It was 0530 on Saturday 16 December 1944 – a date that would change the history of the rest of the 20th century. They were coming out of their Siegfried Line fortifications at last.

NOTES

73　In the winter of 1944 Marshall had introduced a summary of all top Japanese intercepts, bound in a black book. In February 1944 he started sending 'Black Book Ultra' to President Roosevelt.

74　One reason was that Germany transferred the production to the occupied and supposedly allied countries, such as Czechoslovakia (Skoda) and France (Renault), which the Allies were reluctant to bomb. The Czech Skoda works, for example, turned out a quarter of all German armoured vehicles, and the head of Renault was forced to commit suicide at the end of the war because of this collaboration.

75　In the last months of the war, Japanese and German submarines conveyed some of Germany's greatest military secrets, including atomic bomb research, to Japan.

76　Von Ribbentrop's son, an officer in the SS, attended public school in the UK, and was almost certainly the only public school man serving in the premier SS division, *Die Leibstandarte Adolf Hitler*. Later, von Ribbentrop Jr took part in the Battle of the Bulge.

77　By the 'old territory' he meant Germany's pre-war 1939 boundaries, with the Russians in East Prussia and the Allies on the Siegfried Line.

78　Some 800 trains were sent to such townships as Wittlich, Gerolstein and Kyllburg during the run up to the attack – something of which Allied Intelligence were aware.

79　The Meuse was the last natural barrier in the Ardennes. Once it had been crossed by the Germans, they would have had a clear run across the flat Belgian plain to the strategic supply port of Antwerp, their ultimate objective. The British role in stopping the Germans in this area has never been detailed in full. As Montgomery ruefully said afterwards: 'The less said about the Ardennes the better.'

80　A whole book could be written on how American domestic political issues affected the conduct of the war in Europe from 1942 onwards.

3

Breakthrough

We're Americans . . . We're supposed to win.

Mel Brooks, *Playboy*, 1985

While the Germans waited, here and there the unsuspecting cannon-fodder went on attacking the West Wall, even though those at the top already knew their efforts were wasted.

Devers' forgotten US Seventh Army[81] had reached the German frontier and the Siegfried Line. A couple of days earlier its 45th Infantry Division (known as 'The Thunderbirds' on account of their divisional patch) had paused before Lembach, the first German village on the other side of the French border.

Then Colonel Dwight Funk, commander of the 158th Artillery Battalion, had telephoned his superior, Colonel Walter O'Brien, commanding the 157th Battalion of 'The Thunderbirds'. He snapped happily, 'Colonel, from where we are, we can put a barrage across the border. Say the word and we can toss a concentration into Germany.' O'Brien did not hesitate. 'What are you waiting for?' he yelled over the field telephone. 'Fire away!'

Now before dawn on this Saturday, the victorious infantrymen of the 'Thunderbirds' Division were probing the Siegfried Line defences for the first time.[82] They would be back, but not until three months later, and by then most of the division's men would be dead or wounded.

Fortunately for these first platoons and companies of the 'Thunderbirds', the initial German defences in the wooded, hilly terrain were lightly held. As the Divisional History of the 45th states: 'The ease with which the border was breached gave no indication of the bitter fighting which lay ahead.' Now, however, the attackers had already perfected a simple routine to 'take out' these initial defences. It was done by using the enemy's own routine against him. The history of the 'Thunderbirds' notes:

It was observed . . . that the enemy would remain within the concrete bunkers until notified of the approach of enemy troops. As hostile elements came into view, the outpost would sound a whistle and the German troops would leave their pillbox to man their posts in an elaborate series of communication and firing trenches attached to each strongpoint. Only the machine-guns in the bunkers remained inside the fortifications themselves.

This was a procedure which the attackers turned against the Germans. As soon as the Siegfried Line position came in sight, the infantry commander called down an artillery, mortar or tank-gun barrage on both the pillbox and the communication trench. This prevented the enemy from making use of these positions. Now the infantry turned their rifles on both the communication trench and the firing slits of the pillbox.

Some bold infantryman, eager for desperate glory – and possible death – would work his way towards the pillbox. If he made it that far, so that he was in the dead ground, he would draw one last deep breath, raise himself and bolt madly for the air vent on top of the pillbox. If he survived, he would drop one of those terrible phosphorous grenades the Americans used down the opening.

The Germans inside usually panicked. Choked by the acrid, white, blinding fumes, trying to beat the burning pellets from their clothes and flesh (they could only be put out by cutting off the oxygen supply; otherwise they burned right down to the bone), they rushed outside into the communication trench. This was already well covered by mortar and rifle fire. Caught in the open with no place to go, 'the Germans', as the Divisional History feelingly put it, 'either surrendered or died'.

By the time the 'Thunderbirds' Division was overtaken by events and was forced to withdraw from the Siegfried Line, the veterans of Italy and southern France had opened a gap of 1,700 yards and had penetrated Hitler's West Wall to a depth of 1,200 yards. But it had taken the whole division, some 15,000-strong, and four days of fighting to capture a mere seven pillboxes. Still, they were through, and the Seventh Army could mark up its first triumph on the Siegfried Line. That Saturday morning's edition of *The Stars and Stripes* headlined their modest triumph: '7th Smashes Into Germany'.

At the other end of the long Siegfried Line front, totally unaware of what was coming their way in a few short hours, another veteran US division, the 2nd 'Indianhead' Infantry, did the same. Finally, after weeks of trying, they captured the key crossroads leading to the Hürtgen defences. 'Heartbreak Crossroads' the GIs called the Wahlerscheid crossroads north of Monschau, where the Germans were currently targetting the northern flank of their great 'surprise' offensive. But this day it was the Americans who did the 'surprising'.

During the night, with any sound they made muffled by a damp mist, two battalions of the 2nd Infantry moved into the German positions and found the enemy asleep in their trenches and pillboxes. The leading units did not wait for the 'Krauts' to wake up. They moved in. Rapidly they took the *Zollhaus*, the customs post on the Belgo-German border that had held them up for so long. Here they found seventy-six sleepy German soldiers who obligingly surrendered. Thereafter, they rolled up pillbox after pillbox, using the new techniques they had learned in November. Just before dawn they had finished the job. At the extremely modest cost of one man killed, one missing and seventeen wounded, the 'Indianhead' men had taken all of their objectives. 'Heartbreak Crossroads' were American at last.

But then they became aware of the first flickering, pink lights on the horizon. In the icy wind now blowing over the crossroads, they could hear the rumble of artillery. They stared in puzzlement. Something was going on in the area of Monschau – something big. But what the Sam Hill was it?

Captain MacDonald, the future chronicler of the Battle of the Bulge, was there at dawn. He was leading his 'I' Company to the attack through the green US 99th 'Checkerboard' Division, when he too heard the angry rumble of artillery. But he first knew something was seriously wrong when the greenhorns of the 99th began to filter through the misty, green fortresses opposite the Siegfried Line.

There were about 200 of them, all disorganised and frightened. They told the 22-year-old captain that they had been hit hard by attacking 'Krauts', had taken severe losses, and were not sticking around to have another crack at the advancing enemy. An anxious MacDonald tried to persuade them, but only two volunteered to stay and hold.

Now the trouble really began. Dug in, waiting for the enemy to come over the opposite ridge, and as the angry snap-and-crack of small arms fire grew louder, MacDonald called for covering fire. But he did not have much luck. Apparently his fellow company commanders of the 2nd Infantry were doing the same thing. The 'Krauts' were attacking everywhere. MacDonald wrote later:

> Wave after wave of fanatically screaming German infantry stormed over the slight, tree-covered rise by the three platoons. A continuous hail of fire exuded from their weapons, answered by volley after volley from the defenders. Germans fell left and right. The few rounds of artillery we did succeed in bringing down caught the attackers in the draw to our front, and we could hear their screams of pain when the small arms fire slackened. But they still came on.

Ammunition began to run out. MacDonald informed battalion. The answer he got was a curt 'hold at all costs'. The sensitive future author wondered if Battalion HQ really knew what those words meant. 'We must hold until every last man was killed or captured. Company I's last stand!

And what is to be gained? Nothing. But time. Time born of the bodies of men. *Time!*'

All around MacDonald's embattled positions, 88mm shells began to explode in massive, earth-shaking thumps, followed by bursts of angry red and yellow flame. The great, white-painted monsters, well over fifty tons, started to nose their way through the snow-laden firs, knocking them over, snapping them effortlessly like puny matchsticks.

'For God's sake, Cap'n,' one of his platoon commanders, nearly at the end of his tether, sobbed over the field telephone, 'get those tanks down here. Do something, for God's sake. Those bastards are sittin' seventy-five yards away, pumping 88s into our foxholes . . . like we was sittin' ducks. *For God's sake!*'

But the young officer, on this first day of his combat career, could do nothing. The Shermans sent to support their attack had turned tail and scuttled for the safety of the rear. All he could yell back above the tremendous racket was, 'For God's sake hold . . . We've got to hold.'

The time for holding was already over, however. Men started to abandon their positions. They drifted back in twos and threes. Their faces wore 'vague, blank expressions'. When MacDonald looked at them, they avoided his gaze, lowered their eyes, looked the other way. His company was falling apart.

Ignoring the slugs slicing the air all around him, MacDonald rose to his feet. Like a player in some sort of catching game in the schoolyard, he flapped his outstretched hands at them angrily. He tried to wave them back to their positions, but to no avail. They had had enough. The men of the 'Indianhead', veterans and greenhorns alike, had used up all their courage and determination. Dazed and zombie-like, they wandered off towards the rear, finally disappearing into the green Ardennes forest.

Half an hour later, what was left of 'I' Company were running for their lives. Over the chatter and rattle of one of their machine-gunners, still defiantly trying to hold the attackers back, MacDonald heard his superior, Lieutenant Wilson, yell 'Withdraw'. MacDonald later recalled:

> I wanted to obey, but I was caught in the crossfire of the heavy machine-gun and the attackers. I gritted my teeth and waited for a lull in the firing. None came. I jumped from the hole and ran blindly toward the rear. Bullets snipped at my heels. The tank saw we were running again and opened up with renewed vigor, the big shells snapping the tops from the trees around us as if they were matchsticks. But I saw no one fall.

Dusk was now approaching, and MacDonald and his survivors knew they would not make Rocherath and Krinkelt.[83] They plunged blindly into the trees. MacDonald recalled:

I slipped and fell face down in the snow. I rose and fell again. I cursed my slick overshoes. I found myself not caring if the Germans did fire. My feet were soaked. Perspiration covered my body and my mouth was dry. I wanted a cigarette. I felt we were like helpless little bugs scurrying blindly about, now that some monster had lifted the log under which we had been hiding. I wondered if it would not be better to be killed and perhaps that would be an end to everything.

Along the whole length of the Siegfried Line, young soldiers were fighting, dying, giving in to despair, running for their lives, suffering the ignominy of raising their hands in surrender. Middleton's VIII Corps, veterans and greenhorns alike, collapsed. It all seemed hopeless. Outnumbered four to one by the best troops Germany still had, led by the elite of the Third Reich's military commanders, it seemed to many of them that they did not stand a chance.

Colonel Dupuy, the professional military historian who wrote the history of the ill-fated US 106th Infantry Division, which had been in the line for exactly five days, stated:

Let's get down to hard facts. Panic, sheer unreasoning panic flamed that road[84] all day and into the night. Everyone, it seemed, who had an excuse and many who had none was going west that day – west from Schoenberg, west from St Vith too. Jeeps, trucks, tanks, guns and great lumbering Corps Artillery vehicles, which took three-quarters of the road – some of them double-banking. Now and again vehicles were weaving into a third line, now and again crashing into ditches. All this on a two-lane highway. Again this was what the Seventh Armored Division [ordered up to help out] was bucking . . .

In other words, the situation was totally, hopelessly confused and desperate.

The feelings of the average soldier – one who had been taken up by the military machine back in the States, carried halfway round the world, and dumped in this 'asshole of the world' – might well be expressed in the words of Mel Brooks. The Jewish comic and film-maker described his own experiences in a *Playboy* interview forty years later:

Then one day they put us all in trucks, drove us to the railroad station, put us in a locked train with the windows blacked out. We get off the train, we get on a boat. We get off the boat, we get into trucks. We get out of the trucks. We start walking. Suddenly all around us *Waauhwaahwaauh!* Sirens! Tiger tanks! We're surrounded by the Germans. It's the Battle of the Bulge! Hands up! 'Wait,' I say, 'we've just left Oklahoma. We're Americans. We're supposed to win.' *Very* scary, but we escaped . . . And then *they* started shooting. 'Incoming Mail.' Bullshit! Only Burt Lancaster says that. We said, 'Oh God, Oh Christ!' Who knows, he might help. He was Jewish too . . . MOTHER!

Funny, perhaps. But it was not so funny for the 20,000 young Americans killed, wounded or captured in those first three days of the attack across the Our-Sauer rivers line.

The 'surprise' German counter-attack in the Ardennes (which obviously went seriously wrong for Eisenhower) marked the end of the first Allied campaign against the Siegfried Line. Since 13 September it had taken nearly one million Allied fighting men to penetrate it in half a dozen places – from Geilenkirchen in the north, around Aachen-Hürtgen in the centre, down to the Seventh Army area in Lorraine.

At best, these penetrations, so hard won, had not gone deeper than a dozen miles or so (near Juelich). Nor had any really war-winning stretch been conquered, save for the stretch in the Eifel around the Hürtgen Forest, hardly ideal terrain for a massive final thrust. And the cost in young lives had been frightening.

During this first campaign, the US First Army lost 7,024 men killed, wounded or missing, plus another 4,860 taken prisoner. The Ninth Army's losses (and it had come comparatively late to the battle) were 1,135 dead, 6,864 wounded or missing, and a further 2,093 captured. To this must be added another 11,000 American casualties suffered by outfits serving under British or Canadian command, bringing the total American losses on the front to 68,000 men. There were a further 50,672 non-battle casualties in the First Army, and 20,787 in the Ninth. In the Saar and later West Wall battles, Patton's Third Army lost 67,956 men, in both battle and non-battle casualties. All this resulted in a grand total, for three and a half months of battling for a breakthrough in the Siegfried Line, of 200,000 men, the population of a good-sized British or American city.

Looking back now, it is clear that the Germans dominated the 1944 Battle of the Siegfried Line the whole way, just as they brought it to an abrupt end with their attack on 16 December. Although they never really held the initiative, but were forced to react to Allied initiatives, they did determine the outcome of the West Wall battle, defending with meagre and ad hoc forces, while they built up the counter-attack force for the drive out of the Line into the Ardennes.

Admittedly the Germans had sustained grievous losses too, but not as many as the attackers. Yet, after ninety-six days of siege warfare, Model's soldiers had come out fighting. It was Middleton's VIII Corps that broke in the Ardennes and started to fall back on that Saturday. It would be the start of America's 'Gettysburg of the 20th century', the biggest and longest land battle US forces fought in World War Two, indeed in the whole of the 20th century. Whose victory was it in the end?

The young men in field-grey and olive drab, slogging it out in the snow and the forests of the Ardennes, did not bother themselves with such questions. They had other things on their minds – such as surviving.

And on the heights and ridges of the Eifel, now covered with a thick layer of snow, the Great Wall of Germany fell silent. It was almost as if some huge, primeval, predatory creature was resting, and waiting – waiting for the young men to come again. Of that there was no doubt. They would be back.

NOTES

81 The US Seventh Army had been raised by Patton for the invasion of Sicily in 1943. After Patton had been dismissed from his command, because of the famous 'slapping incident', the Seventh was taken over by General 'Sandy' Patch. He was a quiet man with none of the flamboyant Patton's dash and colour. He was certainly no good at providing 'copy' for journalists. As a result, the Seventh became the 'Forgotten Army'.

82 Within three days their attack was ordered stopped, and the 45th would be pulling back to face the unknown 'Battle of the Bulge' (Operation NORTHWIND).

83 Two Belgian villages, among the first to be attacked. Two months later Krinkelt was the last piece of Belgian territory to be re-liberated, five months after the Allies had entered the country.

84 The same road taken by Colonel 'Buck' Lanham's 22nd Infantry when they first attacked the Siegfried Line three long months earlier.

BOOK 3

January to March 1945

We can still lose this war.

General Patton, 4 January 1945

1

The Limeys take a Hand Again

See '45 and survive.

GI quip

On the morning of Tuesday 16 January 1945, the soldiers of two American armies, the First and the Third, were struggling to link up, through waist-deep snow and slick, icy roads against stiff German opposition. Their objective was the little, wrecked Belgian border town of Houffalize, from where Hemingway had set out on his adventures. It did not matter that the First and Third Armies had already linked up at LaRoche a few days earlier, symbolising the end of the Battle of the Bulge. For there the meeting, duly photographed in a whirling snowstorm, had been with the Black Watch of the British Army and the 'Rail-Splitters' of Geilenkirchen fame. This time the world had to know that it was American soldiers under American generals who had been doing the fighting.[85]

For thirty-one days the Allied troops, mostly American, had waged an infantry war in the worst conditions Europe had experienced in a quarter of a century. The weather had been consistently bleak, the ground covered by a thick blanket of snow. In constant sub-zero temperatures, the infantry had plodded into battle time after time, their faces like old leather, turned brick-red by the howling wind filled with razor-sharp particles of frozen snow. For the most part it had been a 'footslogger's' war. The Allied air forces had made brief appearances over Christmas and New Year. As for the armoured vehicles, they had slid and skidded on the Belgian roads, cleared of snow by the engineers' bulldozers, only to be turned into solid sheets of treacherous ice. All in all, the fighting, the killing, and the suffering had, as usual, been the lot of the PBI (the Poor Bloody Infantry).

Now Houffalize, the last town of any size in the area before the German border and the West Wall, was being pounded by Britain's latest secret weapon – the proximity fuse, a radar-directed shell with unprecedented accuracy and deadly effect.

Still, Field Marshal Model tried desperately to hold on to the crossroads town. Following a considerable struggle with Hitler for permission to withdraw and save his remaining armour, he had secured it, and for the past five days he had been making the '*Amis*' pay a high price for their attempt to take Houffalize, the town through which that armour was now escaping.

British war correspondent R W Thompson of the *Sunday Times*, who was following the Americans, advancing at a slow mile per day, noted the beauty of the snow-covered Ardennes hills. But he also noted:

> With every mile forward, this loveliness becomes a menace and a horror to fight with all the energy each man can muster ... Up every hill the troops are manhandling the heavy trucks trying to gain a wheel grip even with chains. Here and there the tracked vehicles slither hopelessly to subside deep into the ditches ... But all the time bulldozers are working, clearing and breaking up the snow and ice to powder, and civilians are smashing away with picks and shovels, while every man with a spade digs down to the earthy roadside banks beneath the snow to shovel soil for the wheels that must grip ... their ears are blasted constantly by shock as heavy guns roar and splash this white world with bursts of flame.

While Thompson reported the Americans' desperate efforts to link up, and as the photographers from the US Signal Corps waited impatiently to get their shots of what would be called 'this historic event', Patton and his driver, Sergeant Mims, set off from Patton's HQ in Luxembourg to view the newly liberated town. As always, Patton would not miss a chance for personal publicity.

Thirty-one days earlier, the two of them had set off from Nancy into the unknown. Bradley, Patton's one-time subordinate, had welcomed him with open arms – Patton and his Third Army had been the only US outfit under his command, now that Montgomery was (albeit secretly) running the First and Ninth Armies.

Patton had revelled in his new found power, especially as Bradley had been so pathetically grateful. Together they had created the legend of the 'Siege and Relief' of Bastogne and its 'Battered Bastards', now to be called for all time 'Nuts City'.[86]

Patton had even agreed to resign with Bradley if Montgomery was ever given overall command of American troops again, as he had been in Normandy. But the previous Sunday, Monty had blotted his copybook with his vain, supercilious account of how *he* had won the Battle of the Bulge. The 'little fart Monty', as Patton styled the Field Marshal, was out of the running and Patton was going to enjoy his second symbolic victory at Houffalize.

The drive to Houffalize, which turned out to have been 'extremely well liberated', as Patton put it, turned into something of a battlefield tour. At one point the General ordered Mims to stop and pick up a German machine-gunner at the side of the road, who appeared to want to surrender. When Mims spoke to the man he did not reply. The driver touched the German. To his horror, the man tumbled over slowly, still retaining his posture with his arms spread wide, holding a belt of cartridges for his MG 42. He had been hit and had instantly frozen to death.

This was typical of the drive in such weather conditions, but it was unnerving nevertheless. A short time later Patton ordered his driver to stop again so that he could investigate what appeared to be a line of black-purple twigs sticking above the surface of the glistening snow. Were they part of a new type of mine, the General wondered. They were not. They were the toes of a dead soldier whose boots had been looted after he was hit. Even the hardboiled 'Ole Blood an' Guts' admitted to his staff later that it had been 'a nasty sight'. The last act in the Battle of the Bulge was being played out in a kind of refrigerator, it seemed, that turned the dead instantly to the colour of mature claret.

But while Patton drove on into the ruined city, wondering whether he should have put some colour film into his camera to photograph the corpses as they really appeared (Patton was always taking photographs of men killed in action), his boss. Eisenhower, far away in Paris, was contemplating what to do next with Patton. A visiting general, Everett Hughes, an old tittle-tattle and intimate crony of both Ike and 'Georgie', was told by the Supreme Commander: 'Everett, George is a very great soldier and I must get Marshall to do something for him before the war is over.'[87]

Although Eisenhower knew that Patton, 'the Liberator of the Battered Bastards of Bastogne', would have to play a greater role in the coming second battle for the West Wall, he also had to consider the British and, in particular, the now (among the US Army) hated Montgomery.

In the end Eisenhower decided that he would let Montgomery go ahead with his second crack at the Siegfried Line in the north. There the British would attack a triangular section of German territory, roughly twenty miles long on each side, called the Heinsberg Salient and defended by three main lines of fortifications that were 'offshoots' of the Siegfried Line.

The first comprised a continuous line of trenches and weapons pits, covered by barbed wire and minefields, with a reserve position to the rear. One and a half miles behind the reserve position was the second line. The third extended from the Siegfried Line to the small town of Heinsberg and a short distance beyond it. This whole formidable position was held by two German infantry divisions, supported by 156 guns and eighteen assault guns, plus a weapon just as deadly, but still unknown to the British – murderous, waterlogged terrain.

Even as it stood, the Heinsberg Salient was not going to be an easy position to crack, although Montgomery had two infantry divisions, one armoured and the 1st Commando Brigade, at his disposal. The 43rd Infantry Division under General 'Butcher' Thomas had been fighting since Normandy, and was tremendously experienced. Despite appalling casualties, it had never failed Thomas in the end. The other division, the 52nd Lowland, was less experienced. It had trained for most of the war as a mountain division, only to go into action in October 1944, not in the mountains of Norway as the men anticipated, but at the *lowest* point of northern Europe – the Dutch Walcheren Islands. However, it retained most of its original personnel, and had not been weakened by a mass influx of 19-year-old reinforcements with, at most, three months' infantry training.

On the whole, those of the division who had been recruited in Scotland (many were Englishmen posing as Scots) were tough little men. Products of the Depression and the dole, they had survived the 1930s with 'a bag of fish an' taties' or 'penny ducks', combined with their native cunning. The Army had filled them out, giving them brawn and muscle. But the Army had not been able to break their vicious, trigger-happy tempers (especially when drunk) and they were formidable opponents. If a prisoner did not surrender sharply enough, 'the Jocks', as they were universally called, did not give 'old Jerry' a second chance. When the official company report read 'no prisoners taken', everyone knew why.

The men of the 1st Special Brigade, the Commandos, were not only tough, they were disciplined too. Most of them were older than the average soldier, and had been fighting since the 1940 raids in the Arctic Circle. They had learned to be controlled, deliver their attack where least expected, and, as their commanding officer put it in his standard maxim: 'React quickly on first contact with the enemy and hold your fire until you can be certain to kill.'

On the whole, both veterans and green replacements were a hardy lot, who expected little from army life, and were not disappointed when that was what they got. They were happy with the simple pleasures that came their way infrequently – a NAAFI issue of a bottle of beer, an egg fried on a shovel, a buckshee tin of fifty fags.

They spoke their own lingo, dating back to the days when the 'old sweats got their knees brown' in some far-flung corner of the Empire, upon which the sun never set. For them, young and old, 'dollai' meant mad, 'dhoby' to wash, a man was a 'wallah', a woman a 'bint', and 'char' was that indispensable beverage without which the average 'squaddie' could not function – tea.

In the last few months in Europe, they had added some new words: 'zig-zag' meant drunk and 'jig-jag' to copulate. Anything found or looted was declared 'liberated', perhaps after the official name of their army, 'The British Liberation Army' – the BLA. As the wags cracked, those initials also indicated their future fate, Burma Looms Ahead.

Now these young men, rigidly constrained in their class and regimental system, and with nicknames like 'Hell's Last Issue' (The Highland Light Infantry) and 'Pontius Pilate's Bodyguard' (The Royal Scots), would bear the brunt of the first battle of the second campaign against the Great Wall of Germany.

At 0730 on Tuesday 16 January 1945 the Jock infantry in their camouflage smocks started to advance through a milky white fog. With bayonets fixed, the first wave waded through the knee-high tendrils of mist, waiting for the first high-pitched scream of a German MG 42.

It came soon enough. But when it did, that first startling burst of fire – one thousand rounds per minute – made even the 'old sweats' jump. Now, as the Jocks of the 4/5th Royal Scots Fusiliers began to cross the first stream and climb the high bank on the other side, the Germans opened up from a house to their immediate front. Suddenly the Jocks were galvanised into violent action. Ignoring the barbed wire and mines, they doubled forward. Men began to go down on all sides. Still they kept moving, ignoring the pitiful cries of their wounded comrades and the angry shouts, 'stretcher-bearer . . . for Chrissake stretcher-bearer'. Now there was a stark choice – piss or get off the pot.

Fusilier Dennis Donnini, a 19-year-old member of that assault wave with only seven months in the Army, was one of those hit. Struck in the head, he tumbled into a frozen ditch unconscious. To those who left him behind, it must have seemed that Dennis had done his bit. Besides, why should he do any more? His father was not even British; he was an Italian ice-cream merchant from the North of England, who had never been naturalised, and had already lost one of his three sons killed in action.

Young Donnini must have thought differently. He regained consciousness. Struggling to his feet, his head pouring blood, he staggered on for thirty yards. He came up to the first defended German house, paused, and flung a grenade through the window. A stream of black smoke poured through the shattered window. There were screams of panic, shouts of anger. A few moments later, the German occupiers fled panic-stricken deeper into the pillbox line.

Donnini and a handful of men still on their feet from the decimated platoon pushed on. Under murderous machine-gun fire, they doubled across a field. Panting frantically, their lungs working like bellows, they flung themselves into the shelter of a barn. But not Donnini. Weakening visibly, he went on and brought in a wounded Jock. Still the brave young man, with his dark, flashing eyes, was not finished. He grabbed a Bren gun and single-handedly charged the German trenches a hundred yards away.

Firing from the hip, he was hit again. He dropped to one knee, panting hectically. Still he went on firing. He forced himself to his feet. But now his luck was running out fast. A German threw a stick grenade at him when he was only ten yards from the trench. He disappeared for an instant in the ugly burst of violet light. When he reappeared, his comrades could see him sinking, his legs giving way beneath him like those of a new-born foal. He was finished. Later he was awarded the British Empire's highest award for bravery in the field, the Victoria Cross – posthumously.

Donnini was not the only one. A day or so later, the Commandos of the 1st Special Brigade were pinned down at the first fortified position they attacked just outside the village of St Joostburg. The men in the green berets lay in the snow, their wounded lying alongside them. Lance Corporal Eric Harden of the Royal Army Medical Corps (which did not enjoy a good reputation in the Army due to the fact that wounded men believed the RAMC stole their possessions when they were unconscious) volunteered to go out and pick up the wounded Commandos.

Permission was given and Harden doubled forward 120 yards under intense rifle and machine-gun fire. He reached the wounded, and bandaged up an officer and three other ranks. But the young corporal's devotion to duty did not end there. He started to drag the most seriously wounded soldier back. He yelped and stopped. The men watching him gasped. He had been hit. Harden had a painful wound in his side. But that did not stop him. He recovered after a few moments and continued in his perilous rescue attempt. Once back in his own position, a swearing, angry medical officer ordered him to stay where he was; he was not to go out again.

Harden refused point blank. He took a volunteer party of stretcher-bearers not once, but twice, to bring in the wounded, weakening notice-ably due to loss of blood. Then, finally, he started to bring in the Com-mando officer who had been waiting for a long time, alone with his agony. Despite this, he had ordered that he was to be brought in last.

But now Harden's luck had finally run out. On his way back with the wounded officer, the young medic was hit in the head. He went down as if poleaxed, and this time for good. He too was awarded the Victoria Cross – again posthumously.

So it went on. Countless men were killed or wounded, some winning the VC, the most noble award of all, for a few square miles of sodden, snowbound fields that today are cow pastures, and which few if any British could point to on a map.

The first German line of defence was taken. The second too. The Commandos, fighting their way through the massed, confused German positions, discovered they were completely lost. The only prisoner they had taken was no help – he was as lost as they were. Even when gently 'squeezed', he could reveal nothing of his comrades' positions. All he could say, repeating it like some litany learned in childhood was: 'I wish to die for the Führer. I wish to die for the Führer.' Whether the irate Commandos granted his wish is not recorded. They blundered on through the smoke and fog of battle. Tracer zig-zagged crazily back and forth like swarms of angry red hornets as they ran for the first line of German-occupied houses.

Medical Officer, Captain Moore, found his way into tiny cellar. In the flickering flame of a stump of candle he could just make out a filthy confusion of 'old and withered people, huddled together under ragged sheets and blankets'. Some were German. Others were Dutch, brought across the nearby border to work on the local farms. One of these, a young woman, was in the throes of giving birth.

Forgetting the battle raging all around him, Captain Moore went to work to deliver a 'tiny Dutch boy', while his orderlies handed over their greatcoats 'to keep the poor girl warm'. It was a brief moment of humanity in the midst of bloody, violent death.

Germans were everywhere – armed and unarmed. Trooper Wheeler, left behind to hold a newly captured cellar while his comrades pushed on, was suddenly confronted by half a dozen 'shadowy figures'. They were not wearing the Commandos' green berets, but German helmets. Wheeler reckoned that his pals were playing a trick on him.

'You can't frighten me, you silly buggers,' he called out.

'Can't we?' came the reply in German-accented English.

Moments later Wheeler went 'into the bag' as a German prisoner of war.

Farther up the line a jeep with three Commandos in it ran into the enemy positions in the dark. It was brought to an abrupt halt by the deadly steel wire stretched across the road, which fortunately struck the iron stanchion on the jeep's bonnet, placed there with the express purpose of preventing the wire from decapitating the vehicle's occupants.

Corporal Selby, the driver, reacted in true Commando style. He swung the jeep round in a tight circle. But he was out of luck. Before the Germans could react, or the two passengers could leap from the little open vehicle, it went over a mine. Its rear axle flew up and disintegrated in the explosion. Selby was thrown out, his leg fractured and a shoulder badly injured.

Commando Connolly, who had been in the back of the jeep, fled into the darkness, chased by angry German small arms fire. Later that night, utterly exhausted, he reached his own lines. He drank the tea, fortified with rum, that was offered him, and then asked for Selby. He was told that the 'Corp' had disappeared, and later the unfortunate NCO was posted 'missing believed killed'. Two and a half days later, a sentry sighted 'a figure crawling on the road half-way between the two front lines'.

It was Corporal Selby. He was covered with caked blood and was terribly emaciated. A dirty, improvised tourniquet was wrapped round his injured leg. He had been out in the open, in sub-zero temperatures, without food or water for sixty hours. During that time he had been seriously wounded. Yet he had managed to observe many enemy positions, and now insisted on reporting to the troop Intelligence officer before he finally received the blessing of a shot of morphia and oblivion.

By 24 January the Jocks had closed on their objective, Heinsberg. They had endured thirty hours of constant shellfire and mortaring. Some of them had broken down. After all, most were reinforcements, aged 19, and, increasingly, as young as 18. But still they pushed on against the guns of the West Wall.

The King's Own Scottish Borderers had already suffered too many casualties. Now their B Company, commanded by Major Hogg, came under heavy fire. Hogg fell, badly wounded. Before he passed out completely, he requested a smokescreen to conceal his trapped survivors. The gunners could not help. They asked for coordinates. By then Hogg had collapsed. The sergeant major took over. Not for long. He was badly hit, as was the second-in-command, killed outright by a mortar bomb. Company communications with the rear, and especially with the waiting gunners, seemed to have broken down altogether. It looked as though the KOSB 'B' Company was doomed.

Then, suddenly, a clear, calm voice with a Scottish accent cut through the confused static of the gunner's set. It was that of Lance-Corporal Alexander Leitch, the sole surviving NCO of Company HQ. The gunners did not know it, but he was completely alone in the smoking ruins of a bunker. Leitch called for smoke, just as his unconscious CO had done, but this time he could give the coordinates the gunners needed for their 'shoot'.

Soon smoke engulfed the survivors' positions and they were able to pull back. Now the stretcher-bearers pushed their way across the pitted, smoking, lunar landscape, and began to pick up those who could not use their legs. Leitch watched calmly until they were ready to go, before asking if they would be coming back. Surprised, the medics asked why. As calm as ever, Leitch said: 'I think I have been wounded in both legs.' He had – hit in one, which was badly mangled; shell fragments had nearly severed the other, now hanging by a strip of flesh.

Half an hour later, as they started to work on the half-dead radio operator, the King's Own Scottish Borderers followed the Royal Scots into the shattered, smoking little town of Heinsberg. The British attack on the Great Wall of Germany had succeeded, at a cost of just under 1,000 men.[88]

Now Field Marshal Montgomery, once a hero, now the villain of the Battle of the Bulge, prepared to face up to the main defences of the Siegfried Line. He would attack through the Reichswald Forest on the Dutch-German border. The aim was to break through in the Cleves-Goch-Udem-Calcar area. Once that had been achieved, the British and Canadian Armies would head for the Rhine, from where the 'little fart', as Patton habitually now called him, would launch his great set-piece assault over the river.

The terrain, the Siegfried Line defences, and the German Army were going to present Montgomery with problems enough. But when the Field Marshal had begun to plan the great assault months earlier, he had not realised that he would be faced with even worse problems within his own camp – the American generals.

NOTES

85   Montgomery had just revealed that *he* had commanded the bulk of US troops (including the First Army) in the Battle of the Bulge, and had helped with his British XXX Corps to stop the German advance on the Meuse. That announcement effectively brought an end to the 'special relationship' of which the British were (and still are) so proud, especially between the top military commanders.

86   Bastogne was never surrounded, and up to the time Patton 'relieved' it, there had been more defenders than attackers. When the US commander replied to a German surrender demand with his celebrated 'Nuts' (many thought he said something more graphic), the local people thought it was a reference to their annual nut fair. Now, however, they have been making a good living from 'Nuts City' and its wartime 'siege' for more than fifty years.

87   Later Hughes flew hastily to Patton's HQ to tell his friend what Ike had said. But Patton was too busy running down his fellow American commanders and, as Hughes noted in his diary, discussed 'his prowess as cocksman. He is good – so *he* says.' During the campaign, Patton appears to have had three mistresses – one French, one English, and his niece, Jean Gordon, who committed suicide after Patton's death.

88   In the 52nd Division, to which were added a couple of hundred non-battle casualties. There were, of course, casualties in the other units involved. Soon the British would be losing the equivalent of a battalion (approximately 1,000 men) a day.

Into the West Wall Again

We're gonna hang our washing on the Siegfried Line – if the Siegfried Line's still there.

Wartime marching song

On the border between Belgium and Germany, they hesitated and waited again, just as they had the previous September. This time they were more cautious. The GIs' motto was 'See '45 and survive'. The Battle of the Bulge was just ended, and now the brass wanted them to attack again, although the assault divisions were down to seventy percent of their official strength in riflemen.

Up in the Ardennes, where the Third Army waited for the 'Victor of Bastogne' to give the word, the weather was terrible. It seemed as if winter would never end. Heavy new snow fell every day. Patton's engineers fought desperately to keep the battered system open. The blacks of the 'Red Ball Express' battled six-foot drifts to bring up supplies. MPs guiding them were found frozen to death at their isolated crossroads posts.

In the village of Lanzerath, once SS Peiper's objective in the heady first days of the German assault, Staff-Sergeant Giles and his US engineer company worked flat out to build a new bridge over the Our. Patton's infantry would need it in a few days' time. 'It's a bitch,' he wrote in his diary. 'The river is 189 feet here and the chasm is 100 feet deep. The weather is lousy – snowing and blowing. And we had plenty of artillery fire. That's my idea of a real T.S. [tough shit]. It's round the clock boys and don't spare the horses.'

US Medic, Lester Atwell, not far away in the German village of Kobscheid on the other side of the river, noted on that same day: 'The captain paced up and down in silence, impatiently awaiting the word to move up farther. Attacking the Siegfried Line, I thought, and prayed suddenly, "God, don't let this be a slaughter. Help them. End this."'

Atwell was not only afraid of what lay ahead, he was worried too by the present. In his own infantry division, and in others slated for the second American attack into the Siegfried Line, riflemen were falling sick by the hundreds and then by the thousands. Severe respiratory infection was decimating whole companies. Frostbite and trenchfoot were another cause of anxiety. Men were losing their toes, their feet, even whole legs when gangrene set in. By the time the Third Army attack got under way, the medics would have to deal with the equivalent of a whole infantry division of sick US riflemen – some 14,000 in all – who were so crippled they would never return to front-line duty.

The tension in the Ardennes-Eifel mounted. And the snow continued to fall in solid sheets.

Three weeks earlier, while his army had still been battling hard on the outskirts of Bastogne, Patton had confided to his diary the dire thought that 'we can still lose this war'. Now his mood had changed dramatically. Despite all the difficulties, he was wildly optimistic. The weather, the state of his troops' health, the fact that he would be attacking the Siegfried Line, which had hitherto proved itself capable of withstanding and repulsing every Allied attack, did not seem to concern him.

His success in the Ardennes had provided plenty of the favourable headlines he craved back in the States, and had brought him back into the limelight. Sacked by Eisenhower in Sicily, turned out to pasture, kept under wraps for most of the invasion, left with the unproductive right flank in Lorraine, he had still always believed (as he wrote on New Year's Eve 1943 in Sicily): 'My destiny is sure and I am a fool and a coward even to have doubted it. I don't any more ... Now for some more success ... Destiny will keep me floating down the stream of fate.'

The prose was purple. But the sentiment meant a great deal to Patton. And for all his faults and self-indulgence, he did know when the time was ripe for him. He was realistic enough. Now that time had come.

For once Eisenhower was supporting him. He had fallen out with Montgomery. As Eisenhower told the *Telegraph* correspondent, Cornelius Ryan, long after the war: 'He [Montgomery] got so damn personal to make sure that the Americans and me, in particular, had no credit, had nothing to do with the war, that eventually I just stopped communicating with him.'

For his part, Bradley was so pathetically grateful to Patton for his help in the Bulge, that he would do anything to support the Third Army commander and ensure that the hated Montgomery did not win any of the kudos associated with the final victory in Germany in 1945. When one of Eisenhower's staff suggested that Patton would have to give up some of his divisions in the Ardennes-Eifel to assist Montgomery in his great attack to the north, Bradley told him that if SHAEF wanted 'to destroy the whole operation' they could do it and be damned. But he added bitterly, 'Eisenhower must realise ... much more than a tactical operation was involved ... the prestige of the American Army was at stake.'

Now Bradley badly needed Patton if he was going to retain control of a fighting army, which would restore his reputation in the Bulge. Patton knew this, and on 12 January he had snorted to Bradley: 'I don't really care where we attack.' It was a sentiment with which Bradley agreed wholeheartedly. Once Patton was engaged, Eisenhower would be less likely to allow Montgomery his head in the north, which would inevitably mean that the two northern armies of Bradley's 12th Army Group, Simpson's Ninth and Hodges' First, would come under the British Field Marshal's control.

Both men were overjoyed when Eisenhower agreed on 23 January that Patton should be allowed to engage in what the former called 'aggressive defense' in the Eifel-Ardennes. It was the green light Patton was waiting for. In the hands of 'Ole Blood an' Guts', 'aggressive defense' would become a full-scale campaign. Perhaps Eisenhower too knew that.

By that last week of January, Patton had thirteen divisions of his Third Army, some of the best in the entire US military, abreast of the three frontier rivers between France, Belgium and Germany – the Our, the Sauer and the Moselle. They could be used to crack the Siegfried Line between St Vith in the north and Saarlautern in the south. And Bradley was quite sure that this was what Patton intended.

As Patton had stated to him categorically: 'I am the oldest combat leader in age and experience in the United States Army in Europe, and if I have to go on the defensive, I want to be relieved.' He would use his old 'rock-soup' method to get round Ike's restrictions. He had explained the tactic to his amused staff back in 1944. 'A tramp once went to a house and asked for some boiling water to make "rock soup". The lady was interested and gave him the water into which the tramp placed two polished, white stones. He then asked if he might have some potatoes and carrots to flavour it a little, and finally ended up with some meat. In other words,' Patton explained with a chuckle, 'in order to attack, we'll have to pretend to reconnoiter, then reinforce the reconnaissance and finally put on the attack.' In this manner he would cock a snook at Ike's restrictions, and naturally put Monty off his mark too.

Patton's plan, which would be put into operation on 29 January, would be started by the veteran 4th 'Ivy Leaf' Division. One battalion would cross the Our river almost where the original division had crossed back in September 1944. Once the crossing had been accomplished, the battalion would be followed by the whole division, and then the rest of the US VIII Corps. To the south, its neighbour, the III Corps, would then assault the Sauer river, followed by XII Corps a week later. On 19 February Patton's final corps, the XX, would enter the frontier battle for the Siegfried Line.

Thus Patton felt his whole army would be involved in the 'armored reconnaissance' to which Eisenhower believed he was committed. Then Patton would see what Eisenhower would do. With luck, the Supreme Commander would conclude that his Third Army was so deeply committed to the West Wall attack and beyond into the Eifel, that he would be unable to do anything but accept Patton's *fait accompli*.

The plan was brash and bold, typical of 'Ole Blood an' Guts'. More importantly for the outcome of the war, and for the future of Western Europe, it was also typical of the way wartime army commanders of Patton's ilk had lost contact with reality. They were running the war as if it was a private battle, independent of the agreed overall strategy and any political considerations.

For if Patton's ruse worked (and it seems to have been little more than that[89]), it would drag the whole of the Allied *Schwerpunkt* farther south than intended. Originally, even before the invasion, it had been agreed that the major Allied thrust into the Reich would take place in the north. The drive would be for the Ruhr, the industrial heart of Germany, and then on to Berlin. But that thrust would inevitably come under Montgomery's command. For the British Field Marshal was the senior Allied officer in the area, currently with a British, a Canadian and an attached American army (the Ninth) under his command. This would have been anathema to the US top brass, especially Bradley.

Now, if Patton's plan worked, the mass of the American armies in Europe, in both the 12th and the 6th Army Groups, might well end the war fighting for the splendid mountain scenery of Bavaria and the Austrian Alps (they did). But this would give the Red Army the time and opportunity to capture the glittering prizes of Berlin, Vienna and Prague. The result would be Russian domination of Central Europe – both military and political.

What was being planned between Patton and Bradley (apparently behind Ike's back) in the rundown Hotel Alpha, Bradley's HQ in the shabby provincial capital of Luxembourg, could well determine the political destiny of Central Europe for the rest of the 20th century.

While the snow continued to fall in that remote border country, the young men along the river line crowded the cobbled streets and half-wrecked villages of the front-line area. The whole countryside was a chaotic, confused mess of Sherman tanks, White halftracks, 'deuce-and-a-half' trucks, great 8-inch howitzers – their tracks can still be found in the fields and forests to this day. It was a great mass of olive-drab machinery, clogging every field, every little farmyard, every country road – and all pointing in one direction. Germany.

The troops waited, nervous and jumpy, paying enormous sums for hard liquor, smoking too much, writing their 'last letters', filling out their will forms, and worrying about who would receive their $10,000 GI insurance pay-out if . . .

Among them, there were not many veterans now. The winter fighting had taken its toll. The ranks of the assault infantry were filled with men recruited from the military police, the air corps, and 18-year-old draftees from the United States. Soon black faces would appear – volunteers from the Service of Supply, who had given up their precious stripes to serve with the infantry, in an army that was still rigidly segregated.

They froze in the poorly heated ruins. They squatted in their foxholes, in wooden shacks, hastily erected for them by the engineers. They stripped and checked their weapons. The machine-gunners ensured that every third slug in the long ammo. belts they carried in little olive-drab metal boxes was tracer. Veterans changed their underwear despite the cold and the difficulties. They knew if they were hit, and soiled clothing came into contact with a wound, they might end up with gas gangrene. Others put metal shaving mirrors or, even better, thick Bibles into their breast pockets. They had all heard of the GI whose life had been saved by his Bible. Somehow, the GI in question always seemed to belong to another outfit.

On the morning of Monday 29 January 1945 the guns opened up. The old song of death broke out once more. As the assault battalion of the 4th Infantry moved forward, it started to snow. Behind them the sky flushed a dull red. It was like the door of some gigantic oven opening . . . a strange fluttering . . . a roar . . . the noise of an express train racing through an empty, midnight station at top speed. Then the US barrage was plastering the heights beyond the Siegfried Line.

Awed and open-mouthed like village yokels, shocked by the rending noise, the infantry moved up the slopes and into the old battlefield of the previous September. Others slid and stumbled across the frozen Our, while the blinding snow continued to fall relentlessly. Then they found themselves back where they had been before, in what must have seemed to the veterans like another age. Schweiler, the location of 'Schloss Hemingstein', was recaptured. A day later Bleialf followed. On to Buchet, from where Colonel 'Buck' Lanham's 22nd Infantry had first launched their attack against the 'Black Man' fortifications of the West Wall.

Lieutenant George Wilson, one of the three surviving officers in his battalion from the September attack by the 4th Division, was 'appalled' by the fighting, which seemed to go on for ever, 'Many bodies still lay where they'd fallen, partly covered by blankets or snow. One long, wide, gradual hillside was strewn with the carcasses of burned-out Sherman tanks and a few German tiger tanks. Evidently our losses had been several times greater than those of the enemy.'

From the same spot, where he had watched the attack on the 'Verdun of the Eifel' five months earlier, Wilson observed the 22nd's 2nd Battalion attack Brandscheid once again:

The infantry advanced by fire and movement supported by artillery and the fire of tanks, and with the use of hand grenades and flame-throwers when the men got close enough. Some pillboxes had grenades thrown down their smoke stacks; others had their apertures blasted by flame-throwers. At least one was plowed under by a bulldozing tank. The Germans should never have started this business. We proved again that fortifications can be taken.

Then it was over and his own F Company headed for the main assault on the nearby county town, Prüm. Wilson never made it. His company commander was killed and he was wounded in the foot. That left only one veteran still on active service from those heady days of the previous Fall when the smell of victory had been in the air.

But the Americans were not finished with Brandscheid yet. By now the unlucky, veteran US 90th Division was coming up to take over from the 4th in the area. They passed through the frontier positions where the US 106th Division, the 'Golden Lions' (from their shoulder patch), had surrendered the previous December, the largest surrender of American fighting men since the Civil War. One Private recalled that Bleialf looked 'eerie . . . like a million ghosts of previous campaigns had passed through it'.

But the men of the 90th were not worried about ghosts. They were too busy dealing with the enemy. They passed easily through what they thought were abandoned West Wall positions. But shortly afterwards the 'dead' pillboxes and bunkers sprang back to life. Captain Colby, a 90th veteran, later recounted: 'Whole platoons of infantrymen disappeared as a result of the German tactic of giving up a pillbox easily, then subjecting it to pre-sighted artillery and mortar fire, forcing the attackers inside for shelter. Then they covered the doorway with fire, surrounding the pillbox after dark and blowing it up. The men soon learned it was safer outside the fortifications than inside.'

The regimental chaplain, Father Murphy, recorded: 'The pillboxes are really a death trap. You're helpless when you get in them.'

There were even 'death traps' outside the bunkers. At Brandscheid, right in the middle of a changeover between the 4th and 90th Divisions, the Germans caught the Americans completely off-guard. The enemy attacked in full company strength. In the confusion of the handover, the attackers pushed right into the centre of the shattered hamlet. Hand-to-hand fighting developed. It was savage, with no quarter expected or given. In the end the Americans drove off the Germans, but the cost had been high. In the initial US attack and the resulting German counter-attack, the 22nd Infantry Regiment's Third Battalion lost half of its strength. The casualties incurred by the 90th Division were not recorded. The 'Verdun of the Eifel' was living up to its awesome, bloody reputation.

But these new GIs who had come to fight a second time in the Siegfried Line were different from their predecessors. This time there were no Hershey bars or chewing gum for the local German kids, no coffee or canned rations for the women, no 'Camels' for the old men. These GIs were bitter and brutal. The 'goodies' were replaced by blows, kicks, and threats with rifles levelled.

Without ceremony, the few remaining civilians were turfed out of their humble cottages and rundown farms. They were followed by the '*Amis*', eager to get out of the cold and wind. In the village of Winterspelt, the old people still remember how the 108 remaining villagers, including the bedridden and the sick, were crammed into two small houses. In Auw the GIs moved in, using the terrified civilians as human shields, before taking over what was left of the hamlet. In Elcherrath, the first village to be captured in the new offensive, the soldiers threw everything out into the village street. They smashed pictures, tore down curtains, stole anything that looked valuable. Then they set fire to anything they did not want. It seemed to the terrified citizens that the '*Amis*' took a malicious pleasure in these cruel, wanton acts.

Young Johannes Nobuesch, who was there at Elcherrath, later wrote: 'Perhaps it was the destruction and carnage the Americans had seen in north Belgium and Luxembourg that caused them to do these things. Perhaps, too, Goebbels' propaganda, which declared that every German home should become a fortress, played a part. At all events, the results of their actions on the border were catastrophic.'

They were. Although the German people 'longed for peace', as Nobuesch put it, the German soldiers, or most of them, fought with desperate, sometimes fanatical, courage. In the following three months, until the Allies finally reached and crossed the Rhine, the German Army would suffer as much as a third of its total casualties of the 1944-45 campaign in Western Europe. It goes without saying that Allied casualties were correspondingly high. The great blood-letting on the Siegfried Line had begun again.

The soldiers did not seem to notice. Those who had survived the bitter fighting of the Bulge had become hard, even brutal, as Nobuesch suspected. It had been a cruel six weeks, which the survivors would remember for the rest of their lives. With the possible exception of the Hürtgen Forest, the US Army had not engaged in such a bitter battle, before or since. The aim now was simply to kill Germans.

Watching the gunners blasting away at German pillboxes in the Eifel below Prum, Captain Colby of the 90th Division admired the artillerymen's blase technique as they fired at their targets with huge 155mm guns. 'The shell struck the pillbox and covered it with a sheet of flame . . . A perfect smoke ring popped out of an air vent at the top.'

Colby was 'thrilled', even more so when the lieutenent in charge said: 'There ain't anyone left inside. If there is, his brains are scrambled.' Then he added: 'Aw hell, let's blast some more before the fun starts. You wanna fire one?'

Colby later recalled: 'How could I refuse?' The artillery officer zeroed the huge gun in for him and Colby fired. He could not miss. When the artilleryman moved away, he and his infantrymen moved forward to view his handiwork and found 'only dead and dazed men inside the pillboxes'.

Without any feeling for the men he had just killed, he commented: 'No matter how many pillboxes or bunkers there might be, the fact was that man had built them and man was tearing them down. The elaborate system of "Dragon's Teeth" proved to be worthless and brought from us exclamations of amazement at the labor the Germans had expended.'

It was a view shared by Patton, who came up to the Eifel from Luxembourg City to check how his infantry were doing in their attack on the Great Wall of Germany. After inspecting a captured bunker (it had been taken through the back door), he pontificated that it showed 'the utter futility of fixed defenses . . . In war the only sure defense is offense and the efficiency of offense depends on the warlike souls of those conducting it.'

It was evident Patton had learned nothing from the last half year of frontal attacks on the Siegfried Line. He adhered to the theory of attack, attack and attack again, which was already outdated by the time of the Civil War nearly a century earlier, and which had caused so many young American lives to be needlessly thrown away.

Whatever Patton thought, the bloody, sometimes pointless attacks on the West Wall would continue for another two months before, surprisingly, no less a person than 'Ole Blood an' Guts' himself showed that there was another way to combat a fortified position effectively.

But that was in the future. In this first week of February 1945, Patton was more concerned with the continuation of his 'armored reconnaissance'. He had partly broken through the West Wall in the Bleialf-Prum area. Would he now be allowed to use his other eleven divisions in attacks across the Sauer, the Saar and even the Moselle? For suddenly Eisenhower's Supreme Headquarters and Bradley had gone strangely silent. What was going on at Versailles? Were they turning a blind eye to his activities in the Eifel? Should he just go with his original plan? Or had Monty and his political boss, Churchill, got at 'the best general the British had', as Patton often scornfully dubbed Ike?

For a day or two, now that his bridgehead over the Our river seemed firmly established, Patton concerned himself with the planning for his other attacks. He went to visit portly, bespectacled General Eddy, commanding his XII Corps. Eddy's corps was scheduled to attack across the Sauer river in the Wallendorf-Echternach region, where the Americans had been forced to withdraw the previous September, on 6 February. Now Patton urged his corps commander to bring forward the date of his attack. 'Make it the 4th,' he told Eddy.

Eddy, who suffered from high blood pressure and other complaints which he concealed from Patton, exploded, 'Godammit, General, you never give me time to get ready ... The trouble is you have no appreciation of the time and space factor in this war.'

Patton was in no mood to argue. He had to get the second attack under way before Eisenhower could stop it. He snapped back at the red-faced corps commander, whom he had already threatened to sack more than once if he did not obey orders, 'Is that so? If I had any appreciation of it, we'd still be sitting on the Seine.'

Reluctantly Eddy gave in, though he knew there was going to be trouble, especially when his brave, but green, 76th Infantry Division attempted to cross the river at Echternach. 4 February it would be.

That day Patton decided to take a calculated risk. He called Bradley's main HQ at Namur in Belgium to clear the 4 February deadline with his boss. Bradley was not there. According to his Chief-of-Staff, he was at Versailles, attending a conference with Eisenhower. Patton must have breathed a sigh of relief. General Lev Allen, the Chief-of-Staff, he could deal with. He was one of the 'hawks', who favoured Patton's decision to give priority to American troops, whether Eisenhower liked it or not. Nor was he concerned about the effect on Montgomery's grandiose plan to make the major thrust in the north. Allen said he could see no objections to either Patton's plan or the date proposed.

Patton's relief was short-lived. One hour later Allen called back. In a small, subdued voice, he said: 'No dice, George. You are to commit nothing ... pending further orders.'

Patton was stunned. He turned to a waiting Eddy, his jaw set and angry. He told the corps commander to suspend all operations for the time being. Shortly afterwards he called a conference of his own staff. 'This doesn't sound good to me,' he told them. 'I'm afraid we're going to be halted again in the middle of an attack in order to start another one, you know where, that has little promise of success. [Patton presumably referred to Montgomery's attack in the north.] I have the sneaking suspicion that SHAEF is out as usual to exalt the Field Marshal.'

Angry at being held up like this, Patton embarked on a whirlwind tour of his front, checking and criticising, venting his wrath on everyone from corporal to commanding general. He told one general that, if he did not get his troops across the Moselle soon, he would make the general *personally* swim the fast-flowing river.

At the HQ of the 94th Division on the Saar, he went into a blind rage when he learned from the divisional commander, General Malony, that the outfit's ratio of combat to non-combat casualties was the worst in the whole of his Third Army. He told Malony: 'If you don't do something to improve this situation, you'll be a non-combat casualty yourself – and pretty damned soon!'

This was typical of George S Patton. His mood was not improved when

Bradley called him when he returned to his command post. Without preamble, Bradley said: 'Monty did it again. You and Hodges will go on the defensive while Montgomery will resume the offensive in the north.'

Hastily, anticipating Patton's explosive reaction, Bradley added: 'It wasn't Ike this time. Orders came from the Combined Chiefs . . . Brooke [the British Chief-of-Staff] even got General Marshall [American Chief-of-Staff] to go along with him. I don't know what made *him* agree. Probably he's anxious to get those fourteen British divisions sitting on their butts in Belgium back into action.'[90]

'What are they trying to accomplish?' Patton asked.

'Montgomery wants to secure a wide stretch of the Rhine as quickly as possible, so that we would have a quick entry if Germany collapsed suddenly.'

'Horseshit!' Patton snorted in disgust. 'I'm convinced that we have a much better chance to get to the Rhine first with our present attack. When are the British supposed to jump off?'

'Probably on the 10th,' Bradley answered.

'I doubt if Monty will be ready by the 10th,' Patton remarked. 'But what are we supposed to be doing in the meantime?'

Bradley, who had his own plans, which Patton apparently did not know about,[91] replied after a moment: 'You can continue your attack until February 10th . . . and maybe after that even, provided your casualties aren't excessive and you have enough ammunition left.'

It was not much, but Patton was glad of the crumbs. He knew that even Ike, his protege, was afraid of the austere General Marshall. He was too, he had to admit. Once in Marshall's presence, he had been unable to pinpoint the location of some of his troops on a map. The Chief-of-Staff had chewed him out, an army commander, in the presence of other commanders, like a shavetail second looey (or 'sixty-day wonder'). When Marshall said 'Stop', he meant it.

But Patton still had ten days left, ten precious days in which to get his army involved in the fighting in Germany. The battle for the Siegfried Line could carry on.

NOTES

89 It is very likely that Eisenhower knew all along what Bradley and Patton were planning and agreed with them. But he kept his nose out of the supposedly 'secret plot' for the sake of Anglo-American unity.

90 While Montgomery knew the US troops fighting alongside his own, visiting them often, and remembering the names of their divisional and regimental commanders, American commanding officers, such as Bradley, almost never came to see the British Army. Five of the divisions, 'sitting on their butts in Belgium', had saved Bradley's bacon the previous month in the Ardennes, and were currently up in Germany ready to launch a massive, 200,000-strong attack on the Siegfried Line.

91   It is likely that Bradley was planning advances of both his First and Third
     Armies to the Rhine. Here they would join up between Cologne and Mainz,
     and major crossings of the great river would follow. This would take the
     wind out of Montgomery's planned crossing, which was going to be attended
     by everyone, from Eisenhower to Churchill's daughter, Mary.

3

Reichswald and Green Devils

Stand to attention, gentlemen, for the bloody para-boys.

Brigadier Essame, February 1945

On 1 February 1945, unknown as yet to Patton, his hated rival, Montgomery, had also received the green light to go into action. But this one had come from the Supreme Commander himself. Eisenhower had agreed to allow the Field Marshal to use both the First Canadian Army (which was eighty percent made up of British troops) and the British Second Army in the main assault on the northern Siegfried Line positions.

Crerar, the commanding general of the First Canadian Army, was informed immediately, and that day he called a press conference to brief the scores of correspondents who were now attached to his nearly half a million-strong force. Crerar's reaction to his new task is not on record. The 57-year-old general was a retiring man. As one of the pressmen reported: 'He is no flaming personality . . . no Montgomery. But he has proved . . . that he would have cool judgement and old nerves in the hard hours when great decisions are in the scales.'

Now General Crerar would need all the cool he could muster. For he was to command the greatest army in Canadian military history, even if it was mostly British, in a battle that was going to be extremely tricky.

In the Dutch town of Tilburg, Crerar briefed the journalists on Operations VERITABLE and GRENADE, that would begin from Nijmegen, sweep through the Reichswald Forest and into the undulating farmland and wooded countryside beyond, clearing the area between the Maas (Meuse) and the Rhine.

This operation may be protracted and the fighting tough and trying. All ranks are confident, however, that we will carry through to a successful conclusion the great task which we have been given the responsibility and honour to fulfil.

To some of his more cynical listeners Crerar must have sounded more confident than he had a right to be. It was not just the matter of the battle to come and its associated problems, but also the 'Canucks', as the British called them. In general, the Canadians had had an unlucky war. Their first years of the great conflict had been spent in relative inaction in England. Then, in 1942, had come Dieppe, where a whole Canadian infantry division had been virtually wiped out.

Their losses in Normandy had been equally heavy, and Crerar's ponderous staff work had allowed too many of the enemy to escape the bloodbath of the Falaise Gap in August 1944.

It was not that the Canadians were not bold and brave; they were. By the autumn of 1944 the 2nd and 3rd Canadian Infantry Divisions had lost 8,211 and 9,263 casualties respectively, the highest casualty rate among Montgomery's forces at that time.[92]

That had brought not only military but also political problems. Canadian manpower in Europe was running out, and as all Canadian soldiers overseas were volunteers, any bloodletting on the continent created heated discussion back home. Crerar could not afford high casualty rates. It was for that reason that Montgomery had been forced to bolster the 'Canadian' Army ('Canadian' in name only) with so many British divisions.

This apart, Montgomery did not like Crerar. He was always having to consult the Canadian Prime Minister before he could make what to Monty seemed purely military decisions, and in the Field Marshal's opinion, the Canadian commander was experienced, yet too set in his ways – a product of trench warfare and the type of thinking that went with it back in World War One.

The task of breaking through the fortifications of the Siegfried Line, which constituted the first major obstacle, was, therefore, given to Horrocks' British XXX Corps, with the Canadian 2nd and 3rd Infantry Divisions attached. 'Jorrocks' had been continuously in battle since 1940 and had been seriously wounded during his five years in combat. If anyone could break through, Montgomery reasoned, it would the the XXX Corps commander.

Now the huge Canadian First Army, plus General Hodges' First Army and General Simpson's Ninth on their right flank, waited. Soon the two American armies would be going into action, too, in an attempt finally to break through their sections of the West Wall and into the open, Rhenish plain beyond. Well over a million Allied fighting men were preparing for the key battle of what remained of the war in Europe.

For most of them the great issues were not of much importance. They had been told what some of them were, but the 'big picture' tended to fade in the face of personal considerations. In essence, these boiled down to 'Will I survive?'

Medic Lester Atwell, attached to the US 87th Infantry Division, noted in his diary in the first week of February: 'This is the part of the war I have dreaded most . . . I have always thought the Krauts would fight like the very devils for every inch of German soil . . . I dreaded this Siegfried Line.' Later, when his CO told the men that they were indeed going to assault the West Wall, Atwell recorded that he prayed: 'God, don't let this be a slaughter. Help them. *End* this! In my imagination I saw them running, being hit, reeling back. But I couldn't pin my mind down. I was hearing the voices of English men and women in the smoky little pub in Stone singing "We'll hang out our washing on the Siegfried Line . . ."'

A British tank officer, who had moved up into the battle area that same week, was not so fanciful. All the same, as he viewed the Reichswald in the dusk, he too was not so happy about the prospect of what lay before him. He later wrote: 'In the valley clustered the houses of a few scruffy villages which marked the Dutch-German border, and beyond loomed the forbidding bulk of the Reichswald. It was not a pleasing prospect, and as the rain poured down, we could imagine what the mud was going to be like in the low-lying ground before us.'

Major Fergusson of the Black Watch, an infantry commander who would end the war having fought on three continents, felt very much the same: 'At last it was the Siegfried Line and many of us felt a new fear. There was just a hope that the coming battle might be the last of the war. The enemy would not lightly yield the Siegfried Line. He might well make his last stand in it.'

Lieutenant John Foley, the commander of a troop of Churchill tanks, viewing the front that day wrote: 'The Reichswald looked sombre and uninviting, the black trunks of the trees seeming as solid as if carved from granite.' His companion remarked: 'There it is. That's the objective for the first day. The Germans think that the forest is an anti-tank obstacle. Maybe it is too.'

A third officer on the scene was not too sure. Knowing that they had to breach the outer defences of the West Wall before they even entered the forest, he said: 'We've got to reach it first.'

Later Foley briefed his men, and a senior NCO asked him why they were launching their attack so late (half past ten in the morning). Foley replied with studied sang froid that it was a gentlemanly hour to begin a battle, adding with a feigned yawn: 'Oh well, I'll probably sleep until nine-ish, a leisurely wash and shave, some breakfast, and then heigh-ho for the Start Line.' Foley ruefully commented later: 'It was a nice dream – while it lasted.'

The Allies' fiercest opponents in the battle were what General Rennie, commander of the British 51st Highland Division and soon himself to be killed in action, called 'those bloody little para-boys'. In the Reichswald there were six battalions of them facing the First Canadian Army. They were paras in name only. Most had never been inside an aeroplane, never mind jumped from one. But they had all absorbed the ethos and sense of duty that went with belonging to the elite *Fallschirmjäger*, the victors of the Low Countries in 1940 and Crete in 1941.

One para commander typically told each new recruit to his formation: 'From the moment a man volunteers and joins my regiment, he enters a new order of humanity. He is ruled by one law only, that of our unit. He must give up personal weaknesses and ambitions, and realise that our battle is for the existence of the whole German nation.'

One Allied Intelligence officer and future newspaper columnist, Milton Schulman of the Canadian Army, summed up their qualities: 'Their faith in their Führer and their cause had not died . . . They had not given in to despair and hoplessness . . . The bulk of them had received not more than three months' [infantry] training. But they possessed two other compensating virtues – youth and a faith.'

There was also a parachute outfit, which was to become the backbone of the German defence, facing Patton in the Prum area and soon to be engaged with his 4th Infantry Division. This was General Heilmann's 5th Parachute Division. After the Battle of the Bulge, Heilman's 'Green Devils' (as they believed the Allied troops called them – they did not) had been reduced to 1,500 men, and were outnumbered ten to one by the Americans.

Nevertheless, Ludwig Heilman, hero of the Battle of Monte Cassino, was undismayed. As he prepared for Patton's renewed onslaught, he and his commanders (only one of whom had any parachute combat experience) assessed their chances. One of them, First Lieutenant Oscar Kauschmann, remarked: 'Eighty to a hundred *"Ami"* tanks against ten of our self-propelled guns. Not bad, eh?' And he concluded: 'At all events they [the Americans] way outnumber us – *haushoch Uberlegen.*'[93]

Still, as their commander reassured them: 'The village houses have got stout cellars. Let them winkle us out.' It is perhaps not surprising that one of the participants in the last pre-battle conference, Colonel Groeschke, left for his regimental command post thinking, 'I had the impression that we felt superior in our inferiority.'

But the situation of the defenders, though they lacked numbers, was not as bad as some of them thought. The terrain they would defend was a series of rugged, sometimes wooded, heights, stretching back as far as the Moselle. Along the Sauer, which would be the site of Patton's next crossing, the heights concealed some of the most formidable West Wall fortifications (including the 'Cat's Head'). From that point, there was line after line of mixed concrete bunkers from the pre-war period, and new ones of logs and earth, constructed the previous September.

The last county town before one reached the Moselle was Wittlich. From here von Rundstedt had commanded the great 1940 offensive. It had no fewer than fifteen defensive lines protecting it. And on the as yet unfinished *Autobahn* leading eastwards from Wittlich there were ramps used to fire the V1s, already being deployed in a ground role.[94]

Whatever the German rank and file thought of their chances in the coming battle against the Anglo-Americans, their senior officers were not very impressed by the enemy. An assessment, made by the German 1st Parachute Army at the time and later captured, maintained:

The great victories in northern France have had a very positive effect on the morale of British and Canadian forces. However, it must not be overlooked that English army units can only achieve results when they are assisted by large-scale air support. If they lack this, then there is a great lack of offensive spirit in their soldiers. In summation, it must be stated that Anglo-American leadership in battle is based on superiority in materiel. An attack without strong artillery, aerial and armoured support is unthinkable . . . However, the English receive very good training, and even with the losses they have suffered so far, the reinforcements reaching the front from England are still well trained.

In a final, patriotic and nationalistic flourish, the author of the assessment maintained: 'Of course, one cannot compare the fighting spirit of the English or American soldier with that of the German. The German is far superior to them . . . The best example of this was at Arnhem, where the 1st English Airborne Division was decisively defeated by our ground troops because the English lacked their usual air and artillery superiority.'

Some of this, of course, was no doubt intended to boost the spirits of waverers and defeatists among the German ranks. Unfortunately for the Allies, however, many of the Germans who were now about to make their final stand in the Siegfried Line believed their own propaganda. All they needed was to hold out – and they could, even if the enemy did come in superior numbers – and then the Führer would step in 'at five minutes to midnight' with his new 'wonder weapons' and transform the situation in Germany's favour in the matter of a day.

Right to the very end, when the victorious Allies were within sight of the Rhine itself, German prisoners would assert vehemently that Germany could still win the war. Indeed, so brave and fanatically desperate was the resistance of those 'bloody little para-boys', that when they finally surrendered, Brigadier Essame of the British 43rd Division, incurred the wrath of the London press when he ordered his staff to stand to attention and salute the survivors as they were led off to the POW cages.

Patton was unfazed by the strength of the defences he was about to attack or the determination of the defenders. Unlike Montgomery, who had been appalled by the way British generals had wasted precious lives in World War One, he cared little about losses, so long as objectives were achieved.[95]

Thirty-six hours before his attack in the Eifel was to kick off, Patton told his corps commanders that Monty had been given priority again, and that 'up to February 10th Third Army will make an all-out effort on the Siegfried Line in the Eifel . . . That is, we are to make a strong assault in order to draw off as much enemy strength as possible from Montgomery.' Once again, Patton could not resist making a dig at the 'little limey fart', though in this case 'the fart' would scarcely be aware that Patton's Third Army was to attack. How could he be if, as Patton seemed to be saying, his efforts were to be kept under wraps?

After lengthy discussions about how the three corps of the Third Army involved should attack (naturally Patton's plan prevailed), the commander swore his generals to secrecy. He said: 'If those gentlemen up north [he meant Montgomery] find out what we're going to do, they'll grab some of our divisions. Let them learn about it when they see it on their maps.'

That was how the war in Europe was conducted in 1945.

By now the German defenders were aware of what was afoot. Patton's army had gone over to radio silence – a sure indication that something big was brewing. From their positions on the heights, observers in the Siegfried Line bunkers could watch the '*Amis*' preparations on the flat Luxembourg delta plain across the Sauer. Although Patton had boasted that his 90th Division had knocked out 120 pillboxes in as many minutes, the same 90th had lost a good score or so men, taken in a surprise German counter-attack that had recaptured Brandscheid. Those POWs were now being urgently squeezed for information.

Patton's surprise attack was not greatly helped by the American propaganda leaflets being fired across the Sauer into the positions of the German 80th Corps defending the area. On the evening of Tuesday 6 February the Nobuesch family, sheltering in the little hamlet of Niederraden, were surprised by the appearance of an HQ sergeant they knew. He swung himself off his bicycle, flushed and excited. He had come from his post bringing with him an '*Ami* leaflet'. He explained that the Americans had been firing them and smoke markers (presumably to range in their artillery) all afternoon. Sixteen-year-old Johannes, a future university professor, read the text excitedly. It read: 'Comrades of the 915 Regiment [the German outfit defending that section of the West Wall]. We're coming. Leave your bunkers and foxholes and surrender.'

Johannes' mother suddenly turned 'white as chalk', and put out the petroleum lantern. In the echoing silence, broken only by the slow rat-tat-tat of a US machine-gun, sounding like an angry woodpecker, young Nobuesch asked himself if it was just '*Ami*' propaganda, or were they really coming?

The 80th Corps obviously thought they were. That evening the commander reported to army group: 'We can expect attacks on both sides of Wallendorf. They will reach as far as Echternach. And they will be more than reconnaissance thrusts.'

Already engaged in the effort against any further penetrations by the Fourth Infantry Division, with support from the US 87th and 90th Divisions in the Bleialf-Prum area, the German 80th Corps now took up the challenge facing them on the Sauer. The High Command agreed that its subordinate corps should put its troops on an alert footing. That night, at about the time the German NCO was bringing his propaganda leaflet to the Nobuesch household, 80th Corps issued the electrifying order to all its front-line troops: '*Alarmstufe Eins*' (Red Alert).

Four hours later, at one o'clock in the morning Wednesday, American artillery in Luxembourg opened up with a tremendous roar. The bombardment was bigger than that which had launched the German 'suprise' attack of 16 December 1944. The 80th Corps' Intelligence had guessed right – the '*Amis*' were coming across the Sauer and, to the south, the Moselle. But unlike the Americans in December, caught completely off- guard, the German defenders were waiting behind their walls of steel and concrete.

Not far away in Germany, Colonel Mabry of the 2nd Battalion, 8th Infantry, Fourth Infantry Division conferred with his officers on the next day's attack. On the floor, oblivious to his surroundings in the little Eifel cottage, Captain Robert Fellers, an old friend of the colonel's, slept the sleep of the just. A veteran of the Utah Beach landings on D-Day, one of only a handful left in the Fourth, he had just returned from a well earned furlough in Paris. Moments earlier, to the accompaniment of ribald comments from his fellow officers, Fellers had got down in the corner next to the stove, and immediately fell into a deep slumber. Now he snored gently as the weary battalion staff discussed their plans.

Just as Mabry stepped over to the field telephone to call one of his company commanders for information, there was a roar like a huge sheet being ripped apart. He ducked instinctively as a German shell exploded in the muddy, cobbled yard outside.

Blast swept through the open door. It carried with it razor-sharp silver slivers of an exploded shell casing. Mabry yelped in pain. He had been hit. So had most of his officers. The splinters had come through the thick wall by way of the hole made for the stovepipe. It was those that had wounded the battalion's officers.

Pulling himself together and wiping the blood away, Mabry bent to waken Fellers, apparently still sound asleep. He shook the captain. Nothing happened. Then Fellers' head rolled to one side. Mabry gasped. The whole of the back of his head was one bloody mess. Mabry could even see Fellers' brain through a gaping, gory wound. The captain was dead.

Moved, Mabry said to his officers: 'How remarkable the way death comes. On Utah, where all hell was let loose, Fellers didn't even get a scratch. And here . . .'

The battalion commander looked down at the dead man for the last time before the medics bore him away to wait for the 'meat wagon', and in a small voice, he said: 'Do you think we should take this as an omen, gentlemen?'[96]

NOTES

92   Losses had been equally high among 'Canadian Loan' officers attached to British divisions to make up for losses of infantry commanders.
93   Literally, 'house-high superiority'.
94   The ramps are still there today, overlooked and forgotten. Interestingly enough, there is a former US missile base on the next hillside.
95   Most of the American top brass (Eisenhower, Bradley, etc.) had not taken part in World War One, indeed in any war prior to the present one. Younger generals had come in at the last stage, when victory was in the air, and the bloody battle of attrition in the trenches was all but over. Patton *had* been wounded, but, to his chagrin, it was in the buttocks.
96   For Mabry in particular it was. He was relieved the next day, though he continued in the Service, as a general in Korea and Vietnam.

4

Across the Sauer Once More

Do you think we should take this as an omen, gentlemen?

Colonel Mabry, 4th US Infantry Division

It was still dark, but already they were pushing the thirty-eight *Luftwaffe* rubber boats, that the engineers had found somewhere in Luxembourg, into the icy, fast-flowing waters of the Sauer on either side of the ruined medieval bridge that led into Germany.

Exactly ninety days earlier, the greenhorns of the 76th Infantry Division had still been training against a simulated enemy in the peaceful hills of Wisconsin. Now, together with the veterans of the 5th and 80th Infantry Divisions of the Third Army, they were going to be blooded in an assault crossing of the border river.

It was not going to be easy. Even the greenest of the new troops realised that. In daylight they could clearly see how tough it was going to be. They were out on the flood plain in full view of the 'Krauts'. On the other side of the Sauer, the enemy were hidden in their deep bunkers, including the notorious 'Cat's Head', on the steep, wooded heights. Consequently, the enemy knew everything about their plans, whereas they knew nothing of the enemy's. One of the handful of survivors of the first wave stated afterwards: 'So help me, the job seemed at first too much for human beings to accomplish.'

Now the 'job' – and a bloody one it would turn out to be – was getting under way. In summer the Sauer, at this spot, could be waded across relatively easily.[97] In winter on the other hand, when the snow on the hills started to melt, the river became a raging torrent, swollen from ninety to 180 feet across, the current running at twelve miles an hour. The 'new boys' were facing the toughest task of any in Patton's 12th Corps.

As the 'long Toms', the great 155 US cannon, thundered, trying to knock out all known German positions on the far side, the 76th's lead company set off at zero one hundred hours precisely on the morning of 7 February. In one of the first of the flimsy rubber boats, Private Harry Goede watched as enemy tracer came zipping low over the water to meet them in a lethal morse. Behind him, a boat was hit and sank immediately. Nobody could be saved. The men were too weighed down by their equipment. The next instant, Goede's own boat was raked by vicious German MG 42 fire. Frantically the infantry, some using their rifle butts as paddles, tried to steer it away from the murderous volley.

It was no use. Goede's comrades panicked and swamped the boat. It started to sink. Goede did not hesitate. It was every man for himself now. He went over the side. Many of the others did the same. But the shock of hitting the icy water took their strength away – that and their equipment. The current started to sweep them away, screaming and shrieking, waving their arms madly for help that did not come.

Goede, who was a strong swimmer, heard someone shout for help nearby. He fought against the current and swam to the drowning medic, who was weighed down by his satchels full of equipment. Somehow he got hold of him and started to haul. In the light of the German verey flares falling slowly over that terrible scene, and bathing everything in their ghastly, unreal light, Goede towed the medic towards the opposite bank.

Without their weapons, and trembling with cold and fear, the two men hid among the frozen reeds on the German side of the river, and watched the slaughter, as the enemy fire swept the river and began to fall on the men waiting on the other bank. Both knew that they were watching a massacre.

Only one boatload, eight men in total, reached the German side. Thirty-five of the thirty-six *Luftwaffe* boats were lost. At other places, two assault companies lost fifty percent of their effectives in the space of an hour. Of nearly a score of officers, only five survived.

Above all, the survivors knew they had to get away from the river. Soaked and miserable, with water squelching in their boots, they began to advance up the slopes, in and through the German pillboxes, towards the Ferschweiler plateau that dominated the left side of the road leading to the ultimate objective, Bitburg.

Others moved towards the nearest small town, Irrel, some five kilometres away. Here they knew that waiting for them was the second great fortification of the Siegfried Line, the 'Cat's Head' which Hitler had visited in person during his 1939 tour of the West Wall. It was not a prospect that gave them much encouragement.

Nevertheless, perhaps sufficiently green and gung-ho that they did not fully appreciate the difficulties, they advanced in small groups, clambering up the heights in the glowing darkness, cut startlingly every now and again by the angry zip of tracer. Sergeant Bliss and Private Meyer, cut off from their platoon, were two such brave men. Caught in the open by rifle fire, they went to ground, only to discover that the 'cave' they had found in the rock was not a cave at all, and that they were 'on top of what later turned out to be a seven-room pillbox full of Heinies'.

Private Ulrich's platoon had been wiped out just after they had got into the boats. With his rifle torn from his hands, and dazed and temporarily blinded by the vivid flashes of exploding shells, Ulrich wandered off crazily into the woods. German machine-gunners spotted him. They ripped off an angry burst in his direction. Terrified, he dropped to the ground. Later, he reported, not without humour: 'I couldn't see anyone else from my outfit. I felt all alone . . . It seemed to me that I was the only Yank in Germany, and the whole *Wehrmacht* was zeroing in on me.'

That terrible night it was the same for virtually every GI who had survived. No one felt he belonged to a cohesive outfit. Officers were in short supply. As usual, they had been the first to be knocked out. Now the few intact formations, small as they mostly were, were led by sergeants, even by private soldiers.

Sergeant John Shepherd of a heavy weapons platoon was one unsung hero of the night-crossing of the Sauer. In the confusion, his superior had been badly wounded. Now Shepherd took over. He was not too happy in his new role, but he knew he had to carry out the orders given to the wounded officer. Above the crazy snap and crack of the small arms battle, he shouted at his men: 'We've got to protect the battalion's left flank, guys.'

A GI wisecracked: 'Hell, Sarge, you mean right up there with those mean old Krauts?'

That was exactly what Shepherd meant. So they set off up the heights until they finally disappeared into the fog and confusion of war. Nearly a week later, a proud Sergeant Shepherd could report to his commanding officer that 'the men held their positions for five days'. The rookies had indeed succeeded in beating off the threat to the battalion's flank.

Elsewhere that day, the Germans counter-attacked what was left of the lead companies with three tanks and infantry sheltering behind the metal monsters. Sergeant Charles Smith, in charge at the spot, watched in horror as the first tank came rumbling to within twenty yards of his foxhole line. Back in Wisconsin he had heard what German tankers did to dug-in infantry who would not surrender. They positioned themselves over the foxholes, then they whirled round and round, gunning their great tank engines. Either the walls of the foxhole crumbled, burying the terrified infantry alive, or the noxious exhaust gases choked them to death.

Smith need not have worried about what to do. Near him, Private Lyle Corcoran sprang to his feet in full view of the tank. The sole remaining bazookaman raised his rocket launcher. Calmly he waited until the tank turned broadside on. Then he fired. Once. Twice. At that range, he could not miss. The Mark IV shuddered to a violent stop. Next moment it was burning fiercely and the German attack came to an abrupt halt.

Some of the greenhorns of the little platoon were not so lucky. Sergeant Guido Fenice watched horrified as the second tank 'ran over some of our men in a foxhole. There were about seven German soldiers running alongside the tank, firing at them with a pistol. They shot one down, so I grabbed his gun and continued to fire. Then the tank got bogged down in the mud.'

The defenders were not slow to take advantage of the situation. A sergeant and two privates dashed forward. They lobbed grenades into the tank's open turret. It burst into flames. That was the end of the German attack. Their infantry fled back to the cover of their pillboxes, while the remaining tank scuttled for the shelter of the woods. For the time being the greenhorns were safe.

Neither of the 5th or 80th Divisions on the 76th's left flank was doing much good. Both ran into serious trouble, with the 5th, veterans of a dozen river crossings under fire, managing to get only sixteen frightened men across on the first night of the assault. Again organisation fell apart, as the Germans pounded hell out of the Americans. Within minutes, it was every man for himself and the devil take the hindmost.

One medic, Private Harold Garman, found himself trapped in a boat filled with wounded in mid-stream and still under fire. Those who had not been hit dived over the side and left the wounded to their fate. Garman, however, stayed. He slipped into the water and, under intense fire, started to push the battered boat with its moaning, groaning wounded back towards land. Slugs twitched and jerked the surface all around him, but by some miracle he made it.

Later, when Patton presented the young medic with the Congressional Medal of Honor for his gallantry, he asked him why he had done it. In Patton's words, Garman 'looked surprised and said, "Well, *someone* had to do it, Sir".'

Now German artillery pounded the US-held side of the Sauer. Just beyond the river bank was the great monastery and basilica dedicated to St Willibrod, the 9th-century English monk, who sallied forth from here to convert the heathen Germans. It must have seemed to the Americans who knew this, that the saint had not done much of a job.

Despite everything, US engineers worked all-out to repair boats, communications, bridge foundations, and so on, to support the handful of troops from XII Corps who had managed to cross the Sauer and were holding the small bridgehead at the other side. And it was not only the enemy artillery they had to contend with. The Germans were trying to float mines to destroy cross-river communications, and here and there, German aircraft zoomed in at treetop height to shoot up the '*Amis*'.

Priority was given to getting a phone wire across the river so that the US commanders could obtain information about what was going on and how they might help the stranded infantry. But, as was the case with bridging operations, the men with the signal wires were not doing too well.

Two brave men volunteered to swim the line across the Sauer, still whipped to a white frenzy by German shells and slugs. But they could get no farther than half-way. Their progress was barred by the deadly German floating mines.

The US Signals Corps tried again. A marksman shot a line with a bazooka. But the German shell-fire soon blew the line apart.

Desperate now for information and news of casualties from the men trapped on the other side of the river, the frustrated Americans tried a new tactic. Smoke pots were set up along the key stretch of the bank, not far from the twin-towered basilica. As soon as the smokescreen started to engulf the water, more volunteers swam across with a new line, this one weighted so that it sank out of sight.

They made it just in time. The Germans had guessed what was going on behind the blanket of smoke, and they floated more mines on the river. One exploded directly above the cable. But it had sunk to fifteen feet below the surface and survived.

At last the relieved Americans had a phone link. Messages began to flood back and forth across the Sauer. Food, ammunition and medical supplies were urgently needed by the trapped men, who were now forming a thin screen on the far side. Oil for cleaning their weapons was also urgently requested.

General Schmidt, the 76th Division's commander, ordered all available artillery spotter planes into action. He had a novel use for the unarmed Piper Cubs. There was still no bridge across the river, and boats were in short supply, so he planned to use the light, single-wing planes to ferry ammo. and the like.[98]

As soon as it was light, the pilots took off. They joked that they were 'dicing with fate', but in fact they really were. As they came in low, the pilots dropped the urgently needed supplies as if they were World War One aviators. They came under intense German rifle and machine-gun fire.

'We were getting pretty short of ammunition and food when the Piper Cubs started dropping stuff to us,' Sergeant Williams of the 76th recalled later. 'The first bundles landed out in open fields under snipers' fire, but later they hit the edge of the woods where we were.' Lieutenant Robert Seiter was one soldier on the far side of the river who was glad to see the spotter planes on that deadly and confused first morning of the assault.

His men were down to half a K-ration per man. The water situation was even worse. Their canteens were virtually empty, and the men did not dare go down to the river to fill up. 'There's some water in my canteen,' he told a rescue party some days later, 'that drained through a blanket over my foxhole. Tastes a little like dye. But it's not bad. Our Halazone tablets purified it.'

Some of the trapped men were without food for nearly two days. This despite the courageous efforts of men like PFC Lowell, who risked his life by rushing into no-man's-land under intense enemy machine-gun fire to pull in bundles of food and ammunition; or pilot Captain Dean, who was decorated in the field by Corps Commander General Eddy for having flown three supply missions across the Sauer in the face of murderous enemy fire.

General Eddy was not the only high-ranking officer who made an appearance on the Sauer front that week. No less a person than the Army Commander, General Patton, did too. In fact, he ventured farther than the rest of the brass, and materialised among his startled troops on the other side of the river. How he did it is the stuff of legends.

One grey, overcast day Patton's jeep raced across a makeshift pontoon bridge constructed by the engineers of the 5th Division under the cover of a thick smokescreen. The hard-pressed infantrymen, to their surprise, found none other than 'Ole Blood an' Guts' himself in their midst, spick and span, from lacquered helmet with its three outsize stars to the famous pistols. Word spread rapidly that, unable to cross the Sauer by conventional methods, the 'Old Man' had swum it.

The Stars and Stripes later reported: 'A fighting front is the breeding place for wild stories. Here is one from this sector. Out of the misty night appeared General George S Patton Jr. "Call back the boats!" he screamed. "They make too high a silhouette. *We will swim!*" They [the troops] hesitated. The general acted. He waded deep into the river and struck out with a powerful crawl. Halfway to the other side, he turned his head and waved. The inspired troops dove in and swam across.'

For once Patton, who had always threatened that he would close down *The Stripes* if he had the power to do so, must have been gratified. It was one more legend to add to the collection concerning his prowess in the war. Soon the days of those legends would be abruptly terminated. But in due course, new admirers would come along and turn Patton into the greatest US military figure of World War Two.

But, the day after he had supposedly crossed the Sauer in such an impressive manner, Patton was concerned with more prosaic matters. Together with General 'Red' Irwin of the 5th Infantry Division, one of the real veterans in the field, he inspected the section of the West Wall through which Irwin's 'Fighting 5th' had broken. They had used the only really effective technique for taking the bunkers – by attacking from the rear.

Staring at the blasted, blackened rear doors[99] of one of the larger hillside bunkers, Patton observed: 'Now I know the Germans are crazy.' He shook his head ruefully. 'You know there are times when I'm sorry the word "defense" was ever invented. From the Great Wall of China to the Maginot Line, *nothing . . . anywhere . . . ever* has been successfully defended.'

The military historian must, with a few exceptions, agree with General Patton.

The two generals stood there on that cold February day, with the guns thundering threateningly in the background. What Patton did not understand was that there were still a lot of Germans who believed, rightly or wrongly, that the Great Wall of Germany could withstand the onslaughts of the Allies – and win.

But in many ways Patton was right, at least as far as the Siegfried Line above the Sauer river was concerned. The second biggest bunker of them all, the 'Cat's Head', which had cost so much and had taken two solid years to build, surrendered, or rather was abandoned, without a fight. A few American shells landed on the heights where the great bunker stood just behind the small town of Irrel, and that was enough. During the night, most of the eighty-four men manning it disappeared towards the east, and only a handful remained to surrender to the 76th.

As it was supposed to be mined and booby-trapped, only the bolder souls among the American victors dared venture close to its steel cupolas. So it was that the entrances to this massive bunker, with its several storeys, forty-five rooms, automatic flame-throwers, machine-guns, air conditioning, etc., were finally sealed up with explosives by the French Occupation Forces nearly three years later. Then it was forgotten, just like the other West Wall bunkers that still dot the heights of the Ferschweiler plateau.[100]

Still, the Siegfried Line complex, which stretched back for nearly thirty miles, would not be finally conquered until 10 March, when Patton's favourite armoured division, the 4th, was within sight of its ultimate objective, the Rhine.

After three days of continual attacks, the greenhorns of the 76th still found themselves tackling a score of pillboxes a day. What the divisional history later called the 'rats' nests' were discovered to number forty per square mile, one every forty yards. In addition, there were a hundred other fortified positions, trenches and minefields in the Ferschweiler heights alone. As one reinforcement, brought up on 11 February commented as he viewed the battlefield from the Luxembourg side: 'Holy Jesus, what detail!'

A full-scale attack, planned by a lieutenant-colonel no less, was launched against a single pillbox that had held up the whole of the 15,000-strong division. A fifteen-minute barrage, fired by a full-strength artillery battalion, fell on it. That was followed by a large-scale mortar 'stonk', which ended when a single green flare sailed into the grey heavens. This was the signal for the specially picked assault squad to attack the bunker.

As they rushed forward bravely, the leading troops stumbled over a cunningly concealed tripwire. All around mines started to explode in flashes of angry, violet light. The young officer leading the assault stumbled. He had been hit. But he recovered and continued running forward, ducking like the others, as if braving torrential rain. Now the assault infantry were about twenty-five yards from the obstinate pillbox.

The machine-guns covering their rush forward ceased firing. It would have been too dangerous for them to continue – they would have hit their own buddies.

The assault force was on its own. A soldier rushed forward. He dropped his satchel charge against the steel door of the large front embrasure. Madly he pelted for cover, slugs slicing the air all around him. The explosive went up with a great roar. But when the smoke cleared, the tense, waiting, watching American infantry saw that only part of the metal door was gone. It still barred their entry.

Another brave volunteer rushed forward to complete the task. But his charge also failed to explode properly. A sergeant cursed. Before anyone could stop him, he darted forward, grenades clutched in both hands. He grunted and tossed them through the hole made by the first satchel charge. That did it.

The garrison had had enough. Fifteen of them had held up an entire US division for more than a day, and had stalled 15,000 young American fighting men. Now they came out, hands held high above their heads, gibbering with fear, frantically crying in a quivering voice: '*Kamerad . . . bitte nicht schiessen . . . bitte.*'

NOTES

97 The author has done it.
98 A month later Patton toyed with the idea of using Piper Cubs to ferry assault troops across the Rhine. It is obvious where he got the idea from.
99 These entrances were usually concealed or protected by steel doors. In some cases the garrison would have to enter by a series of steel hand-holes, descending into a narrow, concealed gully.
100 Nearly thirty years later, the Irrel voluntary fire brigade started to excavate the place and found the bunker exactly as it was when it had been so hurriedly abandoned in February 1945. Soon it might well become a tourist attraction, as the forts of the Maginot Line have. *Sic transit . . .*

5

Patton Goes it Alone

*Goddamit, Brad, why the hell won't SHAEF leave us alone? I'd
rather fight the Hun than Ike and Monty all the time.*

General George S Patton to General Bradley, February 1945

While the 4th Infantry Division fought its way into Prum against
Heilmann's paras, and Patton's favourite 4th Armored Division edged its
way through the Siegfried Line to Bitburg, ready for its dash to the Rhine,
the bulk of Patton's Third Army rested. After a week of bitter combat,
assaulting pillboxes that numbered some forty per square mile, the
survivors of the 76th Infantry were brought back across the Sauer to be
fed, watered and cleaned in preparation for the next stage of the drive into
the West Wall.

The divisional history of the 76th records: 'All that could be seen in
those dirty, whiskered faces, in the sag of wet shoulders, in the shuffle of
mud-caked feet, was the weariness of men who had lived in continuous
danger, little food and less sleep for nearly a week – complete, utter
fatigue.'

Several hundred infantrymen trekked to an open field near one of the
riverside Luxembourg villages. Here a quartermaster shower unit had
been set up. Stripped naked, apparently unconcerned that they were
being watched by a score of local women and children, they dropped their
stained uniforms in the mud. These would be cleaned later. They shuffled
in their flapping boots into tents, where they surrendered their skinny,
filthy bodies to hot water and soap, before being deloused with DDT,
wielded by syringe-bearing, masked blacks. Life – civilised life – could be
resumed, for a while anyway. One is quoted in the history as saying: 'I had
to travel through France, Belgium and most of Luxembourg to get a
chance of hot water and soap. But boy it's worth it!'

Other victorious soldiers settled down where they had been fighting.
Sergeant Giles found himself in a desolate stretch of the battlefield –
'nothing but stumps of pine trees, limbs all blown off, upper halves
splintered' – and found it 'weird, spooky and gave you the creeps.' But
what was to come when the offensive restarted worried him more.

I dreaded this Siegfried Line. I still dread the Rhine. It stands to reason that they have their backs to the wall, and that lunatic Hitler will fight to the last German is dead before he gives up.

Another veteran, Atwell the medic, and his comrades no longer cared where they were or what was going to happen to them. In the shell-shattered village Catholic church, which housed their field dressing centre, they lazed and watched Abbott and Costello in 'Lost in a Harem', and Rita Hayworth in 'Cover Girl' over and over again, until the chaplain protested. Immediately after the war Atwell wrote:

At that time no one seemed to care about anything. Sentences went unfinished, listening faces were loose and vacant; everyone yawned, sprawled, wrote letters in a desultory fashion ... The men hung around the sacristy, crawling over each other like puppies: 'Go wan, ya f . . . . . Aah, ya f . . . . . . Git yer feet off me, greasy bastard! ... Ah'm telling you boy, if Ah ever gits home for a furlough, they're gonna have to burn the woods and sif' the ashes agen to find me!'

It was the familiar, drained mood of men after combat; men collecting their nervous strength, adjusting once more, preparing for the strain, mental and physical, of the next battle – and that battle would surely come.

Patton took his first furlough of the campaign. He spent a few days in Paris, where he was assured by the manager of the Folies Bergères that the establishment was his home, 'for a rest', whenever he was in Paris. 'I can imagine no more restless place than the Folies, full of about a hundred practically naked women,' he confided to his diary that day. Next day he enjoyed another of his favourite pursuits, hunting, but retired with a bad case of food poisoning. Being Patton, he suspected that someone was trying to do away with him. The day after that, his suspicious mind told him that his telephone was being tapped.

It was characteristic of the General that, as the future of Europe hung in the balance, he believed that all of his fellow top generals were out to stop him. They would even murder him if they had to. Montgomery was still 'the little fart', always trying to obstruct his Third Army. Eisenhower was 'yellow' and only interested in the post-war Presidency. Bradley and the First Army Commander, Hodges, were 'nothings'. Even his own corps commanders were insubordinate and no good. He wrote in his diary: I have to battle for every yard. It is not the enemy who is trying to stop me; it is them.'

Patton probably knew that the best way finally to deal with the Siegfried Line was by turning its hinge, just as the Germans had done with the Maginot Line back in 1940. They had swung open the door by coming through the Ardennes and swinging back the hinge to the north of the Maginot. It was obvious that this was what Montgomery was trying to do to the north of the Siegfried Line in the Reichswald.

Patton's successful attempt to break through the West Wall in the Eifel had made no decisive impact on the 400-mile long series of fortifications. So far the Germans had been able to contain his penetration. There had not been the wholesale withdrawals to the Rhine that there would undoubtedly be in the north, once Montgomery broke through the Line. Then the Germans would have to retreat – or be captured, trapped in their bunkers and pillboxes.

What Patton needed, therefore, in the third week of February 1945, was permission to continue his attack, especially over the Moselle, with the US First Army on his left and Patch's Seventh Army on his right, supporting his massive, all-American drive to the Rhine. But he knew this was not the agreed strategy. In his opinion, events, circumstances and personalities shaped strategy, not some obscure staff officer in a safe office a thousand miles away. What did Marshall in Washington or Eisenhower in Versailles know of the real situation at the front? In an impassioned outburst, referring to the current strategy that gave prominence to Montgomery in the north, he told Bradley: 'That's a fine plan all right, General. It sounds impressive on paper. But it is sure one hell-of-a-note to have this war run 5,000 miles away from here [in Washington]. We are trying to fight the enemy according to the situation on the ground. Not on a map or by theory . . . Third Army wants to fight. It wants to get this goddam war over with.'

Patton put forward a proposal, which did not itself seem particularly radical. After all, it involved one armoured division and one German city. Unwittingly, perhaps, he had hit on a plan that would at last completely break the power of the Siegfried Line. Now he suggested 'we can take Trier[101] in two days . . . The Hun can't stop us now!'

Patton did not know it at the time, but he would soon be in a position to upstage Montgomery in the north. The outcome of his suggested course of action would be politically disastrous, but that was of no concern to Patton. He would have restored the prestige of the American Army; the Americans, not the British, would win the kudos of victory. Montgomery would be reduced to not much more than flank guard to the conquering 'Yanks'. And Patton and his Third Army would, naturally, be the authors of the victory soon to be won. Long after Bradley, Simpson, Hodges, even Eisenhower were forgotten, the Great American Public would remember George S Patton Jr. 'Ole Blood an' Guts' was going to make damned sure of that.

In the Reichswald the slogging match continued. The attack had started in the rain. Seven days later the rain was still falling in relentless, soul-destroying, fury, turning the battlefield into a quagmire – reminiscent of the worst conditions in World War One.

The defenders had actually helped by blowing the Roer dams opposite Simpson's Ninth US Army, under Montgomery's command, in the north. The resulting flood had stopped Simpson's attack dead and had inundated the plain beyond the Reichswald. The *Sunday Times* war correspondent, R W Thompson, noted that the battlefield had become 'practically a naval action. The tops of houses, the turrets of derelict tanks, smitten tree trunks and the branches of telegraph poles and all the fearful garbage of war gave shape to all this desolation of water. Otherwise, it might almost have been the sea.'

The soldiers of Horrocks' XXX Corps, in the forefront of the attack, quipped that they were 'the water rats' (a play on the 'desert rats' of the war in North Africa). They went into battle in small boats, and at night formed their 'laagers' on islands of mud.

It could take up to eighteen hours to transport food supplies to these isolated outposts. At one stage, all Horrocks could provide for his entire 200,000 men was a mere 500 cans of self-heating soup. When trying to take up rations, as Quartermaster Captain J Moore of the East Lancs recalled: 'No roads could be seen, or even signs of any. It was just a lake . . . We could have got through because I had a pretty good idea where the submerged road was, but our luck ran out and Bean, the driver, ran into one of the Jerry slit trenches. No one would stop to help – you couldn't blame them. So I got out and tried to make my way on foot. The water was up to my thighs and the Dukws gave me their wash, but I survived.' He did, but that particular company of the East Lancs did not get their hot bully stew that day.

Deprived of their armoured protection, the long-suffering PBI ploughed through the mud and water against the bunkers and pillboxes of the 'bloody para boys'. They also fought mines, the most feared weapon of the war as far as the footsloggers were concerned. Their only weapon against it was the bayonet, deployed in a hit-or-miss prodding operation. Mines came in all shapes and sizes, from the Teller, almost as big as a dustbin lid, to the 'deballocker', the small anti-personnel mine that did exactly what its nickname suggested.

Even engineers, armed with the right equipment, could not find the new plastic, wood- and glass-encased, or the booby-trap mines.[102] Alf Jones of the Royal Engineers maintained: 'The mines of the bloody Reichswald were the worst of the whole sodding war as far as I'm concerned . . . All the poor sods of the infantry could do was to prod for them under the water with the bullets cutting the air just above their heads. No picnic, I can tell you.'

The costs were prohibitive, with the British and the Canadians suffering 1,500 serious casualties every day. They were flooding the military hospitals in Belgium, and even back in the UK. The official Canadian military historian, Colonel Stacey, wrote after the war:

Let no one misconceive the severity of the fighting during those final months. In this, the twilight of the gods, the defenders of the Reich displayed the recklessness of fanaticism and the courage of despair. In the contests west of the Rhine in particular, they fought with special ferocity, rendering the battle of the Reichswald and the Hochwald grimly memorable in the annals of this war.

Canadian casualties were especially horrendous. The all-volunteer Canadian Army in Europe was rapidly running out of 'bodies'. Desertions at the Canadian ports of embarkation were widespread. The embittered volunteers had to live, so to speak, off their own fat. Cooks, clerks and drivers were rapidly retrained as infantry. But, unlike the veterans, who knew the rules of battle backwards, they did not survive for long. Even the vets were being worn down by the constant demands placed on them.

Nevertheless, the Canadians did more than their share to break through the Siegfried Line in the last great battle of the war. The tally of VCs awarded in February and March is testimony to their bravery. Sergeant Aubrey Cousins, together with a handful of soldiers, held off a concerted attack by Rennie's 'bloody para boys'. Once the Germans had gone to ground, Cousins became a one-man army. He charged the house held by the enemy, killed twenty of them, and took many more prisoner. He then consolidated his position, told his four exhausted subordinates that he was going 'back to report to the CO', and was shot dead by a German sniper five minutes later.

Major Tiltson of the Canadian Essex Scottish was another hero. Badly wounded in the head as he led his men through a series of barbed-wire entanglements to attack a fortified position, he still commanded his company. He silenced a German machine-gun with a well aimed grenade. Then he was hit again, this time in the hip. He collapsed, but still would not give up, and continued to direct his survivors while they engaged the enemy in hand-to-hand combat.

The German paras rallied. Shouting wildly and screaming curses and war cries, they counter-attacked. By this time the Canadians had lost three quarters of their strength. Still they slogged it out with their attackers. Tiltson, slumped in a waterlogged shell-hole, drifted in and out of consciousness, and tried to encourage his desperate men. He was hit yet again, but refused to be evacuated. Finally the Germans were driven off, then the barely conscious major allowed himself to be carried away on a stretcher. He was awarded the Victoria Cross, but at a high cost. Both of his legs had to be amputated.

In the end the price paid by the First Canadian Army was a high one. They lost 379 officers and 4,935 men. The British suffered even higher casualties, 770 officers and 9,600 men. Most were lost in the final week of February.

Mercifully death at the front usually came swiftly – the crack of a sniper's rifle like a dry twig underfoot on a hot summer's day; the shriek of an 88mm zipping flatly through the air; the high-pitched hysterical scream of an MG 42. The wounded were another matter – faces ashen, eyes wide and wild in shocked disbelief at what was happening to them, they lay in the mud, hearing the angry voices: 'Stretcher-bearer . . . Where the bloody hell is the stretcher-bearer?' Then the wounded soldier would be in the tough, blood-stained hands of the medics, ripping at the khaki with their jack-knives, pressing home syringes of morphia that looked like small tubes of toothpaste, clapping on thick, clumsy, yellow padded bandages in an attempt to staunch the flow of bright red blood.

Box-like ambulances and jeeps bounced across the ruts made by the tanks in the churned up battlefield to a forward dressing station. Harassed medical officers, with blood-stained aprons round their loins, sometimes working by the hissing glare of a petroleum lantern, cut, sliced, patched, bandaged, in an effort to ensure that the wounded man would survive the next stage of his long journey.

Wound tags were pinned on, with the morphia dose and other medical details pencilled on foreheads. Then it was off again towards the west in a strange white haze, nostrils full of the smell of disinfectant and faeces.

Then there were more doctors – senior ones this time – feeling pulses, ripping bandages off roughly, sniffing the gaping wounds of those who had been in the field for a long time for the stench of gangrene. Now a few would be given the 'red disc'. They had hit the jackpot. Their wounds were serious enough for them to be sent back to the UK for further treatment. They had the 'blighty wound'.

The rest would stay behind in the general hospitals in Louvain, Brussels, and Bruges, among other places. They spent the first few days in a drug-induced sleep before the medics went to work on them. Monty needed 'bodies'. The front was running out of infantrymen. So, they were patched up, given the gold 'wound stripe' if they were an 'other rank', and were sent back to who knew what.

Naturally enough, some were reluctant to go back. But many were happy to be reunited with their mates. Here they at least knew where they stood. If they were going to have to fight again, it was better in the company of men they knew and could rely on. One wounded officer, on returning to his battalion, said:

It was a tonic to find oneself again in the free air of good comradeship, cooperation and good-humoured stoicism of the front line after months of jealouses and petty rivalries, so rampant farther back . . . The Company looked a truly amazing sight as they marched into our area. They were loaded down with the usual impediment of ammunition, guns, picks and shovels, but in addition each man had some personal treasure; some had hurricane lamps, some oil house lamps, or an odd oil stove; others carried blankets or baskets, and two sections arrived, each with a joint of pig they had killed the day before, slung across their haversacks. They looked like a motley crew in their camouflage jackets, scarves and weather-beaten faces.

R W Thompson thought they were 'bloody heroes'.

Casualties or not, they were just about through that Siegfried Line many of them had dreaded so much. The teenage infantry had been schoolkids in short pants when their older brothers had boasted in 1939 that they were going to 'hang out our washing on the Siegfried Line. Have you any dirty washing, Mother dear?' Five years earlier there had been failure. Now the 'kids' – who had never really been normal kids, the war had seen to that – had done it.

They were the ones who had broken out of the 'Nijmegen Bottleneck'[103], smashed the Siegfried Line, and cleared the Reichswald and its surrounding area. They had beaten the best of what Germany still had, those 'bloody para boys', better even than the Waffen SS. These had fought like fiends, when attacked by the flame-throwers of the Camerons, crying, 'Come and get us, you English [sic] bastards!'

Montgomery was pleased with them. He was even pleased with the Canadian staff work, although the start of the battle had been a shambles. In fact the Field Marshal seemed generally pleased. He felt he had been given the green light by Eisenhower who had his subordinates, Bradley and Patton, under control once more.

Unfortunately Montgomery was not a very sensitive or perceptive man. He assumed others were like himself. Although he could be cruel – he had sacked his generals without compunction or any remorse even when one had burst into tears at the final interview with the Army Commander – he did not bear grudges. In January he had put Bradley in his place because of his failings in the Battle of the Bulge. Now he expected the American to pull his weight, as he, Montgomery, would have done for the sake of the team.

Of course Montgomery was not completely naive. He knew that not all other generals lived up to his own high standards (after all, he *was* the son of a bishop). After he learned that Eisenhower would agree to a limited Rhine crossing to seize the Ruhr (a plan Montgomery had been advocating since D-Day), he could still write to King George VI's private secretary: 'Now we are all right again. I think Eisenhower has had a bit of a dogfight, and at the Namur Conference on 5 February [at Bradley's HQ], he sided with me against Bradley for the first time. We shall now have to see whether he can keep the ship on a steady course. He has lost his nerve several times before and Bradley & Co. will "get at" him in my absence.'

Montgomery, the one hundred percent professional soldier, did not appreciate what an important role personalities and national prestige were going to play in the final destruction and breakthrough of the Siegfried Line. Bradley, who now hated Monty, was more determined than ever to drag the direction of the main Allied attack into the purely American zone of operations. Unwittingly or otherwise, Eisenhower played straight into Bradley's hands.

The Supreme Commander had been persuaded at the Namur Conference on 4-6 February that if Montgomery was going to be allowed the 'gamble' of a major, narrow-front attack across the Rhine into the Ruhr, all the Allied armies should first line up and be in position along the whole length of the river. As Major Hansen[104], Bradley's aide, adviser and chief propagandist, noted in his secret diary: 'My contention [that is, Bradley's] was that if you were going to advance into Germany on a narrow front . . . you must have advanced to the Rhine all along the line so that you would have a strong defensive position which could be held with minimum troops without much danger of a major German attack.'

The thinking behind this was that the Americans could not risk another 'surprise' attack like the Battle of the Bulge. It still rankled that Bradley had been caught with his pants down in the Ardennes, but there was more to it than that. In suggesting that Patton's Third Army and Hodges' First should advance to the Rhine before Montgomery launched his set-piece crossing, Bradley was attempting to give his two army commanders a major role in the final battle for the Reich. It was something his counterpart, 'Jake' Devers, commander of the Sixth Army Group, wanted too. 'Sandy' Patch, commander of his Seventh Army and de Lattre de Tassigny, leading the 1st Free French Army, should also close to the river.

Montgomery had broken through his section of the West Wall in the north. Hodges and Patton had done so in the centre. In effect, the Siegfried Line had been penetrated on a broad front from Holland to Luxembourg's border with Germany. However, there was still a huge stretch of Hitler's Wall intact, running from south of Trier through the German Saarland and the whole length of Alsace opposite France to Basle on the French-German-Swiss border. It would take a major effort, even in the dying days of the 'Thousand-Year Reich', to capture that great line of fortifications. And it would be unnecessary if a major assault in the north, such as Montgomery's, turned the whole West Wall flank.

Whatever Eisenhower's thoughts, they were of no interest to Patton. He grabbed the chance being offered – albeit indirectly – of getting his Third Army involved in operations again. Indeed, his short furlough in Paris might well have been part of the plan he was forming in his mind to do so. For the Third Army Commander left Paris with more than a dose of food poisoning.

On the surface, he had gone to Paris to relax and enjoy himself. He had visited the Folies, and had had classy chats with Hemingway and his

'Kraut', Marlene Dietrich, about the author's *The Sun Also Rises*, and the fact that the film star's driver had been shot by a GI sentry a couple of days earlier. But there had been more to the Paris visit than that. Patton returned from his short leave with permission to use SHAEF's armoured reserve, the10th US Armored Division. How he obtained it, and the use to which he would put the 10th, was, as his aide, Colonel Charles Codman, noted in his diary for 1 March 1945, 'a bottling operation', the inside story of which 'will I think shed light on the General's implementation of active defense.'

Patton and his Third Army were going places again.

NOTES

101 The old Roman city was the major hub in the Third Army area of operations on the Moselle.
102 They were often linked by trip wires. Lift one and the unfortunate sapper detonated the next one. Others were fitted underneath with matchbox-sized detonators that went off when the sapper thought (wrongly) that he had safely lifted the deadly device.
103 Some British divisions had been in the area since the failed Arnhem attack – so long in fact that one of them, the 49th Infantry Division, was known by other British units as the 'Nijmegen Home Guard'.
104 Like several of Bradley's junior staff officers, he seems to have been virulently anti-British.

6

Trier

I have taken Trier with two divisions. What do you want me to do?
Give it back?

Patton to Eisenhower's HQ, 1 March 1945

No foreign invader must enter the town. Even if we have to beat him to death, strangle him with our own hands, Trier must remain free.

The Führer's specific command, expressed with such brutality, must have electrified Model. The commander of Army Group B, which had overall responsibility for the defence of the Rhineland, and what was left of the Siegfried Line, had no illusions about Adolf Hitler. Although he had remained in favour after the 'Generals' Plot' to kill Hitler in July 1944, the Führer showed no mercy to any commander who let him down.

In recent months, Hitler had had more than one commander court-martialled for abandoning a position, and in a couple of cases in Russia, he had actually had divisional commanders executed. Field Marshal Model knew that he would be no exception. At best he could be sacked, as Hitler had just done to Field Marshal von Rundstedt, relieving him of his position on the grounds of 'old age'. At worst he might end up facing a firing squad.

In a telephone conversation, recorded on 27 February 1945, between Model, the Chief-of-Staff of the 80th Corps and that of another command, Model made his position quite clear. In his harsh, uncompromising manner, he rasped: 'The Führer has declared Trier to be a fortress city. He has ordered the relevant measures should be taken immediately to do this. Trier is to be defended as a fortress. Please convey this order at once to Colonel Bachmann, the local Trier commandant. Report to me what you have done.'

The Chief-of-Staff of the 80th Corps must have been all too aware that Trier ranked with Aachen, being one of the oldest and most historic cities in Germany. Was it to be razed to the ground as Aachen had so nearly been? In any event, he did not accept the Führer's order automatically and without question as so many high-ranking German officers would have done. Instead he protested: 'I can't carry out an order of that kind with troops I currently have available . . . American tanks are already in position in the heights at Pellingen [a village not far from the old Roman city]. One can't create a fortress in a matter of days.'

Model rode roughshod over his objections. 'I've already told the Führer that,' he snapped. 'He's not interested. He has ordered <u>personally</u> that Trier will be defended as a fortress . . . We've got to get on with it.'

The Chief-of-Staff obviously was not lacking in what the Germans call *Zivilcourage*.[105] He snorted back: 'Do what you like. I can't carry out this order. You can't expect me to pass on an order like that which it is impossible to execute. And tell the people at the top [even the angry general did not dare mention Hitler by name] that I can't defend Trier with six thousand drunken *Volkssturm*[106] and their lack of arms.'

Model's response is not on record. But, no doubt after the characteristic outburst of threats and accusations, he realised that the representative of 80 Corps was giving him no more than the hard facts, however unpalatable. If Trier was to be defended in accordance with the Führer's express command, 80 Corps would need regular troops – the best available, the fanatical young men of the Waffen SS.

The 6th SS Mountain Division, plus the Austrian 2nd Mountain, had fought most of their war in the bleak tundra and forests of Finland. There, close to the Arctic Circle, the all-volunteer formation had battled the Russians in an unknown bitter struggle that has never been properly chronicled. The war had been as much against the elements as the 'Ivan' enemy.

In September 1944 the Russians had forced the Finnish allies to surrender, and the full-strength SS division of 15,000 well trained, experienced, hardy young men had withdrawn by boat, truck, train, even by reindeer-drawn sledge. Four months later the 6th SS had been thrown into what has been called the 'Second Battle of the Bulge', the eight-division strong German attack on the American Seventh Army in Alsace. There, it had almost swung the balance in Germany's favour before being withdrawn because of a lack of heavy equipment and high casualties.

But it was still a top outfit, this formation that, together with the 2nd Austrian Mountain Division and an understrength People's Grenadier Division, was going to stop Patton. Its young soldiers were imbued with the overweening arrogance of the SS, and the belief that the Germany of the 'New Order' could still win the war. All that was required of them was that they hold on until the Führer unleashed the promised 'wonder weapons' on the unsuspecting '*Amis*'.

Now, unknown to the rank and file of the Third Army (though Ultra must have informed Patton what was afoot), the 6th and the 2nd Austrian moved into the Saarbrücken-Sarreguemines salient, part of which was still protected by the West Wall, and the rugged terrain of the Saar-Moselle valleys, ready to do battle again with the '*Amis*'.

By this time Patton's Third was six miles from Trier. The way from the north-east had been tough. The US 94th Infantry Division's assault crossing of the Saar had been a total failure. The two assault battalions had been caught midstream by German artillery. A rain of shells had fallen on their little boats. It was the 76th's crossing of the Sauer all over again. The bombardment was too much for the US infantry. They panicked. Paddling furiously, they fled back to their side of the river. Behind them they left a score of boats filled with dead and dying comrades.

In the confusion, elements of the 94th had tangled with Patton's 'borrowed' division, the 10th Armored. A regular fire fight had broken out. It stopped only when someone noticed that Americans were firing on Americans in the woods. That cost the unlucky 94th another half company of infantry.

The two divisions finally succeeded in crossing the Saar. But the Germans were still ready for a fight. After all, the Führer himself was watching them anxiously from his bunker in Berlin. The 6th and 2nd Mountain Divisions attacked, supported by tanks of the 11th German Panzer Division. For a while the 5th Ranger Battalion, the American commandos, were cut off. The SS even had the gall to ask them to surrender – this with the war almost at an end.

The handful of elite Rangers refused. Patton knew that SHAEF would soon be asking for its 10th Armored back, and he pulled out all the stops to save them. They were to be supplied by air, using the same methods as the 76th had employed on the Sauer. All day Piper Cubs from the artillery flew mission after mission to supply the hard-pressed Rangers with ammunition, food and water. In the end the Rangers held, but the cost was high. The PBI was, as usual, paying the butcher's blood bill.

A German minefield was found to be protecting the outlying villages of Pellingen and Ollmuth. The mines stopped the American advance dead. Engineers were rushed up. Employing Trier's anti-tank guns in a ground role, the Germans pounded the brave engineers as they went about their slow, painstaking work. They eventually cleared the field, but they took appalling casualties. Forty percent were killed or wounded.

The 94th, in the lead and supported by tanks, ran into the bunker line of the West Wall, a section dating back to the very beginnings of the Great Wall of Germany. This stopped them in their tracks. All night Germans and Americans fought for the fortifications. Finally the US survivors broke and fled. Those who did not were left to find their own way back. One such straggler, Captain Standish, was discovered three days later, absolutely alone, his company vanished, half-starved and in a state of shock.

Time was running out. Patton hounded General Malony to keep his men moving, even threatening to sack him. Colonel Codman arranged by phone yet another meeting for his boss and the unfortunate Malony. As

Patton's sedan reached the arranged meeting place, an officious MP directed them elsewhere – fortunately for Patton. A sudden, deadly salvo of German shells straddled the original venue. The Germans were tapping the Americans' communication lines. Patton lived to fight another day, and Malony got another earwigging.

Now Morris's tanks were in sight of Trier. Unknown to the 10th Armored Division's commander, the old Roman city was the Americans' for the taking. Most of the regular German troops had withdrawn, the city's artillery defences were mainly flak artillery, manned by Hitler Youth and girls, and the defending infantry consisted of drunken *Volkssturm* men, who were ready to do a runner at the drop of a hat.

At the same time, SHAEF and, it appears, Bradley were breathing down Patton's neck. Bradley had badly needed Patton's successes in the Battle of the Bulge and the January battles, but now that he had Eisenhower's ear, the 12th Army Group Commander was showing signs of envying Patton, who was hogging the headlines. Bradley was feeling left out and started to pressurise Patton. Now he demanded that Patton return the 10th Armored Division to SHAEF's reserve.[107]

But the Third Army Commander maintained that he could not take Trier without the 10th's armour. What was he to do? He decided to try one of his old tricks. He would cut himself off from any communication with the rear – either Bradley's HQ or Eisenhower's SHAEF HQ at Versailles. This was a tactic no other American army commander would have dared to try. Anyone leading 300,000 troops simply did not sever communications with a superior HQ for twenty-four minutes, far less twenty-four hours as Patton did.

In the early hours of 1 March Patton ordered a change in direction of the attack on Trier. He commanded that the 94th Division call a halt to its costly attempt to batter its way through the bunker line of the West Wall. Instead, the 10th's tanks were to make a direct surprise assault into the ancient city of Pellingen.

At first the attack did not go well. The German flank, defending Trier against aerial bombardment, turned their 88mm cannon and quadruple, quick-firing 20mm cannon on the advancing American tanks. Four Shermans were knocked out in quick order, but still the Americans pressed their assault. They liberated an Allied POW camp on the Petrisburg just above Trier. But by the time they had released the skinny, cheering prisoners, many of whom had been captured during the recent fighting for the Siegfried Line, the American point was down to four tanks and five half-tracks. Patton was paying a high price for victory.

Not that Patton was aware of this. He had flown to confer with his VIII Corps commander, General Middleton, in the battered Belgian town of Bastogne. He reckoned that no one at HQ would expect 'Ole Blood an'Guts' to be that far back from the line.

Patton's impatience was evident. Displeased with the progress of his armour, General Morris, commanding the 10th Armored, sent his Chief-of-Staff personally to find out what was going on. This officer did not get far. He was caught in a German mortar barrage, was wounded in the head, and had to be evacuated at the double.

Street-fighting now started up. Officer patrols, ordered out into the debris-strewn streets by City Commandant, Colonel Bachmann, stopped the Americans through sheer bravery and battlecraft. The German Home Guardsmen, on the other hand, formed into battalions with grand names, such as 'Porta Nigra'[108], had already looted the cellars of the 'Moselle Wine Metropolis', as Trier called itself. They stumbled into battle, thought better of it, and raised their hands before being ordered to do so by the 'Amis'.

Rapidly the defences of Germany's oldest city started to crumble. Max Jordan, the war correspondent of New York's German-language paper, *New Yorker Staatszeitung und Herold*, informed his readers: 'Imagine it. Back in December Trier was the center of the German supply system for the Battle of the Bulge . . . Today the inner city is a ruin save for the Porta Nigra.'

Hearing Jordan speak fluent German to a local civilian, an unidentified GI, battleworn and begrimed, put it more succinctly: 'Nix Trier – Trier kaputt!'

The Germans attempted to blow up the bridges over the Moselle, which would have prevented the reinforcement of the 10th Armored by troops from the west, but to no avail. Colonel Jack Richardson – a 'brave son-of-a-bitch' Patton called him – who was under open arrest awaiting court-martial, risked his life to capture the *Römerbrücke* (Roman Bridge) with a bold *coup-de-main* action. What his crime had been no one found out. A few days later he was killed in action, and the charge against him was quietly dropped.

Bachmann used his last carrier pigeon to send a final message. It had none of the heroic defiance of Colonel Wilck's from Aachen six months earlier. It read: 'Trier's remaining garrison completely surrounded. Can't recapture the Romerbrücke with the forces available. Intend to break out after dark.'

That night the guns in Trier fell silent. At the German Seventh Army HQ they prepared a final report on the fighting in the old city. Part of it read: 'They've gone home . . . The 'Porta Nigra' Battalion of Home Guard ran away as soon as the Americans attacked. The 'Ruwer' Battalion [named after a local river] got drunk and couldn't fight.'

Despite this, Goebbels declared on radio five days later, 'Heavy fighting is still taking place in Trier'. But Trier was finished. Colonel Bachmann, who had been intending to 'break out', vanished without trace. Nothing was ever heard of him again. Three thousand of his brave Home Guard went meekly into the American cages.

As for Patton, he felt he had the world at his feet. He had beaten the 'Krauts' even though his superiors had wanted to impede him by taking away the 10th Armored Division. Now, as SHAEF urgently signalled him to by-pass Trier because four divisions would be needed to take the city, and they wanted their 10th Armored back, he could triumphantly radio back: 'Have taken Trier with two divisions. What do you want me to do? Give it back?'

Thursday 1 March saw the start of the most momentous week of the 1945 campaign in Western Europe. The next seven days could determine the shape of the post-war continent. It began with the seemingly unimportant capture of Trier, its only claim to fame the fact that it was Germany's oldest city. It ended on the 7th with the taking of what was described as 'the most important bridge in the world – for a week', the Remagen railway bridge over the Rhine. In the end, those two, apparently unrelated military events would herald a radical change in Allied strategy. It would signal the rapid demise of the Siegfried Line (much more rapid than the experts had anticipated) and a decisive change in the direction of the Allies' last attack into Hitler's Reich.

On the day Trier fell, Eisenhower was not out looking for his 'borrowed' 10th Armored Division, as Patton, hidden and incommunicado in Bastogne, suspected he might be. Rather, he was on his way to 'Big Simp's' HQ to congratulate the commander of the US Ninth Army. General Simpson's Ninth had finally fought its way through the flooded Rhine delta plain, and had captured Moenchen-Gladbach[109], the largest German city to be conquered so far. The operation had gone off 'like a football game, with every play working perfectly'.

As 'Big Simp', his shaven head gleaming as usual, told Eisenhower, Moenchen-Gladbach was only twelve miles from the Rhine. Tomorrow he would launch his Ninth Army in an attempt to capture a bridge over the great river – according to aerial reconnaissance, there were eight of them still intact in his sector of the front.

That news must have pleased Eisenhower. He knew that Patton had barely got through the Siegfried Line. Patch and his Seventh Army still faced a sizeable portion of intact West Wall. Only Hodges' First Army stood a chance of beating Simpson in the race for the Rhine, which is what it was to become for the American generals. As for Montgomery, he did not seem to care whether he seized a bridge or not. His mind was fully occupied with his well planned, set-piece crossing of the Rhine, still three weeks away.

The two generals took a trip to the rear of the line to inspect some 3,000 infantrymen from the division that had just captured Moenchen-Gladbach. Together they slopped through the mud, while the soldiers shouted, 'Hey, there's Ike'. Eisenhower talked to them for five minutes and prepared to turn and leave. Before he realised what was happening, his feet went from under him, and he sat down hard in the mud in his expensive, Savile Row-tailored pants. Nonplussed, the Supreme Commander clambered to his feet, and gave the men the boxer's salute of triumph and the ear-to-ear grin famous to movie audiences all over the free world. What he said later is not recorded, but some of his words to an amused 'Big Simp' are: 'I want to tip you off. In a few days you can expect Prime Minister Churchill. What kind of an automobile have you?'

Simpson replied that he only had a Plymouth. In an expansive mood, Eisenhower said, 'I'll take care of that. Another thing; Churchill likes scotch. Be sure and have a good supply at hand.'

Two days later Montgomery, who did not really want the PM at his HQ at such a crucial time, Churchill and Chief-of-Staff of the British Army, Brooke, set off in two Rolls-Royces to visit Simpson. They met in Maastricht where they prepared to visit the Ninth Army front. Before they left, Simpson asked Churchill discreetly whether he wanted to visit the 'men's room'. The Prime Minister, who had few inhibitions in such matters, replied. 'How far is the West Wall?' When told it was half an hour away, Churchill said the 'men's room' could wait.

The journey was quite eventful. In a forest, Churchill spotted a road sign. It read: THIS WAS THE SIEGFRIED LINE. A hundred yards farther on there was another, bearing a clothes line, and with, in chalk, the words THIS IS THE WASHING.

If Churchill commented, his thoughts are unrecorded. But he must have been in a good mood. After almost six years of 'blood, toil, tears and sweat', the much vaunted Great Wall of Germany was just about finished. To the Ninth Army troops at the roadside he gave his famous V-sign and a strange sort of smile.

The smile was soon explained. A jeep, honking its horn and driven at speed by a flustered GI, overtook the PM's Rolls. The British driver drew up and the immaculate Redcaps guided the American to where Churchill sat. The GI saluted and handed over a small package, which the Prime Minister unwrapped. To everyone's amazement it contained a set of false teeth. Churchill had forgotten them and now, apparently unconcerned at being watched, he popped them into his mouth and ordered his driver on.

As they approached a small Bailey bridge across a ravine, Simpson remarked: 'Mr Churchill, the boundary between Holland and Germany runs under that bridge ahead of us.'

'Stop the car,' Churchill ordered. 'Let's get out.' The PM led the way, followed by Simpson, Brooke and a host of staff officers and correspondents. They passed a tank bearing the legend 'Alcoholic Bitch', and crossed the bridge. They slipped and slithered down the river bank to a long row of 'dragon's teeth'. There they waited until everbody had caught up, including the tense correspondents and photographers, who were getting ready for a shot of the 'Great Man' at the Siegfried Line.

But Churchill had other ideas. 'Gentlemen,' he boomed in that voice that had put so much heart into the British people in the darkest days of the war, 'I'd like to ask you to join me. Let us all urinate in the Great West Wall of Germany.' He wagged a pudgy finger at the photographers, who were already aiming their cameras, 'This is one of those operations connected with this great war,' he added, 'that must not be reproduced graphically.' With that he tugged open his fly buttons.

Brooke was impressed by 'the childish grin of intense satisfaction that spread all over his [Churchill's] face as he looked down at the crucial moment.'

Churchill had pissed on Hitler's Wall at last. It was almost over now.

NOTES

105 Literally, 'civil courage' – the ability to stand up to authority and say one's piece, a quality for which Germans are not noted.
106 The German Home Guard.
107 Bradley's 'envy' is evident in the movie 'Patton'. Now 'General of the Army', he was hired as a special consultant by the film-makers. He made sure that he was portrayed as calm and reasonable, while Patton appeared as a hothead (if also a genius) who had constantly to be kept under control.
108 The famous Roman 'Black Gate' that Napoleon himself had ordered to be restored.
109 Currently the headquarters of the British Army of the Rhine.

7

End Run

Remember me when I am dead and simplify me when I'm dead

Keith Douglas, Royal Armoured Corps, Killed in Action,
Normandy, 1944

On the morning of Wednesday 7 March the first tanks of Patton's 4th
Armored Division reached the Rhine. In just over fifty hours, they had
driven from an obscure flour mill in the Eifel near Bitburg all the way to
the great river.[110] Ten hours later, the men of the 1st Army's 9th Armored
Division were crossing the river by the Remagen Bridge.[111] Later, Hitler
was to lament: 'Two bridgeheads have decided Germany's fate –
Normandy and Remagen.' Patton had been pipped at the post by a
general he despised, the plodding Courtney Hodges, commander of the
First Army.

True to the way in which the American top brass conducted the war in
1945, Patton was called to the phone later that day to speak to General
'Sandy' Patch, commander of the US Seventh Army, now fighting in the
Saar.

'George,' Patch cried, 'I want to congratulate you.'

'What about, Alec?' Patton asked in surprise.

'For being the last army to reach the Rhine,' came the reply.

Patton thought for a moment, then realised what Patch meant.

'Thanks, Alec,' he said pleasantly enough. 'And I want to congratulate
you too.'

Now it was Patch's turn to be surprised. 'For what?' he asked.

Patton let out that high-pitched, snorting laugh of his and answered,
'For being the first army to be kicked off the Rhine.'[112]

It is on record that Patch, who was to die shortly after the war ended,
joined in the laughter.

Now that Hodges had his bridgehead across the Rhine at Remagen,
Patton rationalised with his staff: 'There is no tactical advantage to be
gained by crossing the Rhine now. If that bridge had not been captured,
an assault of the river probably would have been the best thing we could
have done.'

Patton had already dreamt up another campaign for his Third Army. He thought he did not have approval, though in fact Eisenhower had already given Bradley, Patton's envious superior, permission for Patton to go ahead. He told his planners:

Now our most profitable target is the Palatinate. They [the Germans] have got an army group down there holding the Siegfried Line against the US Seventh Army and the Hunsruck[113] Mountains in the north. G-2 reports they haven't got much on that flank as they are counting on the Hunsruck to hold us off . . . Well, we've cracked that kind of terrain before. We did it in the Eifel and we can do it just as fast in the Hunsruck. I don't see any reason why we shouldn't turn the German rear in a matter of days . . . and then we can cross [the Rhine] at will. It will be a cinch.

Thus Patton committed his army, almost as if they were his personal chattels, to do with as he wished. The last attack on the Siegfried Line was about to begin.

'Smiling Albert', as Field Marshal Albert Kesselring, the new German C-in-C in the West was known, guessed what Patton was up to, even before he attacked in the Palatinate (the area between the Moselle and the Rhine). In the second week of March he visited the German Seventh Army in that part to find out for himself what the situation was.

Kesselring was Germany's defence expert. From 1943, though nominally a *Luftwaffe* officer, he had fought the Anglo-Americans the whole length of Italy. He had always relied on strong-minded officers (Colonel Heilmann of the 5th Para had been one of them) and the rugged, mountainous terrain to make the Allies pay dearly for every metre of ground won. Now 'Smiling Albert' was planning the same tactics for the part of the West Wall still in German hands.

The area covered some 6,000 square kilometres. It included the heavily industrialised Saar, and industrial towns, Kesselring knew, lent themselves to defensive battles. Such places could swallow up whole divisions. At the same time, Kesselring realised that after the Ruhr, the Saar was Germany's most important source of industrial strength. It contributed about ten percent of the nation's coal and perhaps as much as twenty percent of her iron and steel. Big chemical and oil plants, such as those of IG Farben at Ludwigshafen and Mannheim manufactured around forty percent of all Germany's chemicals, and at Homburg the synthetic oil plant was one of the few still in production.

Most importantly, however, the area contained the strongest part of the whole West Wall, plus sections of the Maginot Line still in German hands.

It was ironic that the French-built fortified line would in the end be used by Germans to ward off attacks, not only by the Americans, but also by the French of de Lattre's First French Army under Devers' command.

But the big, bluff, eternally optimistic German Field Marshal also saw the inherent dangers in this strong defensive position. He wrote: '. . . the Third Army is building up a fairly strong concentration in front of the right flank of our Seventh Army [in the Saar] . . . continuous heavy assaults against the right wing of our First Army [meant that] an encircling offensive against our only remaining bastion west of the Rhine – the Saar Palatinate – in order to wipe out Army Group G and so by crossing the Rhine to secure a jumping off base for operations against South Germany.'

It has been recorded in US military histories of the 1945 campaign in Europe that Patton later claimed that he had caught the Germans on the hop; that he had surprised the last defenders of the West Wall by cutting across their rear. In fact, the opposite was true. Kesselring had anticipated what Patton's Third Army was going to do. His only problem was that he could do very little to stop Patton.

Colonel-General Paul Hausser, known to the men of his German Seventh Army as 'Papa Hausser', had no reserves and no hope of securing any. He was virtually cut off from the gros of the German Army. The one-eyed SS General, still recovering from wounds he had received in the retreat from Normandy and the Battle of the Bulge, had already told Kesselring's predecessor, Field Marshal von Rundstedt, that successive withdrawals from the Saar-Palatinate offered the only hope of saving the German troops there. Von Rundstedt's response had been stern and unyielding. 'Hold the Saar-Palatinate.'

Kesselring was just as hard as von Rundstedt, but had had much more experience of defensive battles. He was inclined to encourage Hausser to make a fight of it. He wrote in his memoirs: 'The West Wall and the area on its immediate front . . . could not be overrun straight away, and the West Palatinate, with its successive natural positions, presented extraordinary difficulties to the attack and us with opportunities for a mobile defence.' In other words, it was the kind of situation 'Smiling Albert' had been well used to in Italy. There he had virtually worn out the British Eighth Army and the American Fifth Army in eighteen months of 'mobile defence'. Naturally, he could not do the same in Germany, especially given the state the *Wehrmacht* was in at the moment. All the same, he *could* make the Americans pay dearly for their last attack on the West Wall. It was, he concluded, a matter of keeping one's nerve. So, his orders to the troops defending the Wall in the Saar were, as he put it, 'categorical'. They were: 'Hang on.'

Hausser, whose oath of allegiance ('Our Honour is our Loyalty') had once been to his chief, Heinrich Himmler, now seemed no longer to believe in holding on in a losing situation, which could only bring disaster to the 'stubble-hoppers', as the German infantrymen called themselves. He was not nicknamed 'Papa Hausser' for nothing. He protested against Kesselring's order, and told Kesselring he was inviting disaster. Urgently he pleaded to be allowed to withdraw and cross the Rhine before it was too late. 'The policy of all-out defence west of the river,' he told 'Smiling Albert', 'can only end in tremendous losses and probably annihilation.'

For once Kesselring, who was not normally given to self-doubt, hesitated.

'A decision to withdraw behind the Rhine must be made quickly,' Hausser urged.

Kesselring replied. 'Rejected,' he snapped. 'Hold the line.'

Hausser repeated his objections, but Kesselring had made up his mind. His smile had vanished. 'Those are my orders. You must hang on.'

But now even SS generals were not obeying orders without question any more. As soon as Kesselring and his senior staff officers swept out, Hausser turned to his own staff and told his divisional commanders to start preparing for a withdrawal. Their plans should be shared on a strictly 'need to know' basis. But withdraw they would, even if it cost Hausser 'Kopf und Kragen'.[114]

On the same day that the Ludendorff Bridge, weakened by explosives, mines and aerial attacks, finally collapsed into the Rhine, leaving four divisions of 1st Army troops stranded on the other side, Eisenhower visited Patton's Third Army for the first time in nearly three months. The Supreme Commander pontificated to Patton: 'The trouble with you people in Third Army ... you don't appreciate your own greatness. You're not cocky enough. Let the world know what you are doing, otherwise the American soldier will not be appreciated at his full value.'

Later Eisenhower laid it on with a trowel. 'George, you're not only a good general, you are a *lucky* general and, as you will remember, in a general Napoleon prized luck above skill.'

Patton laughed it off. 'Well, that's the first compliment you've paid me in the two and a half years we have served together.'

That night over dinner, one of his staff mused: 'What I can't get over was his [Eisenhower's] statement that Third Army isn't cocky enough. How do you explain it?'

'That's easy,' Patton said, raising his head from his bowl of soup. 'Before long Ike will be running for President. The Third Army represents a lot of votes.' Patton noticed the smiles all round the table and added earnestly: 'You think I'm joking? I'm not. Just wait and see.'

Of course, Patton would be proved right. But by then he would be long dead. As it was, the future President's remarks, and Patton's interpretation of them were indicative of the way things were among the American top brass in Europe that spring. The future of the continent meant little to the American generals. The war was almost won. They had done their job. Now they were looking towards home and future rewards. A dying President Roosevelt was losing his grip in Washington and control over the US Army in Europe. Senior officers could pretty much do what they wanted. And no one knew that better than Patton. He was becoming a law unto himself, and would run his part of the war how he liked – at least until disgrace and death finally caught up with him.

The US Seventh Army, that was going to make the last attack on the Siegfried Line, was 'America's Forgotten Army'. Eisenhower had never used his press apparat to publicise it because of his antipathy to Devers. And 'Sandy' Patch, the Seventh's Commander was not a man for self-promotion. It was thought in some official quarters that the Seventh had had it easy since landing in southern France in August 1944. Its battle north into French Alsace had been dubbed 'the champagne campaign', with booze and broads all the way.

It now seemed all that was going to change. The Seventh Army was boosted up to thirteen divisions, the largest it had ever been, with divisions withdrawn from the American armies in the north – under protest, naturally. And no less a formation than the famous Third Army, whose commander, Patton, had been the Seventh's first leader, was going to support its attack in the Saar-Palatinate. Patton, of course, saw things differently. Thirty-six hours before the Seventh was due to attack the Siegfried Line on 15 March, Patton's Third jumped off on its attack over the Moselle and into the Hunsruck. As far as 'Ole Blood an' Guts' was concerned, the Seventh would have to make out on its own.

The men of the 'Poor Bloody Infantry' knew nothing of these developments. Veteran divisions, such as the 45th Infantry, and the new boys of the 63rd and 70th[115] started to cross the French border into the German Saar.

In their hundreds they marched through the grimy French industrial villages, where German was spoken on both sides of the border, to be greeted with 'Vive l'Amérique' and 'Bravo!'. They were not impressed. These same people had greeted the German invaders enthusiastically back in May 1940, and had worked for them, for good money, throughout the war. Nor were they impressed by the German propaganda leaflets which showered down on them, proclaiming that a hot reception awaited them in the Siegfried Line. They threw them aside (or used them for more basic purposes), and, as the chronicler of the time had it, 'vowed they would hang their washing on the Siegfried Line as promised'.

Their commanders were not so sanguine, however. The generals of the 45th Division knew they would be facing Siegfried Line positions manned by five battalions of the Waffen SS. In most cases, the natural barrier of the Saar river, which had cost Patton's men so dear, lay between the West Wall bunkers or in front of them. In addition, there were miles of 'dragon's teeth', that still presented an effective barrier to a massed tank attack to cover the infantry assault.

The brass of course did not convey their concerns to the assault infantry. They told their men that the bunkers were manned by retreads from the *Luftwaffe* and the Germany Navy, who knew nothing about ground warfare. Lieutenant Chappel of the 70th, for one, was not convinced. He commented later:

> It made no difference whether they knew anything about infantry tactics or not. All they had to do was sit inside the thick, concrete bunkers and pull the trigger of a machine-gun. It was pure suicide to cross the fields swept by perfect enemy fire, but orders were orders and we were going to try it.

One of the 70th's GIs remembered the start of the 'Trailblazers'[116] attack:

> It was dark and it was quiet that night of March 19th. Too quiet! Orders that were customarily barked and yelled were now almost whispers. Soldiers were deep in silent thought as men always are before battle.

Sergeant Rysso of the same division recalled:

> My platoon jumped off first. I had two squads forward and one back. As soon as we started to move, the Krauts threw over a lot of artillery and mortars, but most of it fell back of us. PFC Condict was the first man over the knob of the hill in front of the [Siegfried] Line. When he came back, he was sweating and his face was pale. 'It's going to be rough,' was all he said.
>
> We kept going until the two leading platoons were at the top of the hill. We could all see the dragon's teeth, pillboxes, dugouts and trenches from there. The hill was completely bare as we stood out in plain sight like sore thumbs. The Krauts couldn't help but see us. They waited till we were out on the flat ground and then cut loose.

Even though they were expecting it, the men of the 70th were startled. Tracer zipped towards them. Mortars gave their obscene 'thonk' and whine. In an instant all was confusion and sudden death. Man after man went down. The German defenders even riddled the heaps of manure, that were everywhere, with vicious bursts of fire – just in case the scattering, disorganised '*Amis*' were trying to hide behind them.

The stalled company commanders called for artillery in an attempt to cover their cowering survivors and get them moving again. But the American shells bounced off the thick, concrete skin of the pillboxes like glowing ping-pong balls.

Tanks were whistled up. One of the Shermans turned tail and fled as soon as it breasted the hill and saw the line of fire-spitting bunkers below.

But the rest kept going doggedly, and for a few minutes they slugged it out. Shells whizzed backwards and forwards. As always, the tanks, without the protection of infantry, felt vulnerable. It took only a single German, armed with a throwaway *Panzerfaust*, to creep up on them and blow away tank and crew. The tank commanders lost their nerve. Under the cover of smoke, they started to retreat, telling the stalled, disappointed infantry that the ground was too soft and muddy for the narrow, rubber tracks of their tanks.

Sergeant Rysso knew when he was beaten. Now his first responsibility was to his men. He said later:

Once we had reached temporary safety, I started to recognize the men we had left. Dunn [a medic] made two attempts to go out into the field to get the wounded, but was driven back by machine-gun fire. Then Newton [another medic] went out accompanied by Penland, Dunn, Boering and Mann. Strange to say they drew no fire, even though they were plainly visible to the Germans. They found Palmer dead, Castro with a broken leg, and Jannick unconscious with a hole in his head . . . Cuervo and Condict were also lying on the ground badly wounded. Newton did what he could for the men. He gave them all a shot of morphine and then waited for the litter-bearers to come up.

The names of men killed and wounded are remembered now only by the old men who survived the battle. But the personal, forgotten little tragedies that befell Rysso's platoon were experienced by scores of other outfits in the assault divisions on that March day more than half a century ago.

Here and there the stalled divisions called up the feared 'Jabos', as the Germans called the dive-bombers of TAC Air. They came falling out of the grey sky, racing in at 400 mph to blast away the bunkers with their rockets and light bombs. The heavy aircraft of 'Bomber' Harris's RAF Bomber Command came in, wave after wave, to blast at the fortifications holding up the veteran 45th Division's drive on Homburg.

But still the Germans held their ground, even though some of them were not really frontline infantry material. Men of Company C of the 70th's 274 Infantry Regiment captured a machine-gunner in one of the West Wall bunkers, who 'was so nearly blind that he couldn't see far beyond the end of his gun. He simply pointed the weapon in the general direction of the Americans and pressed the trigger every time he heard the command "Fire!"'

Another 'bedraggled Kraut', left behind when his comrades fled their bunker, tried to surrender. 'For three days,' as the chronicler recalled, 'on the curb, he waved his hand frantically to surrender. But he was totally ignored.' Finally a battalion of the Division set up its headquarters in the village, 'and to make sure that he wasn't overlooked this time, the soldier got the town mayor to walk with him into the command post and finally made it. He became a happy camper in a POW camp.'

There were all too few happy stories to recall. There was too much suffering, misery and sudden death on the battlefield. Sergeant Penland, lying wounded in no-man's-land in front of the West Wall bunkers, recalled:

Out of the corner of my eye, I saw two men supporting a third coming towards the shell crater. I glanced about and recognized Andrews on the right, supporting Darling who had been wounded in the right thigh. I just got out the first word of warning, 'Get down!', when a large-calibre shell screamed over very low and hit directly on the three men. I saw a tremendous flash of flame and a fearful cloud of black smoke. Pieces of men's bodies came flying through the air. The concussion blew me to the bottom of the crater which was filled with mud and water. One man's horribly torn body flew over my head and hit the water beside me. Newton was standing next to me nearest the shell and was blown into the water. I grabbed him to keep him from sinking under. He was covered in blood from the men who had been hit. I asked him if he had been hit. He said he didn't know and crawled to help another man who had been hit, and who was pushing himself toward the water with only his legs. I looked around and saw just a man's chest and hands sticking out of the water. I grabbed to pull him out, thinking possibly he might be still alive and was drowning. When I got him out, though, I saw he was mangled and dead, so I let him slip back into the water.

The Great Wall of Germany was making the Allies pay the highest price in blood for its capture. But, thanks to Patton's Third Army, the German front behind the West Wall in the Saar-Palatinate was rapidly crumbling. His tank divisions were rushing for the Rhine to beat Montgomery at half a dozen different spots. Indeed, the assault and consequent German retreat was so fast that General Ferber, commanding the German Seventh Army under 'Papa' Hausser, found himself directing operations from a post office. As his means of communication he used the civilian telephone network, with female operators reporting on the movements of the '*Amis*'.

Patton brooked no defiance. Any village that did not display the white flag of surrender – even if it was only 'grandpa's long white under-drawers' (as one Third Army officer put it) – was subjected to 'Patton's Third Army Memorial' technique. It was plastered with artillery fire. As Patton saw it, the wrecked village would be a semi-permanent memorial to the fact that he and his army had passed that way.

Things were little different in the Seventh Army's area, as General Patch's divisions slogged their way forward. 'It is difficult to describe the destruction,' General Frederick, commanding the 45th Infantry Division, wrote. 'Scarcely a man-made thing exists in our wake. It is even difficult to find buildings suitable for CPs – this is scorched earth.'

On 20 March a desperate German Army Command threw in 300 planes of every type, including the new jets, in an attempt to stop the triumphant Americans. Flak shot down twenty-five, and the US Air Force downed another eight. They did not try again.

Two days later the Seventh's 'Rainbow Division' struck a mighty, and final, blow at the West Wall. But already the Germans were in retreat.

Those who could, especially the brass, headed for the Rhine. Once across it, they felt they would be able to put off the inevitable for a few more days. But they would have to surrender in the end, and some did there and then. Others slipped quietly to the rear, searching the ruined, abandoned houses for what they called '*Rauberzivil*' (robbers' civvies – rough, shabby civilian clothes), and took a dive as civilians with no discharge papers.

As yet the men of the Seventh Army's assault divisions were not aware of this. Or, if they were, they still remained on their guard. Everyone knew how stupid it would be to get killed now, at the moment of victory. Sergeant Rysso's regiment, the 274th Infantry, for example, was preparing to launch its attack on the West Wall in front of Saarbrücken. They had suffered a great many casualties getting this far, and they were cautious, very cautious indeed.

Colonel Landstrom, its commander, had sent patrols out the previous day, and they had found all the German bunkers and pillboxes to be occupied. On the day after that, an artillery observer spotted what he thought was someone waving a white flag from a church steeple. He ordered the barrage being brought down on the German positions on the other side of the Saar river to be halted. As soon as the firing stopped, the Germans started machine-gunning and mortaring his regimental line again. They had not given up.

The engineers started to drag up the assault boats for the crossing of the Saar and the attack into the West Wall. Landstrom did not relish the prospect of a crossing under fire, but what was he to do? That afternoon he was called by a fellow regimental colonel and told: 'The Commanding General expects us to cross tonight. You are to select the time for the crossing. If you need any assistance, it is ready on call. If you are successful, the Second Battalion will follow you.'

Landstrom took all this in. He knew that 'against us was the most powerful section of the most elaborate system of fortifications ever built in the world. Pillboxes blocked the way for miles. No one tried to think of what could happen while we floundered around in the water right in front of those electrically controlled guns on the other side.'

Some of his officers did not believe the Germans would put up a fight.

They thought the enemy had retreated already, leaving behind just a few machine-gunners. They argued that, instead of a full-scale assault, the CO should limit himself to dispatching a few patrols, as before.

Colonel Landstrom did not share their opinion. He said: 'If we start across, we will complete it. I am not in favour of patrols. Prefer to go all out. The time for crossing will be sometime between midnight and daybreak. We are still receiving fire from enemy 50 and 80mm guns. This points to the same resistance as before.' With that he dismissed his officers back to their outfits. And that was that.

Colonel Wallace Cheeves, an officer of the 70th Division who wrote the account of that last attack on the West Wall, recalled:

The night of March 19th was quiet and peaceful. The warming winds swept from the south and sent patterns of ripples twinkling in the starlight on the river. In foxholes along the shore the men looked up at the sky and waited . . .

NOTES

110 Interviewing the local civilians who had been present when the Americans started their great drive, the author found that they were still surprised that the '*Amis*' had found this obscure mill, buried in a deep, remote valley.
111 Recent research suggests that the hero of that crossing, Lieutenant Timmermann, a German-American, was not even on the bridge that day.
112 Patton was referring to Patch's withdrawal from the positions the Seventh had taken in November 1944.
113 Literally 'the Huns' Back or Ridge', reportedly crossed by the Huns in the 5th century before their defeat by the Franks at Chalons-sur-Marne.
114 Literally, 'Head and Collar', that is, his life.
115 The 70th had since January already suffered nearly 3,000 casualties in the 'Second Battle of the Bulge'.
116 The nickname given to the 70th Division.

Envoi

Even generals sometimes wet their knickers.

Anonymous British Staff Officer

At dawn on Tuesday 20 March 1945 the 70th Infantry Division assaulted the Saar river. In the lead, the men of Colonel Landstrom's regiment landed on the far bank to find that the bunkers and pillboxes they had so feared were empty. The German defenders had slipped away quietly during the night, and were now in full retreat to the Rhine.

Behind them they left a musty emptiness – a mixture of stale, unwashed bodies, the coarse black *marhorka* tobacco they smoked, and despair. At last the Allies could put out their washing on the Siegfried Line. The Great Wall of Germany had been defeated.[117]

Two days later Patton's men started to cross the Rhine above Saarbrücken, the 70th Infantry Division's final objective before it was 'squeezed' out of the war. With a combination of chance, luck and a certain amount of cunning, Patton's 5th Infantry Division managed to get across the river at the wine-producing village of Oppenheim, before the Germans, or for that matter Bradley, Eisenhower or Montgomery were aware of it.

Patton was like a mischievous child, who sensed he ought to be punished for naughtiness, but hoped he would escape without a hiding. With less than a single division of infantry, he had stolen a march on the Field Marshal, whose great set-piece crossing involved massive bombing, and two-division airborne assaults.

When Montgomery launched his attack in the north on the same day, 23 March, Patton himself crossed the Rhine over a pontoon bridge near Oppenheim. As he reached the bank he appeared to slip. He sank to one elegantly clad knee before steadying himself with both hands. When he stood up, his hands were filled with German soil. 'Thus William the Conqueror,' he exclaimed with a smile in the direction of the watching correspondents, who were naturally puzzled by the reference.[118]

Patton later wrote in his diary: 'Drove to the river and went across on a pontoon bridge, stopping in the middle to take a piss in the Rhine.'

Field Marshal Model, 'the Boy Field Marshal' as von Rundstedt liked to call him contemptuously, was the first of the defenders of the West Wall to go. By the time Patton had crossed the Rhine, Model was at the end of his tether. What was left of his Army Group B had been squeezed into what became known as the 'Ruhr Pocket'. Nearly half a million men and women were surrounded by two American armies, the First and the Ninth, and were being pounded daily by their full weight.

Bradley, who had been humiliated by Model in December 1944 at the time of the Battle of the Bulge, wanted revenge. He promised the Bronze Star to any American soldier who brought in the little, monocled, German Field Marshal, whether dead or alive. Model's staff officers urged him to surrender to the 'Amis' while there was still time.

Model refused categorically. He snorted icily: 'A German Field Marshal does not surrender.'

In the second week of April, when it was clear that his shattered armies, trapped in the 'Pocket', would either have to give in or fight to the bitter end, Model and a handful of his most loyal officers 'did a dive', in the terminology of the time, and became 'submarines'. He disappeared into the depths of the forest.

On the morning of 21 April Model and his companions stretched their legs in the cold, early sunlight after a rough night on the ground. One of his staff, a Major Behr, volunteered to go to the nearest village, Wedau, to check whether the enemy had penetrated that far. Model agreed and handed the young officer a few personal possessions to be given to the Frau Generalfeld-Marschall Model ... just in case. Behr drove away. It was the last time he would see his superior.

Around midday Model asked his adjutant, Colonel Pilling, to join him in a stroll through the forest. Neither man said much until Model called a halt. According to a statement made by Pilling in 1951, Model said to him: 'Anything is better than falling into Russian hands.' He drew his pistol. 'You will bury me here.'

After Model had fired the fatal shot, Pilling called Lieutenant Colonel Michael to the lonely glade. Together the two staff officers buried *der Chef* in a shallow grave beneath a large oak tree. They wrapped his body in a greatcoat. They tamped the earth firm and replaced the sods of grass. There was to be no way of identifying the burial place of the only German Field Marshal to commit suicide in World War Two without being under pressure from the Nazi authorities. They left the place unmarked.

But someone – it was never discovered who – returned to the spot later, where Model's grave was half-hidden by fronds and grass, and started to carve identifying marks on a tree trunk, probably with a bayonet. He must have been disturbed, for he did not complete the inscription. Ten years later the single letter 'M' gave Model's son, Hans Georg, the clue he needed to establish the location of his father's final resting place.

In 1955 a small, furtive group of well-off Germans, led by two foresters in their green uniforms, began to dig up Model's remains. They found bits and pieces of skeleton, clad in the mouldy field-grey of the *Wehrmacht*. Hurriedly and with little ceremony,[119] the remains were put into a large car and driven south at speed. The destination was the Eifel – that 'Awful Eifel' to the GIs he had fought ten years earlier.

Later that same day the car and those following reached the Hürtgenwald – the 'Death Factory' of a decade before. They drove through Grosshau and Kleinhau, where Hemingway had reported seeing a 'half-roasted Kraut' being eaten by a 'Kraut dog'. Finally the little convoy stopped outside the *Ehrenfriedhof* (the Cemetery of Honour) at Vossenack, in the heart of the former Siegfried Line. Here Model's bones were reinterred beside those of one of his private soldiers killed in the great battle. A modest stone, exactly the same as hundreds of others, was placed over the grave, and on it was inscribed 'Walter Model – FM'.[120]

The first of the West Wall conquerors to die after Model's suicide was General 'Sandy' Patch of the US Seventh Army. Officially he succumbed to a heart attack, brought on by the strain of the campaign. Those who knew him said that Patch died of 'a broken heart'. He had never got over the death of his son, killed in action. Just before Captain Patch was wounded, he was posted to his father's staff to recover. It was said that General Patch felt that he should have kept his son at headquarters. Instead he allowed him to return to his infantry outfit and he was killed a few days later. The General and his wife never overcame their feelings of guilt, especially in the knowledge that their son's young children, their grandchildren back in the States, would never see their father again.

General George S Patton also had grandchildren waiting for him in the United States. But 'Ole Blood an' Guts' had not wanted to return home. On his first and only leave with his family in July 1945, he shocked them by saying as he left: 'Well, I guess this is goodbye. I won't be seeing you again.' When his daughter protested, Patton added: 'It's too damned bad I wasn't killed before the fighting stopped, but I wasn't. So be it.' It was the last time his children ever saw him.

Six months later Patton was dead – killed from injuries received in a car crash. On 24 December 1945 he was, like Model, buried among his own soldiers in Hamm, just outside Luxembourg City, from where, a year earlier, he had directed the counter-attack during the Battle of the Bulge, and the subsequent drive across the Sauer-Our into the Siegfried Line – a mere twenty miles away as the crow flies.

There is a mystery attached to his last resting place, too. Although three post-war Presidents, including his old boss, Eisenhower, were within a car's ride of Patton's grave, the only 'old comrade' of note who ever came to visit it was Winston Churchill in 1946. It seemed that the man who had brought about the destruction of the West Wall was out of favour. The top brass seemed to want to forget that he had ever existed.

Thus, one by one, the men who had fought the Siegfried Line disappeared from the scene, taken by time and old age. Hodges of the US First Army died at the age of nearly 80 in 1966. Simonds, the young Canadian commander of his country's First Army in the Reichswald, died in 1974. Montgomery, who had been closest to rolling up the whole Great Wall of Germany at Arnhem in September 1944, died in 1976, 'totally gaga, unable to get out a coherent word'.[121]

While the victors of the conflict were dying off, a mystery arose that, in a convoluted manner, links Patton's last resting place with that of his chief opponent, Model. Patton's widow died in 1957. Some time later it was found that her grave at Green Meadows, California was empty. What had become of Beatrice Ayer Patton's ashes?

Back in 1946 Patton's long-suffering, but loving, wife had written to the American Military Authorities requesting permission to be buried with the 'Conqueror of the Siegfried Line'. They refused. Military regulations forbade it, she was informed gently. But the Pattons were a determined breed. Some time after their mother's death, their two children, George and Ruth Ellen, together with their two sons, visited George Patton's grave at Hamm.

On the white wall that surrounds the hilltop cemetery, in which lie thousands of Patton's young soldiers who fought and died in the 'Awful Eifel', the four of them spotted a cat. They never found out what it was doing there, but in Egyptian mythology, the cat is the goddess of happy death. The sighting inspired Patton's daughter. Ruth Ellen opened her purse, took out an envelope containing her mother's ashes and sprinkled them on her father's grave. They were united at last. As always, the Pattons had managed to cock a snook at authority.

But the greatest cock-snooker of them all turned out to be Bradley. He outlived all the generals who had broken the Great Wall of Germany, and he was going to have the last word.

In the same year that a relatively unknown Hungarian-American author, Ladislas Farago, sold the film rights to his biography of Patton (*Patton: Ordeal and Triumph*, 1964), General of the Army Omar Bradley, a widower now aged 73, surprised everyone by remarrying. His new bride, a vivacious, twice-divorced ash-blonde, was 44.

Now, through the new Mrs Bradley's contacts and insistence, the 'GI General', as they had tried to dub the homely, colourless Army Group Commander, found himself having to rub shoulders with movie stars such as James Stewart and Gregory Peck, and an actor-turned-politician, Ronald Reagan.

Patton came back into the life of the elderly general, who many had thought was already dead. Farago's biography was at the film script planning stage, and the man who would produce the film, Frank McCarthy (who had been one of General Marshall's assistants in Washington during World War Two), asked Bradley's advice.

But five-star generals do not come cheap. Kitty Bradley persuaded McCarthy to lease Bradley's war memoir *A Soldier's Story*, published twenty years earlier, as background material for the film. Not only that – she got herself and the General onto the payroll as senior advisers. She negotiated a guaranteed down payment and a percentage of the profits. It was ironic that the long dead Patton would provide a man he despised with a comfortable income for the rest of his life.

Although everyone was impressed by George C Scott's performance as Patton – it is said that President Nixon watched the movie time and time again during his various Vietnam crises – Bradley succeeded in inserting his own opinions, attitudes and, above all, prejudices into the final film. Even if no one noticed at the time, Bradley took his revenge against Patton and Montgomery for all the slights, real or imagined, he had suffered at their hands.

'Monty' was portrayed as man constantly trying to upstage the Americans, and detesting Patton because of the latter's all-American dash and get-up-and-go. From the invasion of Sicily onwards, the Farago-Bradley team maintained, there was a constant rivalry between Patton and the 'little Limey fart'. In reality, the opposite seems to have been the case. In his personal diary, Montgomery does not mention Patton after 28 July 1943. At that time, his only concern was that the famous 'slapping incident' should not be made public.

According to Warwick Castle, the Editor of the British Eighth Army newspaper, the only time he was rebuked by Monty was when he wrote a piece in 1943 stating that Patton was being investigated for having slapped an unfortunate GI who was suffering from combat fatigue. 'He [Mongomery] didn't think it right . . . Patton was a good man and I should have checked back.'

In the matter of the 'race for Messina' between Montgomery and Patton, which was prominently featured in the film, Freddie de Guingand,[122] Monty's Chief-of-Staff, has stated that there was neither a race nor rivalry. 'It was all balls that . . . We were delighted when we heard that Patton had got to Messina first. About that fictitious scene in the film . . . absolute cock! Monty marching at the head of his Highlanders . . . all balls!'

With uncharacteristic subtlety for a man of his nature, Bradley reserved his full venom for his one-time boss-subordinate, Patton. As Farago wrote:

> General Bradley frequently claims credit for ideas and plans in the war which Patton on his part represented as his brainstorms and designs . . . Yet the fact remains, Patton's plans and ideas are fully documented in his contemporary papers, while Bradley's claims to those same

thoughts were published later, in 1951[123] , when Patton was no longer around to contest or reclaim them.

In the film, Bradley, played by the veteran, sincere-looking Karl Malden (who did not look a bit like Bradley) is constantly trying to restrain Patton. More than once he warns him that he is his own worst enemy, a general whose career will end in disgrace if he does not mend his ways. Naturally, that is just what happens, despite Bradley's best efforts to save George from himself. As the movie has it, Patton is a maverick (a notion that has entered American military folk history). And it was Bradley who was the real author of his victories. The rich, upper-class Patton may have achieved a lot, but it was the solid, dependable Bradley, the 'GI General', who won America's war in Europe.

If Patton was slightly 'unhinged' throughout his fighting career in Europe (and the film placed much emphasis on his 'visions' and 'hearing voices', as well as his memories of an earlier incarnation as a 'Roman centurion'), Bradley was the realist during those final, bloody months of 1944-45.

Apparently forgetting that Patton had saved his bacon in the 'Bulge' after the 'surprise' attack out of the Siegfried Line, Bradley wrote after Patton's death: 'Without meaning to detract from his extraordinary achievements, Patton's great and dramatic gains, beginning in Sicily and continuing through Brittany and on across the Seine . . . had been made against little or no opposition.'

Thus judgement was passed on both Montgomery and Patton, and it is the one that remains in the popular imagination because of the success of the film. Either of those supposedly 'rival' generals could have turned the Siegfried Line with a decisive blow to the flank in the north or the south. As it was, Eisenhower, supported by Bradley, was committed to a broad-front attack on the West Wall. In the circumstances on the Western Front in 1944-45, such an attack virtually everywhere could not possibly have succeeded. Still Eisenhower persisted, goaded by Bradley and his constant references to the 'prestige of the American Army', not to mention his own.

As a result, Bradley, who commanded those three US armies attacking the whole length of the West Wall from the French Saar to Holland, won the kudos of victory. The war in Europe was probably prolonged by six months because of the Allies' failure to break through the Siegfried Line. It was a military victory devoid of a political one. And it meant death or personal disaster for some three quarters of a million young American, British, Canadian and French soldiers, forced to throw away their lives in a long, drawn-out, winter campaign that could not have succeeded on the basis of the Eisenhower-Bradley broad-front strategy.

And what of the 'GI General', the commander whose armies did finally break through – at the wrong place? He did not die in bed, as did so many of those old men who had sent the young men to their violent and tragic deaths. According to his ghost writer, Clay Blair: 'Less than ten minutes after receiving the award,[124] as he was being wheeled into the elevator, Bradley, aged 88, died, while Kitty, his aides and about one hundred guests looked on helplessly. He died instantly . . . He apparently felt no pain; there were no convulsions or seizures, merely a quiet passing from life into death.'

Six days later, General of the Army Omar Bradley, Conqueror of the Great Wall of Germany, was buried with full military honours at Arlington National Cemetery.

It was over.

NOTES

117 There are stories of individual bunkers and pillboxes surviving in remote areas right up to the end of the war, but the author has been unable to obtain verification.

118 William the Conqueror slipped when he landed at Hastings in 1066, which was taken as a bad omen by his followers. William rectified the situation by seizing a handful of 'English soil'.

119 When asked about this incident by the author, *Brigadegeneral* Model was understandably reluctant to give too many details.

120 The story did not end there. Some time in 1997 Model's grave (*Grab* 1073/1074) at Vossenack was reopened by person or persons unknown. His remains were removed. Who the grave-robbers were, and what became of the Field Marshal's remains, is a mystery to this day.

121 As one of Montgomery's staff officers told the author just before the Field Marshal's death.

122 De Guignand had no reason to like Montgomery after the war. Monty had dropped him, and would not even allow him to attend the Victory Parade in London.

123 When *A Soldier's Story* was published.

124 The Gold Medal Award from the National Institute of Social Sciences, New York.

Bibliography

Books

Allied Forces, 12th Army Group G-3: *Report of Operations* (*Final After Action Report*), Vol. 5, Wiesbaden, 1948

Astor, Gerald: *A Blood Dimed Tide: The Battle of the Bulge by the Men Who Fought It*, New York, Donald A Fine Inc., 1992

Ayer, Fred Jr: *Before the Colors Fade*, Boston, Houghton Mifflin, 1964

Baldwin, Hanson W: *Battles Lost and Won*, New York, Harper & Row, 1966

——: *Command Decisions*, New York, Harcourt Brace & Co., 1959

Blumenson, Martin: *US Army in World War II: European Theater of Operations - Breakout and Pursuit*, Washington, Office of the Chief of Military History, Dept of the Army, 1961

Bond, Brian: *Britain, France and Belgium, 1939-1940*, London, Brassey's, 1990

Bovy, Marcel: *La Bataille de l'Amblève*, Liège, Les Amitiés Mosanes, 1947

Bradley, Omar N: *A Soldier's Story*, New York, Henry Holt & Co., 1951

Brett-Smith, Richard: *Hitler's Generals*, San Rafael, Presidio Press, 1977

Bryant, Arthur: *Triumph in the West*, New York, Doubleday, 1959

Bullock, Alan: *Hitler: A Study in Tyranny*, New York, Harper, 1953

Calvocaressi, Peter: *Top Secret Ultra*, New York, Pantheon, 1980

Churchill, Winston S: *Triumph and Tragedy*, Boston, Houghton Mifflin, 1953

Codman, Charles R: *Drive*, Boston, Little, Brown & Co., 1957

Cole, Hugh M: *The Ardennes: The Battle of the Bulge* (in USA WWII series), Washington, OCMH, 1965

——: *The Lorraine Campaign*, Washington, Historical Division, Dept of the Army, 1950

Collins, Joseph Lawton: *Lightning Joe: An Autobiography*, Baton Rouge, Louisiana State University Press, 1979

Columbia Broadcasting System: *From D-Day Through Victory in Europe*, New York, CBS, 1945

Cortesi, Lawrence: *Valor in the Bulge*, Zebra Books, 1986

Critchell, Laurence: *Four Stars of Hell*, McMullen, 1947

Davis, Franklin M Jr: *Breakthrough*, Derby Ct, Monarch, 1961

Davis, Kenneth Sydney: *Experience of War: The United States in World War II*, New York, Doubleday, 1965

De Man, Paul: *Wartime Journalism 1939-1943*, Lincoln, University of Nebraska Press, 1988

Downing, David: *The Devil's Virtuosos: German Generals at War*, New York, St Martin's Press, 1977

Draper, Theodore: *The 84th Infantry Division in the Battle of Germany, November 1944-May 1945*, New York, Viking Press, 1947

Dupuy, R Ernest: *St Vith, Lion in the Way*, Washington, The Infantry Journal Press, 1949

Eisenhower, Dwight D: *Crusade in Europe*, Garden City NY, Doubleday, 1948

Eisenhower, John S: *The Bitter Woods*, New York, Putnam's, 1969

Elstob, Peter: *Bastogne: The Road Block*, New York, Ballantine, 1968

——: *Hitler's Last Offensive*, New York, Macmillan, 1971

Esposito, Vincent J: *The West Point Atlas of American Wars*, New York, Frederick A Praeger, 1959

Farago, Ladislas: *Patton: Ordeal and Triumph*, New York, Dell Publishing Co., 1965

Franks, Norman L R: *The Battle of the Airfields: 1st January 1945*, London, W Kimber, 1982

Fussell, Paul: *Wartime: Understanding and Behaviour in the Second World War*, OUP, 1989

Gavin, James M: *On to Berlin: Battles of an Airborne Commander, 1943-1946*, New York, Viking, 1978

Giles, J H: *The G.I. Journal of Sergeant Giles*, New York, Houghton Mifflin

——: *Those Damned Engineers*, New York, Houghton Mifflin

Greenfield, Kent Roberts (ed.): *Command Decisions*, New York, Harcourt Brace, 1959

Greil, Lother: *Die Wahrheit unter Malmédy*, Schild Verlag

Guderian, Heinz: *Panzer Leader*, New York, E P Dutton & Co., 1965

Guingand, Sir Francis de: *Generals at War*, London, Hodder & Stoughton, 1964

Hart, B H Liddell: *The German Generals Talk*, New York, Wm Morrow, 1948

Heffner, Richard D: *A Documentary History of the United States*, New York, The New American Library of World Literature Inc., 1956

Hitler, Adolf: *Hitler's Secret Conversations, 1941-1944* (English translation of *Tischgesprache* by Norman Cameron and R H Stevens), New York, Farrar Straus & Young, 1953

——: *Mein Kampf* (English translation by Ralph Manheim), Boston, Houghton Mifflin, 1943

Horrocks, Sir Brian: *Escape to Action*, New York, St Martin's Press, 1961

Ingersoll, Ralph: *Top Secret*, New York, Harcourt Brace, 1946

Irving, David J C: *The War Between the Generals*, London, Allen Lane, 1981

Jacobsen, H A and Rohwer, J: *Decisive Battles of World War II: The German View*, New York, Putnam's, 1965

Keefer, Louis E: *Scholars in Foxholes: The Story of the Army Specialized Training Program in World War II*, McFarland & Co. Inc., 1988

Knickerbocker, H R; Thompson, Jack; Belden, Jack et al: *Danger Forward*, Atlanta, Albert Love Enterprises, 1947

Lame, G R de: *La Bataille de la Gleize-Stoumont*, Brussels, L'Alliance

Leigh, Randolph: *48,000,000 Tons to Eisenhower*, Washington, The Infantry Journal Press, 1945

Lewin, Ronald: *Ultra Goes to War: The First Account of World War II's Greatest Secret Based on Official Documents*, New York, McGraw Hill, 1978

Liversidge, Douglas: *The Third Front*, London, Souvenir Press

Lyman, Samuel and Marshall, Atwood: *Bastogne: The Story of the First Eight Days*, Zenger Publishing Company, 1946

MacDonald, Charles B: *A Time for Trumpets: The Untold Story of the Battle of the Bulge*, New York, Morrow, 1985

——: *The Siegfried Line*, Washington, OCMH, Dept of the Army, 1963

MacDonald, John: *Great Battlefields of the World*, London, Michael Joseph, 1984

MacKenzie, Fred: *The Men of Bastogne*, New York, McKay, 1968

Manteuffel, A D Hasso von: *Panzer-Division im Zweiten Weltkrieg*, Verdingen am Rhein, Joseph Broich, 1965

Marshall, S L A: *Bastogne: The First Eight Days*, Washington, The Infantry Journal Press, 1946

Merriam, Robert E: *Dark December*, Chicago, Davis, 1947

——: *The Battle of the Ardennes*, London, Souvenir, 1958

Montgomery, Bernard Law: *Normandy to the Baltic: 21st Army Group*, Germany, British Army of the Rhine, 1946

——: *Memoirs*, Cleveland, World Publishing Company, 1958

Morgan, Kay Summersby: *Eisenhower Was My Boss*, Dell

——: *Past Forgetting: My Love Affair with Dwight D Eisenhower*, New York, Simon & Schuster, 1976

Niedermayer, Walter: *Into the Deep Misty Woods of the Ardennes*, Halldin, A G Publishing Company, 1990

Nobecourt, J: *Hitler's Last Gamble*, New York, Schocken, 1969

Pallud, Jean Paul: *After the Battle of the Bulge: Then and Now*, London, Battle of Britain Prints, 1984

Parker, Danny S: *Battle of the Bulge: Hitler's Battle for the Ardennes*, Hippocrene Books Inc., 1991

Patton, George S Jr: *War As I Knew It*, Boston, Houghton Mifflin, 1947

Pergrin, David and Hammel, Eric: *The Story of the 2nd 91st Engineer Combat Battalion Part III*, New York, Ballantine, 1989

Piekalkiewics, Janusz: *Spione, Agenten, Soldaten*, Sud-West Verlag

Pogue, Forrest C: *The Supreme Command*, Washington, OCMH, Dept of the Army, 1954

Rapport, Leonard and Northwood, Arthur Jr: *Rendezvous with Destiny: A History of the 101st Airborne Division*, Washington, Infantry Journal Press, 1948

Rothbrust, Florian K: *Guderian's XIX Panzer Corps & The Battle of France: Breakthrough in the Ardennes May 1940*, Greenwood Publishing Group Inc., 1990

Royster, Charles: *The Destructive War: William Tecumseh Sherman, Stonewall Jackson and the Americans*, New York, Alfred Knopf, 1991

Schulman, Milton: *Defeat in the West*, New York, Ballantine

Speer, Albert: *Inside the Third Reich: Memoirs* (English translation by Richard and Clara Winston), New York, Macmillan, 1970

Stawson, J M: The Battle for the Ardennes, New York, Scribner's, 1972

Toland, John: *Battle: The Story of the Bulge*, New York, Random House, 1959

Weingartner, James J: *Crossroads of Death: The Story of the Malmédy Massacre and Trial*, Berkeley, University of California Press, 1979

Whiting, Charles: *1944: In Combat from Normandy to the Ardennes*, New York, Stein & Day, 1984

——: *The Battle of Hürtgen Forest*

——: *Ardennes: The Secret War*, Jove Publications, 1990

——: *Death of a Division*, New York, Berkeley Publishing, 1991

——: *Massacre at Malmédy: The Unknown Battle of the Bulge*, New York, Stein & Day, 1971

——: *Operation Northwind: The Unknown Battle of the Bulge*, London, Leo Cooper in association with Secker & Warburg, 1986

——: *Skorzeny*, New York, Ballantine

Wilmot, Chester: The Struggle for Europe, Harper & Row, 1952

Young, Donald J: *The Lion's Share*, Aptos, California, Avranches Press, 1990

Articles

Alexander, Martin S: 'Prophet Without Honour? The French High Command and Pierre Taittinger's Report on the Ardennes Defence, March 1940', *War and Society* (Australia), 1986, 4(1), pp 53-77.

Ambrose, Stephen E: 'The Bulge', MHQ: The Quarterly Journal of Military History, 1989 1(3), pp 22-33.

American Legion Magazine series on The Battle of the Bulge, Part I, 'Hitler Plans the Impossible' (January 1966); Part II, 'Disaster and Rection in the Ardennes' (February 1966); Part III, 'The Bulge is Erased' (March 1966).

Blumentritt, Gunther: 'Field Marshal von Rundstedt's Own Story of the Battle of the Bulge', *Collier's*, 3 January 1953.

Cole, Hugh M: 'The Ardennes: Battle of the Bulge' in series USAWWII, Washington, OCMH, 1965, pp 260-4.

Crandell, William F: 'Eisenhower the Strategist: The Battle of the Bulge and the Censure of Joe McCarthy', *Presidential Studies Quarterly*, 1987, 17(3), pp 487-501.

Doherty, John Stephen: 'The Battle Babies: The Saga of the 99th Division', *Saga*, January 1945.

Draper, Theodore: 'Battle in the Bulge', *Infantry Journal* LVI (May 1945), pp 8-17. Per.

Endsley, Mark C: '9th Infantry Division Activated – Glories of Past Are Revived', *Army Information Digest* (March 1966).

Gordon, John: 'The Gunners of Bastogne', Field Artillery Journal 54 (September-October 1986), pp 15-21. Per.

Hartman, Douglas R and Paul, Andrea I: 'The Butler B Miltonberger Collection', *Nebraska History* 1988, 69/4, pp 199-203.

Hood, Barton F: 'Operation Grief', *Military Review* XXXIX (January 1960), pp 37-43. Per.

Karl, Dennis R: 'Drive for Berlin: the Debate Over Strategy in the Invasion of Germany', *American History Illustrated* 1985, 20(4), pp 21-7.

Luttichau, Charles V von: 'The German Counteroffensive in the Ardennes', *Command Decisions*, Washington, GPO, 1960, pp 463-9.

MacDonald, Charles: 'The Neglected Ardennes', *Military Review* XLIII (April 1963), pp 74-89. Per.

——: 'The Battle for Eisenborn Ridge', *The Johns Hopkins Magazine* (December 1959).

Marshall, S L A et al: 'Christmas Eve at Bastogne', *Infantry Journal* LVII (December 1945), pp 8-15. Per.

Matters, James P: 'Murder at Malmédy', *Army* 31 (December 1981), pp 32-5. Per.

Merriam, Robert E: 'Bulgeland Revisited', *Infantry Journal* (December 1949).

Middleton, Drew: 'The Battle that Sealed Germany's Fate', *New York Times Magazine* (16 December 1984).

Peterman, Ivan H: 'They Took the Nazis' Sunday Punch', *Saturday Evening Post* (28 September 1946).

Porch, Douglas: 'French intelligence and the Fall of France, 1939-40', *Intelligence and National Security* (Great Britain), 1989, 4(1), pp 25-8.

Privratsky, Kenneth L: 'Mobility versus Sustainability', *Military Review* 1987.

Raymond, Allen D III: 'The Battle of St Vith', *Armor* (November-December 1944).

Starr, Mark: 'Take no Prisoners', *Newsweek* (29 April 1985).

Stevenson, Charles S: 'A Christmas Card from the General: Bastogne 1944', *Army* 25 (December 1975), pp 24-5. Per.

Thompson, Royce L: 'Ardennes Campaign Statistics, 16 December 1944-19 January 1945', Study OCMH, 28 April 1952, p 29.

US Army 101st Airborne Division: *History of the 101st Airborne Division, 1942-1964*, Mimeo, Ft Campbell, Ky, 1964, pp 42-65.

US Army, European Theater of Operations, Historical Division: Interviews w/Obst Joachim Peiper.

——: Interrogations 10-11, September 1945, p 23 Garland reprint WWII *Military Studies*, Vol. 2.

VanStraten, James G and Kaufman, Lynn W: 'Lessons from Team SNAFU', *Military Review* 1987.

Weingartner, James J: 'Otto Skorzeny and the Laws of War', *Journal of Military History*, v55 (April 1991).

Index